CompTIA®
A+® Complete
Lab Manual

CompTIA®
A+® Complete
Lab Manual

James Pyles

WILEY

John Wiley & Sons, Inc.

Senior Acquisitions Editor: Jeff Kellum
Development Editor: Amy Breguet
Technical Editors: Niall McCarthy and Ian Seaton
Production Editor: Eric Charbonneau
Copy Editor: Linda Recktenwald
Editorial Manager: Pete Gaughan
Production Manager: Tim Tate
Vice President and Executive Group Publisher: Richard Swadley
Vice President and Publisher: Neil Edde
Book Designers: Judy Fung and Bill Gibson
Compositor: Craig Woods, Happenstance Type-O-Rama
Proofreader: S. B. Kleinman
Indexer: Ted Laux
Project Coordinator, Cover: Katherine Crocker
Cover Designer: Ryan Sneed

Dear Reader,

Thank you for choosing *CompTIA A+ Complete Lab Manual*. This book is part of a family of premium-quality Sybex books, all of which are written by outstanding authors who combine practical experience with a gift for teaching.

Sybex was founded in 1976. More than 30 years later, we're still committed to producing consistently exceptional books. With each of our titles, we're working hard to set a new standard for the industry. From the paper we print on to the authors we work with, our goal is to bring you the best books available.

I hope you see all that reflected in these pages. I'd be very interested to hear your comments and get your feedback on how we're doing. Feel free to let me know what you think about this or any other Sybex book by sending me an email at nedde@wiley.com. If you think you've found a technical error in this book, please visit http://sybex.custhelp.com. Customer feedback is critical to our efforts at Sybex.

Best regards,

Neil Edde
Vice President and Publisher
Sybex, an Imprint of Wiley

To my wife, Lin; my children, Michael, David, and Jamie; my daughter-in-law, Kim; and my grandson, Landon, without all of whom my life would be so much dimmer.

Acknowledgments

No one writes a book alone. While my name may be on the cover as the author, a small army of people has been responsible for reviewing every word and image that appears in this book, just like the other editions before it. Sincere thanks go to the fine folks at Sybex, who worked hard arranging for the book you now hold in your hands to come into existence. My special thanks also go to everyone who has been involved in this book and has supported me in this endeavor.

Thanks to my agent at Waterside Publications, Carole McClendon, who always finds the right projects for me at the right time.

Thanks also go to Jeff Kellum, who first introduced me to this series way back when it was called Street Smarts.

Kudos to development editor Amy Breguet for being able to see all of the little details in my writing that needed fixing. Thanks to Niall McCarthy, who was the technical reviewer and kept me on the straight and narrow. Also thanks to copy editor Linda Recktenwald and production editor Eric Charbonneau.

I have also depended again on the gang over at CertForums.co.uk for letting me bounce ideas off their collective heads and presenting some of the puzzles and solutions that added flavor to this book.

Finally, thanks to my wife, Lin, who graciously let me spend incalculable hours in my lair writing this second edition when I should have been mowing the lawn or playing with my grandson.

About the Author

James Pyles, CompTIA A+, CompTIA Network+, has worked as a freelance consultant, technical writer, and editor. He has been involved in numerous Ethernet rollout projects as well as many software and hardware installations. He has provided support services for a city-government IT department and a wireless-network vendor; supported a usability lab for Hewlett-Packard (HP); and served as a technical writer for EmergeCore Networks, Aquent Studios, and Sybase iAnywhere and as a developmental editor for Global Support Content Operations at HP.

His most recent books are *CompTIA A+ Certification Practice Exams (Exams 220-701 & 220-702)* (McGraw-Hill, 2011) and *MCTS Microsoft SharePoint 2010 Configuration Study Guide: Exam 70-667* (Sybex 2010). He has also written *MCTS: Microsoft Office SharePoint Server 2007 Configuration Study Guide: Exam 70-630* (Sybex, 2008), *SharePoint 2007: The Definitive Guide* (O'Reilly, 2007), and *PC Technician Street Smarts, 1st ed.* (Sybex, 2006).

James previously contributed to *Linux Magazine* and *Ubuntu User Magazine*. He has bachelor's degrees in psychology and computer network support and a master's degree in counseling. James currently works as a technical writer for Keynetics, Inc.

Contents at a Glance

Contents

Introduction

The A+ certification was developed by the Computer Technology Industry Association (CompTIA) to provide an industry-wide means of certifying the competency of computer service technicians in the basics of PC support. According to CompTIA, the A+ certification "confirms a technician's ability to perform tasks such as installation, configuration, diagnosing, preventive maintenance, and basic networking."

Most books targeted toward certification candidates present material for you to memorize before the exam, but this book is different. It guides you through procedures and tasks that solidify related concepts, allowing you to devote your memorization efforts to more abstract theories because you've mastered the more practical topics through doing. Even if you do not aspire to become A+ certified, this book will be a valuable primer for your career as a PC technician.

What Is A+ Certification?

The A+ certification was created to offer an introductory step into the complex world of PC and laptop hardware and software support.

In 2006, CompTIA changed the format of the A+ exam to focus on various job roles, all of which can be rolled into the title of PC technician. However, the current exam format has returned to nearly its original form of separating the hardware and software portions of the exam. A+ candidates must take two exams: Exam #220-801, which covers various concepts related to computer hardware, including PC hardware, networking, laptops, and printers; and Exam #220-802, which is more software-oriented, addressing areas such as operating systems, security, mobile devices (an entirely new content area as of the current exam), and troubleshooting.

Obtaining the A+ certification does not mean you can provide sufficient PC support services to a company. In fact, this is just the first step toward true technical knowledge and experience. Hopefully, by obtaining A+ certification you will be able to acquire more computer-support experience and gain an interest in hardware and software maintenance that will lead you to pursue more complex and in-depth knowledge and certifications.

For the latest information on the exam and updates to registration procedures, go to the Pearson VUE website at www.pearsonvue.com/comptia/index.asp. If you have further questions about the scope of the exames or related CompTIA programs, go to CompTIA's website at www.comptia.org.

Is This Book for You?

CompTIA A+ Lab Manual is designed to give you insight into the world of a typical PC support technician by walking you through some of the daily tasks you can expect on the job. Some investment in equipment is advised to get the full value from this book. However, much value can be derived from simply reading through the tasks without performing the steps on live equipment. Organized classes and study groups are the ideal structures for obtaining and practicing with the recommended equipment.

The *CompTIA A+ Complete Study Guide: Exams 220-801 and 220-802* (Sybex, 2012) is a recommended companion to this book in your studies for the CompTIA A+ certification.

How This Book Is Organized

This book is organized into four chapters. Each chapter is separated into individual tasks. The chapters represent broad categories under which related responsibilities are grouped. The tasks within each phase lead you step-by-step through the processes required for successful completion. When performed in order, the tasks in this book approximate those required of a PC technician over an extended period of time. The four chapters and their descriptions follow:

- *Phase 1—Installing Hardware and Software* presents common tasks recommended for most projects involving the installation of hardware and software components on a PC or laptop.

- *Phase 2—Maintaining and Documenting Computer Systems* gives you tools to enable you to provide routine maintenance of computer hardware, operating systems, and peripherals.

- *Phase 3—Networking Computer Systems* shows you how to perform a series of basic networking tasks in a computing environment.

- *Phase 4—Troubleshooting and Restoring Computer Systems* provides real-world computer and network problems for you to solve. These tasks are derived from the trouble tickets acted upon by PC technicians in an actual production environment.

Each task in this book is organized into sections aimed at giving you what you need when you need it. You are first introduced to the task and any key concepts that can assist you in understanding the underlying technology and the overall procedure. The sections that follow each task are described here:

- *Objective*—This section lists the objective that the task covers.

- *Scenario*—This section places you in the shoes of the PC support technician, describing a situation in which you will likely find yourself. The scenario is closely related to and often solved by the task at hand.

- *Scope of Task*—This section is all about preparing for the task. It gives you an idea of how much time is required to complete the task, what setup procedure is needed before beginning, and any concerns or issues to look out for.

- *Procedure*—This is the actual meat of the task itself. This section informs you of the equipment required to perform the task in a lab environment. It also gives you the ordered steps to complete the task.

- *Criteria for Completion*—This final section briefly explains the outcome you should expect after completing the task. Any deviation from the result described is an excellent reason to perform the task again and watch for sources of the variation.

How to Contact the Publisher

Sybex welcomes feedback on all of its titles. Visit the Sybex website at www.sybex.com for book updates and additional certification information. You'll also find forms you can use to submit comments or suggestions regarding this or any other Sybex title.

How to Contact the Author

James Pyles welcomes your questions and comments. You can reach him by email at james.pyles@gmail.com.

The A+ Exam Objectives

The A+ exams are made up of the 220-801 exam and the 220-802 exam. Following are the detailed exam objectives of each test.

 Exam objectives are subject to change at any time without prior notice and at CompTIA's sole discretion. Please visit the A+ Certification page of CompTIA's website (http://certification.comptia.org/getCertified/certifications/a.aspx) for the most current listing of exam objectives.

A+ Certification Exam Objectives: 220-801

The following table lists the domains measured by this examination and the extent to which they are represented on the exam:

Domain	Percentage of Exam
1.0 PC Hardware	40%
2.0 Networking	27%
3.0 Laptops	11%
4.0 Printers	11%
5.0 Operational Procedures	11%

1.0 PC Hardware

1.1 Configure and apply BIOS settings: Task 2.14

- Install firmware upgrades—flash BIOS
- BIOS component information: RAM; hard drive; optical drive; CPU
- BIOS configurations: Boot sequence; enabling and disabling devices; date/time; clock speeds; virtualization support; BIOS security (passwords; drive encryption: TPM; lo-jack)
- Use built-in diagnostics
- Monitoring: Temperature monitoring; fan speeds; intrusion detection/notification; voltage; clock; bus speed

1.2 Differentiate between motherboard components; their purposes; and properties: Task 2.1, 2.15

- Sizes: ATX; Micro-ATX; ITX
- Expansion slots: PCI; PCI-X; PCIe; miniPCI; CNR; AGP2x, 4x, 8x
- RAM slots
- CPU sockets
- Chipsets: North Bridge; South Bridge; CMOS battery
- Jumpers
- Power connections and types
- Fan connectors
- Front panel connectors: USB; audio; power button; power light; drive activity lights; reset button
- Bus speeds

1.3 Compare and contrast RAM types and features: Task 1.2

- Types: DDR; DDR2; DDR3; SDRAM; SODIMM; RAMBUS; DIMM; parity vs. non-parity; ECC vs. non-ECC; RAM configurations (single channel vs. dual channel vs. triple channel); single sided vs. double sided
- RAM compatibility and speed

1.4 Install and configure expansion cards: Task 1.3, 1.4, 1.11

- Sound cards; video cards; network cards; serial and parallel cards; USB cards; FireWire cards; storage cards; modem cards; wireless/cellular cards; TV tuner cards; video capture cards; riser cards

1.5 Install and configure storage devices and use appropriate media: Task 1.5, 1.6, 1.7, 1.8, 1.9, 1.10, 1.13, 1.14, 1.15

- Optical drives: CD-ROM; DVD-ROM; Blu-ray
- Combo drives and burners: CD-RW; DVD-RW; dual layer DVD-RW; BD-R; BD-RE
- Connection types
    - External: USB; FireWire; eSATA; Ethernet
    - Internal SATA; IDE and SCSI: IDE configuration and setup (master; slave; cable select); SCSI IDs (0–15)
    - Hot-swappable drives
- Hard drives: magnetic; 5400 rpm; 7200 rpm; 10,000 rpm; 15,000 rpm
- Solid state/flash drives: CompactFlash; SD; Micro-SD; Mini-SD; xD; SSD
- RAID types: 0; 1; 5; 10
- Floppy drive
- Tape drive
- Media capacity: CD; CD-RW; DVD-RW; DVD; Blu-ray; tape; floppy; DL DVD

1.6 Differentiate among various CPU types and features and select the appropriate cooling method.

- Socket types
    - Intel: LGA, 775, 1155, 1156, 1366
    - AMD: 940, AM2, AM2+, AM3, AM3+, FM1, F
- Characteristics: speeds, cores, cache size/type, hyperthreading, virtualization support, architecture (32-bit vs. 64-bit), integrated GPU
- Cooling: heat sink, fans, thermal paste, liquid-based

1.7 Compare and contrast various connection interfaces and explain their purpose.

- Physical connections
    - USB 1.1 vs. 2.0 vs. 3.0 speed and distance characteristics. Connector types: A, B, mini, micro
    - FireWire 400 vs. FireWire 800 speed and distance characteristics
    - SATA1 vs. SATA2 vs. SATA3, eSATA, IDE speeds
    - Other connector types: serial, parallel, VGA, HDMI, DVI, Audio, RJ-45, RJ-11,
    - Analog vs. digital transmission: VGA vs. HDMI
- Speeds, distances and frequencies of wireless device connections: Bluetooth, IR, RF

1.8 Install an appropriate power supply based on a given scenario: Task 1.5, 2.2, 2.3

- Connector types and their voltages: SATA, Molex, 4/8-pin 12v, PCIe 6/8-pin, 20-pin, 24-pin, floppy
- Specifications: wattage, size, number of connectors, ATX, Micro-ATX; dual-voltage options

1.9 Evaluate and select appropriate components for a custom configuration, to meet customer specifications or needs.

- Graphic/CAD/CAM design workstation: powerful processor, high-end video, maximum RAM
- Audio/video editing workstation: specialized audio and video card, large fast hard drive, dual monitors
- Virtualization workstation: maximum RAM and CPU cores
- Gaming PC: powerful processor, high-end video/specialized GPU, better sound card, high-end cooling
- Home theater PC: surround sound audio, HDMI output, HTPC compact form factor, TV tuner
- Standard thick client: desktop applications, meets recommended requirements for running Windows
- Thin client: basic applications, meets minimum requirements for running Windows
- Home server PC: media streaming, file sharing, print sharing, Gigabit NIC, RAID array

1.10 Given a scenario, evaluate types and features of display devices.

- Types (CRT, LCD, LED, Plasma, Projector, OLED), refresh rates, resolution, native resolution, brightness/lumens, analog vs. digital, privacy/antiglare filters, multiple displays

1.11 Identify connector types and associated cables: Task 2.12

- Display connector types: DVI-D, DVI-I, DVI-A, DisplayPort, RCA, HD15 (i.e. DE15 or DB15), BNC, miniHDMI, RJ-45, miniDin-6
- Display cable types: HDMI, DVI, VGA, component, composite, S-video, RGB, coaxial, Ethernet
- Device connectors and pin arrangements: SATA, eSATA, PATA (IDE, EIDE), floppy, USB, IEEE1394 (SCSI), PS/2, parallel, serial, audio, RJ-45
- Device cable types: SATA, eSATA, IDE, EIDE, floppy, USB, IEEE1394, SCSI (68pin vs. 50pin vs. 25pin), parallel, serial, Ethernet, phone

1.12 Install and configure various peripheral devices: Task 1.16, 2.6, 2.7

- Input devices: mouse, keyboard, touch screen, scanner, barcode reader, KVM, microphone, biometric devices, game pads, joysticks, digitizer

- Multimedia devices: digital cameras, microphone, webcam, camcorder, MIDI enabled devices
- Output devices: printers, speakers, display devices

2.0 Networking

2.1 Identify types of network cables and connectors.

- Fiber. Connectors: SC, ST, and LC
- Twisted Pair. Connectors: RJ-11, RJ-45; wiring standards: T568A, T568B
- Coaxial. Connectors: BNC, F-connector

2.2 Categorize characteristics of connectors and cabling: Task 3.6, 3.7

- Fiber. Types (single-mode vs. multi-mode); speed and transmission limitations
- Twisted pair. Types: STP, UTP, CAT3, CAT5, CAT5e, CAT6, plenum, PVC; speed and transmission limitations
- Coaxial. Types: RG-6, RG-59; speed and transmission limitations

2.3 Explain properties and characteristics of TCP/IP: Task 3.4, 3.6, 3.7

- IP class: Class A, Class B, Class C
- IPv4 vs. IPv6
- Public vs. private vs. APIPA
- Static vs. dynamic
- Client-side DNS
- DHCP
- Subnet mask
- Gateway

2.4 Explain common TCP and UDP ports, protocols, and their purpose.

- Ports: 21 - FTP, 23 - TELNET, 25 - SMTP, 53 - DNS, 80 - HTTP, 110 - POP3, 143 - IMAP, 443 - HTTPS, 3389 - RDP
- Protocols: DHCP, DNS, LDAP, SNMP, SMB, SSH, SFTP
- TCP vs. UDP

2.5 Compare and contrast wireless networking standards and encryption types.

- Standards: 802.11 a/b/g/n; speeds, distances, and frequencies
- Encryption types: WEP, WPA, WPA2, TKIP, AES

2.6 Install, configure, and deploy a SOHO wireless/wired router using appropriate settings: Task 3.17, 3.18

- MAC filtering; channels (1–11); port forwarding, port triggering; SSID broadcast (on/off); wireless encryption; firewall; DHCP (on/off); DMZ; NAT; WPS; basic QoS

2.7 Compare and contrast Internet connection types and features.

- Cable, DSL, dial-up, fiber, satellite, ISDN, cellular (mobile hotspot), line of sight wireless Internet service, WiMAX

2.8 Identify various types of networks.

- LAN, WAN, PAN, MAN
- Topologies: mesh, ring, bus, star, hybrid

2.9 Compare and contrast network devices, their functions, and features.

- Hub, switch, router, access point, bridge, modem, NAS, firewall, VoIP phones, Internet appliance

2.10 Given a scenario, use appropriate networking tools.

- Crimper, multimeter, toner probe, cable tester, loopback plug, punchdown tool

3.0 Laptops

3.1 Install and configure laptop hardware and components: Task 3.12

- Expansion options: express card /34, express card /54, PCMCIA, SODIMM, flash
- Hardware/device replacement: keyboard, hard drive (2.5 vs. 3.5), memory, optical drive, wireless card, Mini-PCIe, screen, DC jack, battery, touchpad, plastics, speaker, system board, CPU

3.2 Compare and contrast the components within the display of a laptop.

- Types: LCD, LED, OLED, plasma
- Wi-Fi antenna connector/placement
- Inverter and its function
- Backlight

3.3 Compare and contrast laptop features.

- Special function keys: dual displays, wireless (on/off), volume settings, screen brightness, Bluetooth (on/off), keyboard backlight
- Docking station vs. port replicator
- Physical laptop lock and cable lock

4.0 Printers

4.1 Explain the differences between the various printer types and summarize the associated imaging process.

- Laser: imaging drum, fuser assembly, transfer belt, transfer roller, pickup rollers, separate pads, duplexing assembly. Imaging process: processing, charging, exposing, developing, transferring, fusing and cleaning.
- Inkjet: ink cartridge, print head, roller, feeder, duplexing assembly, carriage and belt. Calibration.
- Thermal: Feed assembly, heating element, special thermal paper
- Impact: Print head, ribbon, tractor feed, impact paper

4.2 Given a scenario, install, and configure printers: Task 1.27, 1.28, 1.29, 3.5, 3.14

- Use appropriate printer drivers for a given operating system
- Print device sharing: wired (USB, parallel, serial, Ethernet), wireless (Bluetooth, 802.11x, infrared [IR]). Printer hardware print server.
- Printer sharing: sharing local/networked printer via operating system settings

4.3 Given a scenario, perform printer maintenance: Task 2.19, 2.20

- Laser: replacing toner, applying maintenance kit, calibration, cleaning
- Thermal: replace paper, clean heating element, remove debris
- Impact: replace ribbon, replace print head, replace paper

5.0 Operational Procedures

5.1 Given a scenario, use appropriate safety procedures: Task 1.1

- ESD straps
- ESD mats
- Self-grounding
- Equipment grounding
- Personal safety (disconnect power before repairing PC, remove jewelry, lifting techniques, weight limitations, electrical fire safety, CRT safety-proper disposal, cable management)
- Compliance with local government regulations

5.2 Explain environmental impacts and the purpose of environmental controls.

- MSDS documentation for handling and disposal
- Temperature, humidity level awareness and proper ventilation

- Power surges, brownouts, blackouts: battery backup, surge suppressor
- Protection from airborne particles: enclosures, air filters
- Dust and debris: compressed air, vacuums
- Component handling and protection: antistatic bags
- Compliance to local government regulations

5.3 Given a scenario, demonstrate proper communication and professionalism.

- Use proper language: avoid jargon, acronyms, slang when applicable
- Maintain a positive attitude
- Listen and do not interrupt the customer
- Be culturally sensitive
- Be on time (if late contact the customer)
- Avoid distractions: personal calls, talking to co-workers while interacting with customers, personal interruptions
- Dealing with difficult customer or situation
- Avoid arguing with customers and/or being defensive
- Do not minimize customer's problems
- Avoid being judgmental
- Clarify customer statements (ask open ended questions to narrow the scope of the problem, restate the issue or question to verify understanding)
- Set and meet expectations/timeline and communicate status with the customer
- Offer different repair/replacement options if applicable
- Provide proper documentation on the services provided
- Follow up with customer/user at a later date to verify satisfaction
- Deal appropriately with customer's confidential materials: located on a computer, desktop, printer, etc.

5.4 Explain the fundamentals of dealing with prohibited content/activity.

- First response: identify, report through proper channels, data/device preservation
- Use of documentation/documentation changes
- Chain of custody: tracking of evidence/documenting process

A+ Certification Exam Objectives: 220-802

The following table lists the domains measured by this examination and the extent to which they are represented on the exam.

Domain	Percentage of Exam
1.0 Operating Systems	33%
2.0 Security	22%
3.0 Mobile Devices	9%
4.0 Troubleshooting	36%
Total	100%

1.0 Operating Systems

1.1 Compare and contrast the features and requirements of various Microsoft Operating Systems.

- Windows XP Home, Windows XP Professional, Windows XP Media Center, Windows XP 64-bit Professional
- Windows Vista Home Basic, Windows Vista Home Premium, Windows Vista Business, Windows Vista Ultimate, Windows Vista Enterprise
- Windows 7 Starter, Windows 7 Home Premium, Windows 7 Professional, Windows 7 Ultimate, Windows 7 Enterprise
- Features: 32-bit vs. 64-bit; Aero, gadgets, user account control, bit-locker, shadow copy, system restore, ready boost, sidebar, compatibility mode, XP mode, easy transfer, administrative tools, defender, Windows firewall, security center, event viewer, file structure and paths, category view vs. classic view
- Upgrade paths—differences between in place upgrades, compatibility tools, Windows upgrade OS advisor

1.2 Given a scenario, install, and configure the operating system using the most appropriate method: Task 1.17, 1.18, 1.19, 1.20, 1.21, 1.25, 2.4, 2.5, 2.17, 3.2

- Boot methods: USB, CD-ROM, DVD, PXE
- Type of installations: creating image, unattended installation, upgrade, clean install, repair installation, multiboot, remote network installation, image deployment
- Partitioning: dynamic, basic, primary, extended, logical
- File system types/formatting: FAT, FAT32, NTFS, CDFS, quick format vs. full format

- Load alternate third party drivers when necessary
- Workgroup vs. Domain setup
- Time/date/region/language settings
- Driver installation, software and windows updates
- Factory recovery partition

1.3 Given a scenario, use appropriate command line tools: Task 3.4

- Networking: PING, TRACERT, NETSTAT, IPCONFIG, NET, NSLOOKUP, NBT-STAT
- OS: TASKKILL, BOOTREC, SHUTDOWN, TLIST, MD, RD, CD, DEL, FDISK, FORMAT, COPY, XCOPY, ROBOCOPY, DISKPART, SFC, CHKDSK; [command name] /?
- Recovery console: fixboot, fixmbr

1.4 Given a scenario, use appropriate operating system features and tools: Task 1.26, 3.15

- Administrative: computer management, device manager, users and groups, local security policy, performance monitor, services, system configuration, task scheduler, component services, data sources, print management, Windows memory diagnostics, Windows firewall, advanced security
- MSCONFIG: general, boot, services, startup, tools
- Task Manager: applications, processes, performance, networking, users
- Disk management: drive status, mounting, extending partitions, splitting partitions, assigning drive letters, adding drives, adding arrays
- Other: User State Migration tool (USMT), File and Settings Transfer Wizard, Windows Easy Transfer
- Run line utilities: MSCONFIG, REGEDIT, CMD, SERVICES.MSC, MMC, MSTSC, NOTEPAD, EXPLORER, MSINFO32, DXDIAG

1.5 Given a scenario, use Control Panel utilities (the items are organized by "classic view/large icons" in Windows): Task 1.22, 1.23, 1.24, 2.22, 2.23, 2.25, 2.26, 2.27, 4.3

- Common to all Microsoft Operating Systems
- Internet options: Connections, Security, General, Privacy, Programs, Advanced
- Display: Resolution
- User accounts
- Folder options: Sharing, View hidden files, Hide extensions, Layout
- System: Performance (virtual memory), Hardware profiles, Remote settings, System protection
- Security center

- Windows firewall

- Power options: Hibernate, power plans, Sleep/suspend, Standby

- Unique to Windows XP: Add/Remove Programs, network connections, printers and faxes, automatic updates, Network Setup wizard

- Unique to Vista: Tablet PC settings, pen and input devices, offline files, problem reports and solutions, printers

- Unique to Windows 7: HomeGroup, Action center, remote applications and desktop applications, troubleshooting

1.6 Setup and configure Windows networking on a client/desktop: Task 3.1, 3.3, 3.9, 3.10, 3.11, 3.12, 3.13

- HomeGroup, file/print sharing

- WorkGroup vs. domain setup

- Network shares/mapping drives

- Establish networking connections: VPN, dialups, wireless, wired, WWAN (cellular)

- Proxy settings

- Remote desktop

- Home vs. Work vs. Public network settings

- Firewall settings: exceptions, configuration, enabling/disabling Windows firewall

- Configuring an alternative IP address in Windows: IP addressing, subnet mask, DNS, gateway

- Network card properties: half duplex/full duplex/auto, speed, Wake-on-LAN, PoE, QoS

1.7 Perform preventive maintenance procedures using appropriate tools: Task 2.8, 2.9, 2.10, 2.11, 2.13, 4.6

- Best practices: scheduled backups, scheduled check disks, scheduled defragmentation, Windows updates, patch management, driver/firmware updates, antivirus updates

- Tools: Backup, System Restore, Check Disk, recovery image, defrag

1.8 Explain the differences among basic OS security settings.

- User and groups: Administrator, Power user, Guest, Standard user

- NTFS vs. Share permissions: Allow vs. deny, moving vs. copying folders and files, file attributes

- Shared files and folders: administrative shares vs. local shares, permission propagation, inheritance

- System files and folders

- User authentication: single sign-on

1.9 Explain the basics of client-side virtualization.

- Purpose of virtual machines
- Resource requirements
- Emulator requirements
- Security requirements
- Network requirements
- Hypervisor

2.0 Security

2.1 Apply and use common prevention methods: Task 2.16, 3.16, 4.1

- Physical security: lock doors, tailgating, securing physical documents/passwords/shredding, biometrics, badges, key fobs, RFID badge, RSA token, privacy filters, retinal
- Digital security: antivirus, firewalls, antispyware, user authentication/strong passwords, directory permissions
- User education
- Principle of least privilege

2.2 Compare and contrast common security threats: Task 4.4, 4.5

- Social engineering, malware, rootkits, phishing, shoulder surfing, spyware, viruses (worms, Trojans)

2.3 Implement security best practices to secure a workstation: Task 4.4, 4.5

- Setting strong passwords, requiring passwords, restricting user permissions, changing default user names, disabling guest account, screensaver required password, disable autorun

2.4 Given a scenario, use the appropriate data destruction/disposal method: Task 2.24

- Low level format vs. standard format
- Hard drive sanitation and sanitation methods: overwrite, drive wipe
- Physical destruction: shredder, drill, electromagnetic, degaussing tool

2.5 Given a scenario, use the appropriate data destruction/disposal method: Task 3.19

- Change default user-names and passwords
- Changing SSID
- Setting encryption
- Disabling SSID broadcast

- Enable MAC filtering
- Antenna and access point placement
- Radio power levels
- Assign static IP addresses

2.6 Given a scenario, secure a SOHO wired network: Task 2.18

- Change default usernames and passwords
- Enable MAC filtering
- Assign static IP addresses
- Disabling ports
- Physical security

3.0 Mobile Devices

3.1 Explain the basic features of mobile operating systems.

- Android vs. iOS: open source vs. closed source/vendor specific, app source (app store and market), screen orientation (accelerometer/gyroscope), screen calibration, GPS and geotracking

3.2 Establish basic network connectivity and configure email: Task 1.30, 1.31, 3.20, 3.21

- Wireless/cellular data network (enable/disable)
- Bluetooth: enable Bluetooth, enable pairing, find device for pairing, enter appropriate pin code, test connectivity
- Email configuration: server address, POP3, IMAP, port and SSL settings, Exchange, Gmail

3.3 Compare and contrast methods for securing mobile devices.

- Passcode locks, remote wipes, locator applications, remote backup applications, failed login attempts restrictions, antivirus, patching/OS updates

3.4 Compare and contrast hardware differences in regards to tablets and laptops.

- No field serviceable parts
- Typically not upgradeable
- Touch interface: touch flow, multitouch
- Solid state drives

3.5 Execute and configure mobile device synchronization.

- Types of data to synchronize: contacts, programs, email, pictures, music, videos
- Software requirements to install the application on the PC
- Connection types to enable synchronization

4.0 Troubleshooting

4.1 Given a scenario, explain the troubleshooting theory: Task 2.3

- Identify the problem: question the user and identify user changes to computer and perform backups before making changes
- Establish a theory of probable cause (question the obvious)
- Test the theory to determine cause. Once theory is confirmed determine next steps to resolve problem. If theory is not confirmed re-establish new theory or escalate.
- Establish a plan of action to resolve the problem and implement the solution
- Verify full system functionality and if applicable implement preventive measures
- Document findings, actions and outcomes

4.2 Given a scenario, troubleshoot common problems related to motherboards, RAM, CPU and power with appropriate tools: Task 2.21, 4.8, 4.10, 4.15

- Common symptoms: unexpected shutdowns, system lockups, POST code beeps, blank screen on bootup, BIOS time and settings resets, attempts to boot to incorrect device, continuous reboots, no power, overheating, loud noise, intermittent device failure, fans spin-no power to other devices, indicator lights, smoke, burning smell, BSOD
- Tools: multimeter, power supply tester, loopback plugs, POST card

4.3 Given a scenario, troubleshoot hard drives and RAID arrays with appropriate tools: Task 4.17, 4.22, 4.25

- Common symptoms: read/write failure, slow performance, loud clicking noise, failure to boot, drive not recognized, OS not found, RAID not found, RAID stops working, BSOD
- Tools: screwdriver, external enclosures, CHKDSK, CHKDSK, FORMAT, FDISK, file recovery software

4.4 Given a scenario, troubleshoot common video and display issues: Task 4.18

- Common symptoms: VGA mode, no image on screen, overheat shutdown, dead pixels, artifacts, color patterns incorrect, dim image, flickering image, distorted image, discoloration (degaussing), BSOD

4.5 Given a scenario, troubleshoot wired and wireless networks with appropriate tools: Task 3.8, 4.12, 4.13, 4.19, 4.20, 4.21, 4.24

- Common symptoms: no connectivity, APIPA address, limited connectivity, local connectivity, intermittent connectivity, IP conflict, slow transfer speeds, low RF signal
- Tools: cable tester, loopback plug, punch down tools, toner probes, wire strippers, crimper, PING, IPCONFIG, TRACERT, NETSTAT, NBTSTAT, NET, wireless locator

4.6 Given a scenario, troubleshoot operating system problems with appropriate tools: Task 2.28, 4.7, 4.9, 4.15, 4.16, 4.17

- Common symptoms: BSOD, failure to boot, improper shutdown, spontaneous shutdown/restart, RAID not detected during installation, device fails to start, missing dll message, services fails to start, compatibility error, slow system performance, boots to safe mode, file fails to open, missing NTLDR, missing Boot.ini, missing operating system, missing graphical interface, graphical interface fails to load, invalid boot disk
- Tools: fixboot, recovery console, fixmbr, sfc, repair disks, pre-installation environments, MSCONFIG, DEFRAG, REGSRV32, REGEDIT, event viewer, safe mode, command prompt, emergency repair disk, automated system recovery

4.7 Given a scenario, troubleshoot common security issues with appropriate tools and best practices: Task 2.29, 4.2

- Common symptoms: pop-ups, browser redirection, security alerts, slow performance, internet connectivity issues, PC locks up, Windows updates failures, rogue antivirus, spam, renamed system files, files disappearing, file permission changes, hijacked email, access denied
- Tools: anti-virus software, anti-malware software, anti-spyware software, recovery console, system restore, pre-installation environments, event viewer
- Best practices for malware removal
- Identify malware symptoms
- Quarantine infected system
- Disable system restore
- Remediate infected systems
- Update anti-virus software
- Scan and removal techniques (safe mode, pre-installation environment)
- Schedule scans and updates
- Enable system restore and create restore point
- Educate end user

4.8 Given a scenario, troubleshoot, and repair common laptop issues while adhering to the appropriate procedures: Task 4.24

- Common symptoms: no display, dim display, flickering display, sticking keys, intermittent wireless, battery not charging, ghost cursor, no power, num lock indicator lights, no wireless connectivity, no Bluetooth connectivity, cannot display to external monitor

- Disassembling processes for proper re-assembly: document and label cable and screw locations, organize parts, refer to manufacturer documentation, use appropriate hand tools

4.9 Given a scenario, troubleshoot printers with appropriate tools: Task 4.11, 4.12, 4.14, 4.23, 4.26

- Common symptoms: streaks, faded prints, ghost images, toner not fused to the paper, creased paper, paper not feeding, paper jam, no connectivity, garbled characters on paper, vertical lines on page, backed up print queue, low memory errors, access denied, printer will not print, color prints in wrong print color, unable to install printer, error codes

- Tools: maintenance kit, toner vacuum, compressed air, printer spooler

CompTIA®
A+® Complete
Lab Manual

Phase

1

Installing Hardware and Software

Every common task that is performed by a PC technician is hands-on in some way. Although some of the work you do is performed at the keyboard, many of the tasks you will perform in this phase will be spent underneath a desk in someone's cubicle or at a workbench. These are the usual locations for opening a computer case and installing or removing equipment. This phase of the book covers the most common installation tasks for hardware such as RAM, hard drives, and adapter cards. In this phase, you'll also learn how to install and uninstall various types of software, including operating systems and drivers. You will also learn how to work with Bluetooth devices such as printers and mobiles. In general, you'll need at least one PC that you can open up and work with, as well as some common tools. Each task will list the specific requirements you'll need in order to complete the job. This is also true of the software portion of this phase. Now it's time to open the book to the first task, pick up a screwdriver, and get started.

Task 1.1: Preventing ESD Damage

It is amazingly easy to damage the delicate electrical circuitry inside a computer. As a child, you may have rubbed your feet back and forth on a carpet and then touched another person's hand to give them a static shock. What you probably don't realize is that your body carries some electrical potential all of the time. Most of the time, though, the discharge is insufficient to be perceived by the human nervous system. Unfortunately, it is more than enough to fry some components inside a PC. This type of damage can cause maddening intermittent faults in the computer that can seem impossible to diagnose.

Happily, there are precautions you can take to prevent such damage. The most common method (though not recommended as the only method) is to open the PC's access panel and touch the frame of the computer to equalize the electrical potential between you and the computer. This is the "quick and dirty" method of preventing electrostatic discharge (ESD). If you want to do this while working on your own computer, go for it. When you are working with other people's equipment, you'd better stick to safer procedures.

Taking ESD precautions isn't the "sexy" part of PC repair and maintenance, but learning this first will save you one or more migraines as you progress through this book and your career.

Objective

This task covers objective 220:801:5.1.

Scenario

You have a PC on your workbench that needs to have its memory upgraded (see Task 1.2). You are about to remove the screws from the PC case's access panel and take off the panel. You have just been briefed by your supervisor on the proper method of preventing ESD damage to the inside of the computer. All of the necessary equipment has been provided, and you begin going through the necessary precautionary procedures.

 Many desktop computer cases today have latches rather than an access panel held on by screws, but you will likely work on older PCs that will require the use of a screwdriver, so always keep one handy. Throughout the book, I will refer to using a screwdriver to open a PC case.

Scope of Task

Duration

This should only take a few minutes.

Setup

You don't actually have to open the computer for this task; all you'll need to do is set up the ESD precautions.

Caveat

Although this is a single task, you would be wise to perform it every time you open a computer case. The few minutes it takes to implement these procedures could save you hours of trying to figure out some problem caused by a stray static shock or having to replace a motherboard.

Procedure

This lesson will show you how to implement proper ESD procedures.

Equipment Used

You'll need at least an ESD wrist strap, but you can also get an ESD cover for your workbench and a mat to stand on while working on the computer. Always have antistatic bags ready for any components you remove from the computer.

Use your favorite search engine and enter the search string "ESD equipment" or "ESD equipment suppliers" to see the different tools available for taking ESD precautions and where they can be purchased.

Details

This exercise will show you the steps to take to prevent ESD damage while working on a computer.

Taking Steps to Prevent ESD Damage

1. Verify that your workbench is covered with an ESD mat before placing a computer on the bench.

2. Make sure there is an ESD mat where you will be standing while working on a computer.

3. Check to make sure whatever component you are installing is stored in an antistatic bag.

Try not to wear synthetic clothing while working on a computer.

Don't use Styrofoam while working on the computer. If you have to have a cup of coffee, use a ceramic cup (although drinking anything around an open computer is asking for trouble). Passing a piece of Styrofoam over electrical components can damage them.

4. Place an antistatic strap around one of your wrists.

5. Clip the other end of the cable attached to the strap to the frame of the computer.

Another activity that can cause ESD damage is vacuuming the interior of the PC case with an ordinary vacuum cleaner. Use a can of compressed air or a vacuum unit specifically designed to work inside a PC instead. To clean components, use antistatic sprays instead of detergents. Do not spray any liquid onto an internal computer component. Instead, spray the liquid onto a lint-free cloth or swab and then use that to clean the component. Rubbing an eraser inside the case also can build up static.

Criteria for Completion

You will have successfully completed this task when you have secured your work area and yourself with ESD equipment. You are now ready to open the computer case.

Task 1.2: Installing RAM

RAM, or random access memory, is the desktop of the computer. Anytime a PC user wants to open a program to read email, surf the Web, or play a game, that program is loaded into memory from the hard drive and will stay in memory for as long as it's active. How many programs a PC can run at the same time without a noticeable slowdown of performance depends on how much RAM is in the computer. Naturally, the more RAM a computer has, the better.

 The RAM used in desktop PCs is commonly referred to as DRAM (pronounced "DEE-ram"), or dynamic random access memory.

Installing RAM sticks is an extremely common task for a PC technician. You'll likely spend countless hours on the floor or at a workbench, installing or upgrading RAM. Although choosing the correct type of RAM is vitally important, it is fairly simple to research the computer you are working on to discover exactly which type it takes.

Once you have the correct stick of RAM for the computer, all that's left to do is to power down the PC, open it, and install the stick. This task will guide you through the steps necessary to find the appropriate type of RAM for a particular computer and physically install it.

Objective

This task covers objective 220-801:1.3.

Scenario

One of the users in Accounting has recently had installed on her PC new software that is required for a special project she is working on. The application consumes a great deal of memory to run, and she complains that when she tries to work with the software, computer performance slows dramatically. Your supervisor has determined that the user's PC has insufficient RAM to run this piece of software along with the other applications she must access as part of her job. You have been assigned to upgrade the amount of memory in her machine. You will need a computer with access to the Internet to research the type of RAM stick that is correct for the particular PC you'll be working on. You will also need to have a computer in which you can install a RAM stick and the appropriate RAM itself. Make sure you have a screwdriver to remove the side panel of the computer so you can access the interior. You'll need to take the appropriate steps to prevent ESD damage to the sensitive electrical components inside the PC as well as to the RAM stick you are about to install. See Task 1.1 for details about ESD precautions.

Scope of Task

Duration

This task should take about 15–30 minutes.

Setup

All you'll need for this task is a single computer with at least one empty RAM slot, an appropriate stick of RAM, and a screwdriver that will fit the screws holding the side access panel on the PC.

Caveat

Depending on the type of computer you are working on, how the PC's access panel is attached will vary, so the instructions in this task may not be quite the same for your PC. The memory slots can be located on different areas of the motherboard on different computers, so you will have to take a moment to locate them. Some RAM slots can be difficult to reach and require that you remove other components first, making your task a bit harder. The occasional scraped knuckle is to be expected when working inside a PC. This example uses a computer running 64-bit Windows 7 Professional. If you are using a different operating system, the steps you use to test and verify that RAM has been added may not be identical to the steps in this task. When selecting the type of RAM, make sure that you use the correct amount of memory. Also, some motherboards care which memory slots you place the first and second sticks of RAM into, so you may have to switch sticks between slots in order to have the computer recognize all of the RAM installed.

It is very common for modern computers to run 64-bit (x64) operating systems rather than the 32-bit (x86) versions. 64-bit operating systems support much more memory than 32-bit machines. Make sure you verify which type and version of operating system a computer runs before attempting a memory upgrade. For more information, go to http://bit.ly/uyjqdK.

Procedure

In this task, you will learn how to determine which type of memory is correct for a particular PC, open the PC, install an additional stick of RAM on the motherboard, close the PC, and verify that the additional RAM is detected and being used by the computer. Part of locating the right type of RAM involves visiting the website of a commercial memory vendor. It will not be necessary to purchase RAM from this vendor; you will simply visit this site to find the type of RAM your computer uses.

Equipment Used

You should need only a single screwdriver to complete this task, although some PCs come with a latch system that lets you open the panel without any tools at all.

Details

The following sections walk you through determining the computer's manufacturer and model type, using that information to find out what kind of memory is correct for this machine, and installing and testing the additional RAM.

Determining the Correct Type of Memory for a Particular PC

DETERMINING THE MAKE AND MODEL OF A PC

1. Look at the front of the computer.
2. Locate the name of the computer manufacturer and the name and number of the model.

LOCATING THE CORRECT RAM TYPE FOR A COMPUTER

1. Open a web browser on a computer with an Internet connection.
2. In the URL field, type `www.crucial.com`.
3. On the Crucial website, click Memory (RAM) in the overhead menu.
4. Click the Select Manufacturer list to open it.
5. Select the name of the maker of the computer.
6. Click the Select Product Line drop-down arrow.
7. Select the model name of the computer.
8. Click the Select Model drop-down arrow.
9. Select the specific model of the computer.
10. Click the FIND IT button.

11. Locate the specific type and amount of RAM you need.

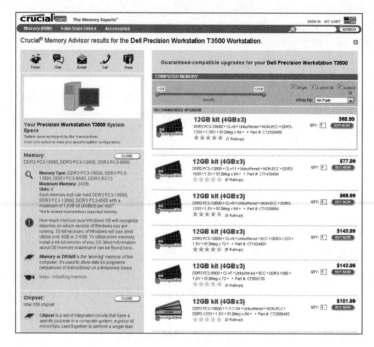

 You can also select the Scan Your System link to view your specific computer specifications and memory requirements, but you will have to download and install the scanner on your PC. The option to scan your system is also available on the Crucial Memory main page. On the Memory main page, you can also shop by memory type or category or directly select the name of a manufacturer.

12. Click the picture of the RAM stick or the More Details link in the desired row.

13. Locate the memory-module details and, if necessary, scroll down and locate the product details.

14. Write down the specific details about the stick of RAM you need.

15. Close the web browser.

Installing a Stick of RAM

OPENING THE CASE

1. Power down your computer and wait until it is completely off.

WARNING   Some technicians feel that for complete safety, the power cord should be unplugged from the computer's power supply as well.

2. Use your screwdriver to remove the screws attaching the access panel to the computer case.

3. Remove the access panel.

4. Before proceeding, take ESD precautions, such as placing an ESD strap on your wrist and attaching the other end to the metal frame of the PC.

INSTALLING A MEMORY STICK

1. Place the PC on its side or in a position that gives you access to the motherboard.

2. Locate the RAM slots.

WARNING   See the following graphic for an example of how to locate RAM slots on a motherboard.

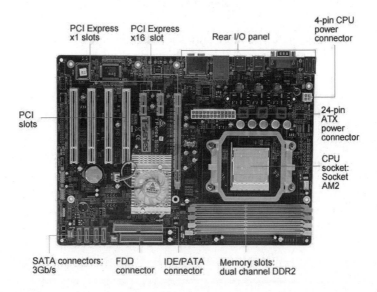

3. Remove the RAM stick from its antistatic bag, being careful not to touch the pins.

4. Pull the latches back from the slot.

5. Position the stick of RAM so that the notch on the stick is appropriately aligned with the tab on the slot, angling the stick so one end of the stick enters the slot first.

6. Slowly but firmly press down the stick of RAM causing first one end of the stick to enter the slot, and then the other, until both latches on the slot click into position.

7. If you are wearing an ESD strap, after removing your hands from inside the PC case, unclip the cord of the strap from the PC frame and remove the strap from your wrist.

8. Replace the access panel.

9. Replace the screws so that the access panel is held firmly to the PC's frame.

10. Return the PC to its original position.

TESTING THE MEMORY

1. Power on the computer.

If you unplugged the power cord, you will need to plug it back in first.

2. Listen for one beep as the computer boots.

Beep codes differ depending on the type of BIOS used in your mother-board. To learn more about different types of BIOS and their associated beep codes, visit www.pchell.com/hardware/beepcodes.shtml or go to your favorite search engine and search for "beep codes."

3. Look for a message on the monitor indicating that the amount of memory on the computer has changed.

4. Follow any instructions you see on the monitor.

5. Allow the computer to continue to boot and the operating system to load.

VERIFYING THE MEMORY

1. On the computer desktop, click the Windows Start button.

2. Right-click Computer and select Properties.

If Computer isn't in your Start menu, it can most likely be found on the desktop.

3. In the System Properties dialog box under System, locate the amount of RAM in the PC.

4. Click Cancel to close the System Properties dialog box.

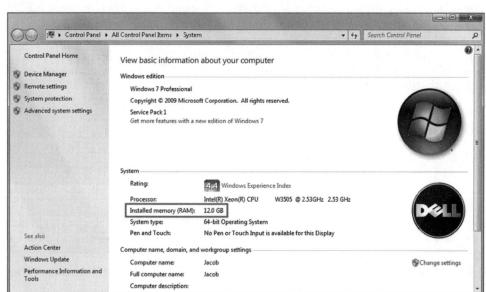

Criteria for Completion

You have completed this task when you have verified that the amount of RAM has increased to the correct amount. This amount will vary depending on how much RAM the computer originally had and how much you added.

Task 1.3: Installing a PCI Card

Despite the popularity and ease of use of USB devices and the ubiquitous use of PCI Express in modern computers, many hardware features of a PC continue to be supported by PCI, or Peripheral Component Interconnect, cards on older PCs. Actually, PCI is an industry standard that describes how data is managed on the PCI bus of a computer's motherboard in terms of clock speed and throughput rate. The PCI bus has replaced the now obsolete Industry Standard Architecture (ISA) expansion bus in modern computers. PCI cards are added to the main circuit board of a computer to add hardware functionality such as a modem, sound card, or network interface card (NIC).

WARNING

PCI Express is the modern standard that has all but replaced the aging PCI bus (see Task 1.4). You'll find an excellent overview of this technology here: http://bit.ly/c34FLr.

Installing or upgrading a PCI card in a computer is a common task for the PC technician; in most cases it is quite easy to do, thanks to Plug and Play (PnP) technology. Older expansion bus cards required the technician to manually configure the I/O and IRQ values for the new card to prevent it from attempting to use resources that were already allocated to another piece of equipment. Configuring I/O and IRQ values is becoming a lost art. Today, this configuration is done automatically for the most part, and all you really need to do is install the card and expect it to work.

Objective

This task covers objective 220-801:1.4.

Scenario

Your company has just opened a small branch office nearby that requires several computers to be networked on a LAN and to have Internet access. One of the computers is an older unit that had a failed NIC. That card has been removed but a replacement was never installed. You have located an appropriate NIC that you can install in a PCI slot on the PC's motherboard. You must travel to the branch office to install the card. You will need to have a PCI card for this task as well as a screwdriver to remove the screws anchoring the side access panel to the computer's metal frame. Finally, you'll need to take the appropriate steps to prevent ESD damage to the sensitive electrical components inside the PC and the new NIC. See Task 1.1 for details.

A local area network, or LAN, is a group of networked computers, printers, and other devices in a single physical location such as a home, office, or suite of offices. For more about what a LAN is, go to http://bit.ly/eRSvLG.

Scope of Task

Duration

This task should take approximately 30 minutes.

Setup

For the general task of installing a PCI card, all you'll need is a single computer with at least one empty PCI slot, a PCI card, and a screwdriver that will fit the screws holding the side access panel on the PC. PCI slot covers are also usually attached to the computer by screws. You may need an additional screwdriver if the screw types for the access panel and the PCI slots are different. Although the task scenario specifies a NIC, you can use any PCI card to perform the actual task on your computer.

For the purpose of installing a NIC and testing network connectivity, you will need two computers networked together through a switch or a router. Most home computer users with two desktop computers have them networked using Ethernet cables connected to a switch. The switch is connected to a DSL or cable modem, which acts as a DHCP server, assigning the computers' IP addresses. For the networking part of the task, this is the type of setup that is required in order to test the success of installing the new NIC.

 To learn more about networking terms such as *DHCP*, *IP address*, and *router*, visit http://bit.ly/AwYJSZ and http://bit.ly/wGUtju. For more about switches, see http://bit.ly/4eCbU. Also see Chapter 3, "Networking Computer Systems," of this book for more about these topics.

In our scenario, the computer is already configured to be recognized by the server that controls the network.

 If you absolutely have no access to a PC that supports PCI, skip ahead to Task 1.4, "Installing a PCI Express Card," since the task is almost the same as installing a PCI card.

Caveat

The same caveats that applied to Task 1.2 apply here in terms of how to actually open the computer's access panel and where the PCI slots are located on your particular motherboard. The procedure for installing the new card is identical regardless of the operating system installed on the machine. The process of testing the card subsequently described uses an older Windows XP computer as an example.

Procedure

In this task, you will learn how to install a PCI card into the PCI slot on a computer's motherboard. You will also learn how to determine if the card is functioning correctly once it's installed.

Equipment Used

You may need a flat-head screwdriver and/or a Phillips screwdriver, depending on the types of screws holding the access panel and PCI slot cover to the computer. As mentioned in Task 1.2, some computer access covers use a latch system that doesn't require the use of a screwdriver. Also, some PCI slot covers are attached by latches that can be opened without a tool.

 If you don't know if your computer has one or more PCI slots, you can search online for "PCI vs. PCI express slots" to see comparative images such as those found at http://bit.ly/mKnRh7.

Details

The following sections guide you through the process of installing a PCI card on a PC and verifying that the card is functioning correctly.

Installing a PCI Card

OPENING THE CASE

1. Power down your computer and wait until it is completely off. For additional safety, unplug the power cord from the back of the computer.
2. Locate your screwdriver, and remove the screws attaching the access panel to the computer case.
3. Remove the access panel, and before putting your hands inside the case, don't forget to take ESD precautions.

INSTALLING THE PCI CARD

1. Locate the PCI slots on the motherboard and select the one you will use.
2. Locate the appropriate screwdriver, and remove the screws attaching the PCI slot cover from the PC's frame.
3. Remove the cover and put it aside.
4. Remove the PCI card from its antistatic container.

 All electronic components should be stored in an antistatic container to prevent ESD damage.

5. Identify the pins on the PCI card; these pins connect the card to the motherboard.
6. Orient the card so that the pins line up correctly with the PCI slot.
7. Identify the Ethernet port on the PCI card; the network or patch cable will be plugged into this Ethernet port.
8. Orient the card so that the NIC's port lines up with the opening in the back of the PC.
9. Gently but firmly press the PCI card into the slot, making sure it is fully engaged.
10. Use the PCI slot cover screw to secure the PCI card to the PC's frame.
11. Replace the access panel.
12. Replace the screws securing the access panel to the PC's frame.
13. Return the PC to its original location, and replace the PC's power cable.

TESTING THE PCI CARD

1. Power on the computer.
2. Wait for the PC to boot and load the operating system.
3. Plug the patch cable into the NIC's port.

The link light on the NIC should go on if the NIC is active and if the other end of the cord is plugged into an active port on a network switch.

4. Click Start ≻ Run.

5. In the Run box, type **cmd** and click OK.

6. When the command emulator opens, type **ipconfig/all** and press Enter.

7. If the output displays the IP address and subnet mask of the PC and other network configuration settings, the PCI NIC is working.

The one exception is if the computer cannot connect to the DHCP server. Windows XP, Vista, and Windows 7 are configured by default to use Automatic Private IP Addressing (APIPA) if the computer cannot acquire a dynamic address. If the address is returned in the 169.254.*x.x* range and the subnet mask is 255.255.0.0, the computer is using APIPA. Consult with your network administrator to find out what subnet mask and IP address range you should expect the computer to acquire. To learn more about APIPA, visit this site: http://bit.ly/F0MxEh.

If the computer hasn't received addressing information, it doesn't necessarily mean that the installation didn't go well. You may have to type **ipconfig/release** and press Enter and then type **ipconfig/renew** and press Enter to acquire an IP address from the DHCP server.

Criteria for Completion

You have completed the task when the PCI NIC functions correctly, allowing network communications between the PC and the rest of the network. You may have installed a different type of PCI card, such as a video or sound card. If so, the criteria for completion is the successful testing and operation of those cards based on their purpose.

Task 1.4: Installing a PCI Express Card

As mentioned in Task 1.3, the PCI standard is aging and is no longer capable of meeting the current needs for speed and performance, particularly in the arena of graphics cards. AGP (Accelerated Graphics Port) cards are also an aging technology having the same issues. The most common reason for an upgrade to a PCI Express (PCIe) graphics card is to let you run games faster and to add TV/DVI (Digital Video Interface) to your computer system.

Fortunately, installing a PCIe graphics card is a relatively simple task, akin to installing a PCI card. The processes are different enough to make creating a separate task worthwhile. To learn more about the PCIe standard, see the URL in the introduction to Task 1.3. Also, Wikipedia provides a good description of the PCIe standards and specifications: http://en.wikipedia.org/wiki/PCI_Express.

Objective

This task covers objective 220-801:1.4.

Scenario

You have a PC in your workshop with a customer request to install a PCIe graphics card. You have been provided with the necessary card, and your only task is to install it and the drivers. The computer's motherboard is current and PCIe-capable. You will need to have available a flat-head screwdriver and/or a Phillips screwdriver to enable you to remove the PC's access panel and to remove the card-slot cover. After the card has been installed, you will need to use the accompanying disc to install the drivers. Be sure to follow ESD precautions to prevent damage to the PC's electronic components (see Task 1.1).

 To find out about device drivers, go to http://bit.ly/gEL101.

Scope of Task

Duration

This should take about 30 minutes.

Setup

You'll need a computer that can connect to the Internet. The computer should have at least one empty PCIe slot, and you'll need a PCIe card and a screwdriver that will fit the screws holding the side access panel on the PC. You may also need a second screwdriver for any screws attaching the PCIe-slot cover to the PC's frame. If you are unsure whether your motherboard supports the PCIe bus standard, check your motherboard manual.

The card may come with additional features such as a heat sink and cooling fan. The fan may need an external power source. Consult the card's documentation for any additional requirements before proceeding.

You will also need the driver disc for the PCIe graphics card. The driver disc should come with the card. Although the scenario specifies a PCIe graphics card, you can use any

PCIe card you have available to complete this task, but make sure you have the drivers for the card. As always, follow ESD precautions while working inside the PC case. You can use a computer running any Microsoft Windows operating system for this task. A Windows XP Professional computer was used for this exercise.

If you are interested in actually installing a PCIe graphics card suitable for gaming but are unsure how to select the right card, visit www.build-gaming-computers.com/gaming-video-card.html for more information.

Caveat

A PCIe card, unlike the older PCI or AGP cards, can fit into a slot its own size or larger on the motherboard but cannot fit into a smaller-sized slot, so verify the size of the card and slot before proceeding. The PCIe bus uses pairs of point-to-point serial links called lanes rather than a shared parallel bus. Depending on the lane speeds supported by the PCIe card and the motherboard, the number of pins on the card can be different. PCIe card and slot types include x1, x4, x8, and x16. Make sure that the lane speeds for the card and motherboard are compatible by checking card and motherboard documentation.

Procedure

This lesson will show you how to install a PCIe graphics card and then install the card's drivers from a disc.

Equipment Used

You'll need a flat-head screwdriver and/or a Phillips screwdriver to remove the screws from the PC access panel and from the PCIe slot cover. Some covers, however, are attached by tabs or latches that require no special tools. Although you may not consider a disc a tool, you'll need to have the card's driver disc handy.

Some expansion cards and other hardware can be installed without a driver disc if Windows already has the drivers available, but this is not guaranteed. Check the documentation that came with the PCIe card to verify the installation instructions.

Details

The following sections guide you through the process of installing a PCIe graphics card on a PC and installing the card's drivers from a disc.

Installing a PCIe Graphics Card

OPENING THE CASE

1. Power down your computer and wait until it is completely off. For additional safety, unplug the power cord from the back of the computer.

2. Locate your screwdriver and remove the screws attaching the access panel to the computer case.

3. Remove the access panel and position the PC on its side. Apply ESD precautions before proceeding.

INSTALLING THE PCIE CARD

1. Locate the PCIe slots on the motherboard and select the one you will use.

2. Locate the appropriate screwdriver and, if necessary, replace the PCIe slot screws to secure the PCIe card.

3. Remove the cover and put it aside. For some cards, you may need to remove more than one slot cover to accommodate the size of the heat sink and fan on the card, if they are present.

4. Remove the PCIe card from its antistatic container, holding it by its edges.

5. Orient the card so that the pins are aligned correctly with the slot.

6. Gently but firmly, push the card into the slot until it is securely installed. Push the plastic slot latch, if present, to the up position to more securely seat the card.

7. Replace the PCIe slot screws to secure the PCIe card.

8. If your card has a fan, verify that the fan is clear of any cables or other obstructions.

9. If your card's documentation states that it requires an external power connection, locate the necessary power cable that came with the card. Connect the correct ends of the cable to the motherboard and to the card.

10. Verify that the card is secure in the slot and that all connections are firm.

11. Replace the PC's access panel, securing it with the accompanying screws, place the PC upright, and replace the PC's power cable.

INSTALLING THE PCIE GRAPHICS CARD DRIVERS

1. Power up the computer.

2. Wait for the computer to completely boot and for the operating system to load, verifying that no error messages occur.

3. Locate the disc containing the drivers for the graphics card.

4. Open the CD/DVD drive, insert the disc, and close the drive.

5. Follow the onscreen instructions for installing the drivers. The instructions will vary depending on the make and model of the graphics card. See Task 1.17 for more information about installing drivers from a disc.

6. When prompted, remove the disc and reboot the computer.

7. After the computer has rebooted and the operating system has loaded, open a web browser and locate the PCIe graphics card manufacturer's website.

8. Locate the current drivers for the card you installed, download and install the most current drivers from the website. The drivers on the disc will almost certainly be out of date. See Task 1.18 for more information on installing drivers from the Internet.

9. Reboot the computer again.

10. When the computer has rebooted and the operating system has loaded, verify the operation of the graphics card by right-clicking the desktop, clicking Properties, clicking Settings, and then configuring the screen resolution to the desired setting.

11. Close all dialog boxes when finished.

Criteria for Completion

You will have successfully completed this task when you have installed the PCIe graphics card and the card's drivers and have verified that the card and the PC are functioning correctly. If you installed a different type of PCIe card, the criteria for completion are the successful testing and operation of the card based on its purpose.

Task 1.5: Installing a Power Supply

The term *power supply* is a bit misleading. A PC's power-supply unit takes the AC current from an electrical wall socket (actually, from the wall socket and through a surge protector if you're smart) and converts it to DC current that the computer can use. Should the power supply fail, however, the PC and its components are about as useful as a box of rocks.

Installing a power supply is pretty straightforward. However, you do need to make sure that the voltage and wattage match the computer's requirements. Unless you buy a bare-bones PC kit, any PC you purchase will have the power supply already installed. You are likely to need to install a power supply only if you're building a computer from scratch. It is more common that you'll replace a power supply that has failed. The original power supply will have the necessary specifications recorded on its case, telling you what you need to know to order a suitable replacement.

WARNING   If you truly don't know what power supply you need, you can look up the computer's requirements on the manufacturer's website or go to the motherboard maker's site and search there.

Replacing a power supply may seem like a daunting task, but it's one of the easiest jobs you'll face as a PC technician.

Objective

This task covers objective 220-801:1.8.

Scenario

You received a trouble ticket stating that the power supply in the HR manager's computer has failed. You have removed the PC from the manager's office and now have it on your workbench. You looked up the computer make and model on the Web and found out the specifications for the appropriate replacement. You pulled the replacement unit from the supply closet and have it on the bench with the computer. You are ready to open the case, remove the old power supply, and install the new one.

Scope of Task

Duration

This task should take about 15 to 20 minutes.

Setup

Ideally, you'll need a PC and an appropriate replacement power supply for the computer. If your power supply doesn't need to be replaced and you want to save yourself the cost of buying a new one, you can just remove the power supply unit from your PC and then reinstall it. You will follow the same steps in either case. As always, take ESD precautions (discussed in Task 1.1) to avoid accidentally damaging electrical components on the motherboard.

Caveat

You can upgrade a PC to use a more robust power supply, especially if you have installed newer components in the computer that are power-hungry. Just make sure that the specifications of the power-supply upgrade match the computer's requirements. Check the motherboard's and power supply's documentation to determine whether you need additional adapters or other equipment to correctly perform the upgrade. It should also go without saying that you will need to completely unplug the power supply from its power source before beginning this exercise.

Procedure

In this task, you will learn how to replace a PC's power supply and verify that the new unit is operational.

Equipment Used

Other than the new power supply, all you'll need is a screwdriver to remove the PC's access panel and the old power supply. To verify that the replacement is successful, you'll need a monitor, keyboard, and mouse attached to the PC when you power it up.

Details

The following exercise will walk you through the process of removing a failed power supply and replacing it with a new unit.

WARNING   Before attempting this exercise, make sure you have powered down the computer and unplugged the power cord from the back of the PC!

Removing and Replacing a Power Supply

REMOVING THE POWER SUPPLY

1. Locate the screwdriver and remove the screws from the PC's access panel and put them aside.
2. Remove the access panel.
3. Locate the power supply.

NOTE   It's virtually impossible to not be able to find a computer's power supply. The back of the power supply contains a large fan and the connector for the power cord and is easily seen on the back of the PC.

4. Make careful notes of how the unit is mounted to the case and how the wires are connected to the motherboard, to the hard drive, to the floppy/CD/DVD/Blu-ray drives, and possibly to the graphics card.

NOTE   Not all power supplies have the same number or type of power connectors. Three is a common number, but your unit may be different. See this site for an example: http://bit.ly/FPr9rU. Note that, depending on the requirements of the replacement unit and your motherboard, you may need additional pin adapters or extensions.

5. Disconnect the power supply's wires from the motherboard.

6. Unscrew the power supply from the PC's frame.

7. Lift the old power supply out of the computer.

INSTALLING THE POWER SUPPLY

1. Locate the replacement power supply.

2. Mount the new unit in the PC frame in the same way the old unit was mounted.

3. Screw the new unit to the computer frame, making sure it is secure.

4. Connect the power supply's wires to the motherboard in the same way the old unit was attached.

5. Make sure the connections are firm.

6. Replace the PC's access panel.

7. Secure the access panel to the PC by replacing the screws.

TESTING THE POWER SUPPLY

1. Verify that a monitor, keyboard, and mouse are attached to the PC.

2. Plug the power cord into the socket on the back of the power supply.

3. Verify that the power cord is plugged into a surge protector that is receiving AC current.

4. Power up the computer and watch the boot process.

5. Check that all disks, CD and DVD drives are working (missing the power to a DVD or second disk will not be immediately obvious after a boot).

See the section 'Replacing a Power Supply in a Computer' in Task 2.3 for further details.

Criteria for Completion

You have successfully completed this task when the PC powers up normally and the operating system loads.

Task 1.6: Installing an IDE Hard Drive

Periodically, hard drives fail (which is why you always back up your computers and servers... right?). If your data is backed up, it's an inconvenience but not a total disaster. You can simply replace the failed unit with a new comparable drive (while you're at it, you might as well put in a hard drive with more capacity). You might also end up installing a second hard drive in a computer, but that depends on your needs and the computing environment in which the PC is located.

There are a few details that you'll need to know to successfully install a hard drive, but it's a fairly routine task. The time-consuming part is reinstalling the operating system and the application software and then restoring the data from your backup tape or external drive.

Installing an operating system is covered in Tasks 1.20 and 1.21, and installing application software is addressed in Task 1.22. The actual restoration of data from backups in a production environment is usually handled by an experienced tech in an IT department, so that task is beyond the scope of this book.

Objective

This task covers objective 220-801: 1.5.

Scenario

You have been directed to install a hard drive in a new computer. The hard drive already has an operating system and application software installed via "ghosting".

It's typical in production environments to configure a hard drive on a master machine and then "ghost" it to other drives and install those drives in PCs. This saves a lot of time in deploying PCs with identical configurations in the company.

The computer is on your workbench, with the hard drive and IDE ribbon cable sitting next to it.

The ribbon cable is used for data transfer. The power cable for the hard drive uses a Molex connector to attach to the drive and typically will be attached to the computer's power supply.

Scope of Task

Duration

This task should take 15 to 30 minutes.

Setup

For this task, you'll need a hard drive and a PC. If you are not in a position to install a new hard drive, you can remove the hard-disk drive (HDD) from the computer and then replace it. As always, take ESD precautions to avoid damaging electrical components in the computer.

Caveat

In this exercise, you will be installing an Integrated Drive Electronics (IDE) hard drive. An IDE drive is also referred to as ATA or PATA (Parallel ATA) drive. Most modern PCs ship with SATA drives onboard, and they have all but replaced PATA drives as a storage standard. However, there are still plenty of PCs that use PATA drives, and the current A+ exam expects you to know how to install these older drives. Installing a SATA drive is only slightly different from installing an IDE drive; however, there are enough differences to require that the process have a task dedicated to such an installation.

Installing a SATA drive is described in Task 1.7.

In the last few years, solid-state drives (SSDs), otherwise known as electronic disk drives, have been entering the mainstream storage drive market, and some computers, such as Apple's MacBook Air, come standard with SSDs. This storage type is covered in the 220-801 objectives under Domain 1.5.

Procedure

In this task, you'll learn how to install an IDE hard drive in a computer.

Equipment Used

You'll need an IDE hard drive and a parallel ribbon cable to connect the hard drive to the motherboard. Besides a screwdriver, you'll also need a pair of needle-nose pliers or a pair of strong tweezers. For testing you will need a monitor, keyboard, and mouse.

Details

The following steps will guide you through the process of installing an IDE hard drive into a PC.

Installing a Hard Drive

INSTALLING THE HARD DRIVE IN A PC

1. Verify that the PC is powered down and unplugged.
2. Locate a screwdriver and remove the screws from the PC's access panel.
3. Remove the access panel.
4. Locate the IDE connectors on the PC's motherboard.

WARNING A motherboard usually has two IDE connectors. One is used for the primary hard drive, which you are installing now. The other is typically used to attach a CD or DVD drive or can be used for a second hard drive.

5. Locate the power cord with the Molex connector for the hard drive; it will be coming out of the power supply.

6. Locate the holes in the hard drive's bay in the computer; this is where you will use screws to attach the hard drive to the bay.

7. Locate the drive jumpers or switches.

NOTE A hard drive needs to be set to perform a specific function, such as master, slave, only drive, or cable select.This is controlled by a set of either jumpers or switches on the hard drive. They are usually located on the part of the drive containing the ribbon and power connectors. A diagram on the hard drive will show you the position for the jumpers or switches for each role. Your drive is most likely set up to function as the only drive in the PC.

8. Locate the jumper or switch diagram on the drive.

9. If the jumpers or switches are set for only the hard drive or master role, move on.

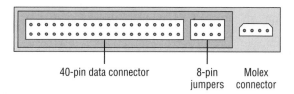

40-pin data connector   8-pin jumpers   Molex connector

10. If the jumpers or switches are not configured correctly, move them to the correct position with your needle-nose pliers or your tweezers.

NOTE You can use your fingernails if you are fairly dexterous, but the chances of dropping a tiny jumper into the bowels of your PC are high.

11. Connect the ribbon cable to the ribbon connector on the hard drive.

12. Connect the hard drive power cable to the power connector on the hard drive.

13. Place the hard drive in its bay, but do not attach it.

NOTE Both of these connectors can fit only one way. Be especially careful connecting the ribbon cable to the hard drive and motherboard, because the pins are thin and easily bent.

Putting one or both hands inside a PC case is difficult; often there isn't very much room for you to work. Make sure all your connections are in place before you mount the hard drive to the PC bay.

Some hard drives mount differently. Instead of installing them from the inside, you must remove the face plate from the front of the PC and slide the hard drive in from the front. However, if this is the case, you will not be able to connect the cables to the drive until after it is mounted in the front loading bay.

Some hard drives mount in trays rather than bays and are secured by pins and a plastic holding arm. These trays are designed to secure a hard drive unit of exact physical dimensions. If you upgrade a computer's hard drive and the drive is even slightly physically larger than the original drive, the new drive may poorly fit in the tray or not fit at all, leaving you with no place to secure the new drive. Before replacing any type of storage drive, verify the computer's requirements, including drive unit dimensions.

14. Connect the ribbon cable to the IDE connector on the motherboard.

15. Use the screws that came with the hard drive to mount the drive into the bay securely.

You could probably leave the hard drive sitting loosely in the bay and finish the installation. PCs don't move around much once they are installed in an office or cubicle, but there is still a risk that the hard drive will fall out of the bay and damage the motherboard if the PC is subsequently kicked or moved.

16. Replace the access panel.

17. Secure the access panel to the PC by replacing the screws.

TESTING THE HARD-DRIVE INSTALLATION

1. Verify that a monitor, keyboard, and mouse are connected to the PC.

2. Make sure the power cord is connected and that the computer is receiving power.

3. Power up the unit and watch the boot process.

Because a ghosted hard drive is used in this scenario, there shouldn't be any issues with hard-drive formatting or loading of software. The computer should boot and load the operating system.

Criteria for Completion

You will have successfully completed the task when the computer boots normally and the operating system loads.

Task 1.7: Installing a SATA Hard Drive

Now that you've experienced the installation of an IDE drive, it's time to move on to some more recent technology. The most common reason to install a SATA drive is that it's the current industry standard, or to upgrade a computer's storage from IDE. As previously mentioned, the installation process isn't much different from installing an IDE drive, but there are enough dissimilarities to warrant a separate task in this book.

While Task 1.6 didn't require you to install an operating system, application software, or data onto the IDE drive because it was ghosted, this task is constructed to end at the point where you would normally begin installing an operating system. Tasks 1.20 and 1.21 describe installing Windows XP and Windows Vista, respectively, so for additional details, you can skip ahead to those tasks. This task does require that you set the BIOS to recognize the new SATA drive, which isn't always a straightforward process.

Objective

This task covers objective 220-801: 1.5.

Scenario

Your company is in the process of conducting a long-term upgrade of the older PCs in each department from IDE to SATA drives. The operating systems, applications, and data are to be reinstalled on the new drives once they are physically upgraded in each computer. You have been tasked to install the SATA drive and then prepare the drive so that the operating system can be reinstalled. The PC is sitting on your workbench and you are ready to begin work.

Scope of Task

Duration

This task should take about 30 minutes.

Setup

For this task, you'll need a SATA hard drive and a PC, including any peripheral equipment necessary to complete the installation process. If you don't have a new SATA hard drive, assuming your computer already has such a drive installed, you can uninstall the drive and reinstall it in the PC. As always, take ESD precautions to avoid damaging electrical components in the computer.

 You can install a SATA drive in a computer that already has an IDE drive installed, as long as your motherboard supports both standards. This lets you enjoy the performance advantages of using SATA for your data-storage partition while continuing to use the IDE drive for the operating system. This configuration, however, is not common because modern computers are shipped standard with SATA drives.

Caveat

As mentioned earlier, installing a SATA drive is only slightly different from installing an IDE drive; however, there are enough differences to require that the process have a task dedicated to such an installation. The major variation is in the type of cables and connectors used; SATA drives have no jumpers because SATA supports only one drive per controller. This means that you don't have to set drives as master and slave or cable select.

There is a jumper block next to the SATA interface connector on SATA 150 Mbps drives, but it is for factory use only. On the SATA 300 Mbps drives, the jumper block next to the SATA connector can be used to force the drive to use 150 Mbps mode. You would use this option only if the motherboard came equipped with an older SATA controller that could accommodate only SATA 150 Mbps drives.

One detail that is sometimes overlooked is using the correct SATA drive cables. Depending on how the SATA drive and the SATA host adapter are oriented in your computer, you may need connectors that are right-angled or straight on one or both ends. Also, make sure the cable is compatible with the SATA standard for your drive, such as SAS-II. Check the documentation for your drive if you're unsure, or go to the manufacturer's website for more information.

If your motherboard does not have a SATA host adapter present, you can add an adapter as a PCIe card into the PC. Before beginning this task, check your computer's motherboard manual for information regarding SATA drive support.

Procedure

In this task, you'll follow the steps required to install a SATA drive in a computer and set the BIOS to recognize the drive.

Equipment Used

You'll need a computer with a monitor, keyboard, and mouse, a SATA hard drive, and separate SATA interface cables and power cables or adapters, which are usually sold separately. You will also need an appropriate screwdriver for removing the PC's access panel as well as for attaching the SATA drive to the PC's frame. Although this task does not require you to install an operating system, if you wish to do so, you'll need an authentic installation disc for the operating system you want to install.

Details

The following steps walk you through the process of installing a SATA drive into a computer and setting the BIOS.

Installing a SATA Hard Drive

INSTALLING THE SATA HARD DRIVE IN A PC

1. Verify that the PC is powered down and unplugged.
2. Locate a screwdriver and remove the screws from the PC's access panel.
3. Remove the access panel.
4. Locate the SATA connector on the PC's motherboard.
5. Locate the SATA drive interface cable.
6. Attach one end of the drive interface cable to the SATA connector on the motherboard and the other end to the cable connector on the drive.

 The connectors on the interface cable can be attached in only one way, preventing you from attaching the cable incorrectly.

7. Locate the SATA drive power cable. Notice that this SATA power cable is very different from the Molex power cable used with IDE hard drives.
8. Attach the SATA drive power cable to the SATA drive.

 Some SATA power connections are mounted next to the SATA host adapter on the motherboard. If the power cable from the power supply is for IDE, you will need a Molex-to-SATA drive power cable adapter, but this is an unlikely occurrence in modern computers.

 Some SATA drives have both a SATA power socket and a 4 pin MOLEX power socket. One or the other should be connected, not both.

9. Place the drive into the drive bay.
10. Locate the mounting screws for the drive and the appropriate screwdriver, and secure the drive to the bay.
11. Locate the mounting screws for the PC's access panel and the appropriate screwdriver, and replace the access panel.
12. Reconnect the power cable to the PC's power supply.

CONFIGURING THE BIOS

1. Verify that a monitor, keyboard, and mouse are connected to the PC.

2. Make sure the power cord is connected and that the computer is receiving power.

3. Power up the unit.

4. When the system begins its startup routine, enter the BIOS setup.

 The BIOS setup may appear automatically, but if it doesn't, you can manually get into the BIOS. Different computers have different ways of entering the BIOS setup, including F1, F2, F10, F11 or Delete key.

5. Select the menu item for the SATA drive and set it to Auto.

 Because BIOS setups vary, there is no standard method for locating specific menus and submenus.

If you used a PCIe SATA host adapter, your BIOS may not recognize the new SATA drive because the PCIe card uses its own BIOS. Consult the documentation for the PCIe adapter. This issue will not affect the SATA drive's functioning or storage capacity. If you have your drive connected to the SATA adapter on the motherboard and your BIOS does not recognize the drive or identifies it as a SCSI drive, install the drivers for the SATA drive and reboot. Consult the drive's documentation for instructions on how to install the drivers.

6. Verify that your computer is set to look first at your CD/DVD drive when booting.

7. Save the settings and exit the BIOS.

8. If you plan to install an operating system, locate the installation disc and place it in the computer's CD/DVD drive.

9. Reboot the computer.

See Task 1.20 for instructions on how to install Windows XP onto the new SATA drive or Task 1.21 to perform the same task using Windows Vista. Continue to one of those tasks if you want to install an operating system onto your new SATA drive and you have an authentic Windows XP or Windows Vista installation disc available.

Criteria for Completion

You will have successfully completed the task when the computer boots normally and it is ready to install an operating system.

Task 1.8: Moving an Operating System to a New SATA Drive with Acronis True Image

Sometimes when you purchase a computer, you have to balance your requirements and desires against how much they will cost. That includes the size of the hard drives in the computer. Unfortunately, if your estimates are wrong, you could find that one or more of the drives in your computer are becoming dangerously close to being filled. If the drive is the storage unit containing the operating system and application software, this is a compelling concern.

Fortunately, it's possible to move the operating system to a larger drive using an application such as Acronis True Image. True Image allows you to make an exact copy of the partitions on the original drive on a new, larger drive and then install and boot from the newer drive.

NOTE   Learn more about Acronis True Image by going to www.acronis.com/homecomputing/products/trueimage/.

When I originally performed this task, it didn't go without a few bumps. For one thing, the documentation for this product was less than complete: it required that I discover what information was missing and then piece together a complete set of instructions. This is also part of the duties of any PC technician, as you'll learn in Phase 4 of this book, "Troubleshooting and Restoring Computer Systems."

Objective

This task covers objective 220-801: 1.5.

Scenario

The primary SATA disk drive on your personal Windows 7 computer is filling up. This drive contains the computer's operating system and application software. All of your data is on a separate SATA drive in the computer. You have purchased a much larger replacement SATA drive and compatible cable and after doing some research determined that you can transfer the operating system and application software from the smaller original drive to the larger replacement drive using Acronis True Image 2011.

You have gone to the Acronis website and purchased and downloaded the Acronis True Image software onto your computer. You have the replacement drive and all of your tools handy and are ready to clone the information from the original drive to the replacement drive.

You'll need to take the appropriate steps to prevent electrostatic discharge damage to the sensitive electrical components inside the PC. See Task 1.1 for details about ESD precautions.

Scope of Task

Duration

Because of the level of difficulty involved in cloning and replacing the primary drive in a computer, this task will take several hours. Much of the time is used during the actual cloning process, during which you, as the technician, will have little to do but watch the progress bar proceed slowly across the screen.

Setup

The ideal setup would be to purchase a larger SATA drive for your lab computer, including a compatible SATA data drive. You also have to purchase Acronis True Image and download it to the computer you plan to use to perform this task. You will also need the tools and equipment necessary to replace the hard drive, which should include ESD protection and a screwdriver if it's required to remove the PC's access panel and/or hard drive. Go to the Acronis website (I provided the link in the previous note) to determine the current price for a single PC license. The computer used in the creation of this task runs Windows 7 Professional.

Caveat

As I previously mentioned, tasks such as this one don't always go as planned, and if the application performs differently than expected, an exercise that should take several hours can end up taking several days in terms of research, contacting customer support, and making modifications to the steps required to accomplish your goal. Pay close attention to the steps listed here. This task was written using Acronis True Image 2011. If you purchase a later version of this software, the steps in this book may not apply. Consult the documentation if you use a different version, and contact the support team at Acronis if necessary.

Procedure

In this task, you will learn how to clone the operating system and application software from one SATA drive to a larger SATA drive, install the replacement drive, and boot from the replacement.

Equipment Used

As previously mentioned, you'll need a PC with a SATA drive installed; access to the Internet; a monitor, keyboard, and mouse; a replacement SATA drive with compatible data cable; and the tools required to install the new drive. Also, Acronis True Image will need to be installed on the computer used for this task.

Details

In this exercise, you will learn the steps involved in cloning the primary SATA drive from a smaller to a bigger SATA storage unit and then replacing the older drive with the newer SATA drive. There are three basic subtasks:

1. Installing the replacement SATA drive as an additional drive in the computer while leaving the original drive in place

2. Installing Acronis True Image and then using it to clone the original drive to the new drive

3. Removing the original drive and replacing it with the larger drive containing the cloned OS and application software.

This exercise assumes that a compatible power cable for the additional SATA drive is available in the computer and you have no need to install one yourself.

WARNING   You may want to refer back to Task 1.7 for additional instructions on how to install a SATA drive.

Cloning a SATA Drive to a Replacement SATA Drive

INSTALLING THE REPLACEMENT DRIVE AS A SECONDARY DRIVE

1. Power down your computer and remove the power cable from the back of the PC.

2. Open the access panel, using a screwdriver if necessary.

3. Look inside the computer and locate an available SATA adapter and power connection as well as a bay or other area to place the new SATA drive temporarily.

4. Using ESD precautions, attach one end of the SATA cable to the SATA adapter on the motherboard and attach the other end to the new SATA drive.

5. Locate the power cable for the SATA adapter you are using for the replacement drive, and attach it to the available connection on the new drive.

6. Secure the drive in the drive bay.

7. Close the access panel on the computer and reattach the power cable.

8. Make sure the monitor, keyboard, and mouse are attached, and power up the computer.

9. When the computer begins its startup routine, enter the BIOS setup.

NOTE   If the BIOS setup doesn't appear automatically, you can manually get into the BIOS. Different computers have different ways of entering the BIOS setup, including F1, F2, F10, F11 or Delete key.

10. In the BIOS, set the SATA channel being used by the replacement drive to Active.

11. Save your BIOS settings and exit, allowing the computer to boot normally.

12. Open a web browser, navigate to the Acronis True Image website using the link provided earlier, and then purchase and download the True Image application for a single PC to your computer.

 As I previously mentioned, purchasing and installing Acronis True Image is a simple task, so the specific steps are not included here.

CLONING FROM ONE SATA DRIVE TO ANOTHER USING ACRONIS TRUE IMAGE

1. Click Start ➢ All Programs ➢ Acronis ➢ Acronis True Image Home 2011 ➢ Tools and Utilities, and then click Add a Hard Disk.

2. If the Windows 7 UAC prompts you regarding opening True Image, click Yes.

3. When the Add a New Disk Wizard opens, select the new replacement disk you added to your computer.

 Although the Add a New Disk Wizard allows you to size the partitions on the disk and select a file system, since you will be cloning the original C drive to this replacement drive, you will not need to do this.

4. Once the new disk is added, go back to Tools and Utilities in the Acronis True Image menu and select Clone Disk.

5. When the Clone Disk Wizard launches, under Clone Mode, choose Automatic (Recommended), and then click Next.

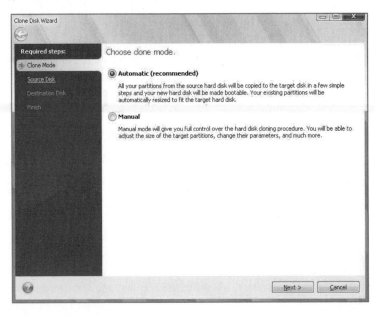

6. Under Source Disk, select the original primary disk drive, which should be Disk 1 in the list (most likely your C drive), and then click Next.

7. Under Destination Disk, select the new replacement disk and then click Next.

8. If you receive a warning saying that all partitions on the destination disk will be deleted, click OK.

9. Click Proceed to begin cloning.

10. When prompted, reboot your computer.

> **NOTE** Once the computer reboots, you will enter a text-only screen, and a set of processes will flash by quickly until you arrive at Operation 4 of 5: Copying Partition. This process can take some time, depending on the size of the partition you are cloning. You will see two progress bars: Current Progress and Total Progress. Wait until the cloning process is complete.

11. When prompted, press any key on the keyboard to shut down the computer.

```
Acronis True Image Home
Synchronizing with operating system:
[●●●●●●●●●●●●●●●●●●●●●●●●●●●●●●] 100%
Congratulations!
You have successfully completed the hard disk cloning procedure.
If you have used the automatic mode or manually configured the new hard
disk as the bootable drive, be sure to make it Primary Master by
switching the appropriate jumpers on it before booting (please see the
guide supplied with your new hard disk for details).

If you plan to remove your old hard disk and are concerned about data priva
cy, please use Acronis DriveCleanser to remove your confidential informatio
n.


Press any key to shut down the computer.
```

INSTALLING AND TESTING THE REPLACEMENT DRIVE AS THE NEW PRIMARY DRIVE

1. Once the PC is completely powered down, remove the power cable and open the access panel.

2. Remove the original primary SATA drive and its data cable, and move the replacement drive with its data cable attached to the primary drive's bay.

3. Connect the replacement drive's SATA data cable to the primary drive's SATA host adapter. Check to make sure it is connected to a power cable.

4. Close the computer's access panel, plug in the power cable, and power up the computer.

5. Enter the BIOS setup and remove the Active setting for the channel previously used by the replacement drive.

6. If necessary, set the primary drive to be the first in boot order.

7. Save and exit the BIOS and allow the computer to boot normally.

8. Once the computer boots into Windows 7, click Start ➢ Computer, and on the Computer screen, verify that the size of the C drive is correct (it should be reflect the size of the new SATA drive you installed).

Criteria for Completion

You will have successfully completed this task when the OS partition has been cloned to a larger, replacement SATA disk, that disk is installed on the SATA channel for the primary drive, and the computer boots into Windows 7 from the replacement drive.

Task 1.9: Installing a SCSI Drive

Installing a SCSI device can be a challenge. It is definitely not a Plug and Play technology. Here are a few things you should know:

When SCSI drives are linked together, they are referred to collectively as a SCSI chain. SCSI chains need to be terminated at both ends.

Either the motherboard of the computer must have an onboard SCSI controller or you need to install an expansion card with a controller before doing anything else.

Not all devices on a SCSI chain have to be drives. A wide variety of SCSI devices are available, many of which are found in engineering laboratories for manufacturing or testing equipment. These SCSI devices can be linked, although for the sake of this exercise, we will be dealing with only SCSI drives on the chain.

Improperly terminating a SCSI chain is probably the most common problem with an installation. If either end of the chain isn't properly terminated, electrical signals hitting an unterminated point will be reflected back along the cable, interfering with normal electrical signals.

Each SCSI device must have a unique ID number in the chain. On some occasions, a specific device needs a particular ID number. Check the manufacturer's documentation before attempting the installation, to avoid any pitfalls. Sometimes you'll run into a SCSI device that has a built-in terminator, meaning that it must be installed at the end of the chain.

Installing a SCSI device is not for the faint of heart, but with proper preparation, it is an accomplishable task.

Objective

This task covers objective 220-801: 1.5.

Scenario

You are assigned to install a SCSI drive in a small, older server. The server has four SCSI drives and one of them has failed. The failed drive has already been removed, and all you are expected to do is configure, install, and terminate the replacement drive. The high-level formatting and all subsequent tasks will be handled by the supervising technician.

Scope of Task

Duration

Because of the level of difficulty in successfully installing a SCSI drive, this task could take from 15 to 30 minutes.

Setup

The ideal setup would be to use an older server with SCSI drives installed. You can some-times "rescue" old servers as they are being decommissioned. More than one starving student has retrieved an ancient server from the recycling heap. Although installing a SCSI drive is quite similar to installing an IDE or SATA drive, there are enough differences to require that you have "the real thing" on hand. As always, take ESD precautions to avoid damaging elec-trical components in the computer.

Caveat

The task includes only the physical installation. Formatting a drive and installing an operating system are separate tasks and not within the scope of this exercise.

Reformatting a hard drive is covered in Task 1.19, and installing an operating system is discussed in Tasks 1.20 and 1.21.

Procedure

In this task, you will learn how to install and terminate a SCSI drive.

Equipment Used

You will need a screwdriver or screwdrivers to open the access panel of the server and mount the SCSI drive in its bay. SCSI drives are linked in chains, so the connector and power cables are already inside the server. The drive is to be connected to the end of the chain, so it must be terminated. In this scenario, the terminator is the last connector on the linking cable. You will need a small pair of needle-nose pliers or tweezers to adjust the jumpers or switches on the drive.

Details

In this exercise, you will learn each step of the process of installing and terminating a SCSI drive in a server.

Remember, only the ends of the chain need to be terminated. If you were installing the drive somewhere in the middle, the termination portion of this task would be unnecessary.

Installing a SCSI Drive

SETTING THE JUMPERS OR SWITCHES

1. Locate the jumpers or switches on the SCSI drive.

2. Locate the diagram on the drive describing what each jumper setting means.

WARNING This part of the task walks you through an example of the default jumper settings on a particular SCSI drive. The drive you are using may require different settings.

3. Set the SCSI ID to an unused number in the chain.

NOTE Narrow SCSI IDs are numbered 0 through 7, with the host adapter usually set to 7. You must select an ID for your drive that is not being used by the adapter or any other devices on the chain. Also, some drives are configured to receive an ID number from the host adapter over the I/O channel.

WARNING Some SCSI devices must be set for a particular ID number. Consult the documentation that came with the drive to see if this is true for your device.

4. Set Motor Start to Disable.
5. Set Delay Motor Start to Disable.
6. Set Write Protect to Disable.
7. Set Parity Check to Enable.
8. Set Terminator Power to Other.

NOTE The Other setting in Step 8 means that another device will provide power to the terminator, even though your drive will be terminated. The host adapter typically provides the terminator power.

INSTALLING THE SCSI DRIVE INTO A SERVER

1. If necessary, power down the server.
2. Remove the power cord from the server's power supply.
3. Use your screwdriver to remove the screws securing the access panel.
4. Remove the access panel.
5. Locate the vacant drive bay in the server.

SCSI devices often use a single connector for both data and power. This task uses a Molex power connector and a separate SCSI data cable.

6. Locate an unused Molex power cable from the power supply.

7. Locate the vacant data connector and terminator on the end of the SCSI cable.

8. Insert the SCSI drive into the bay but do not secure it.

9. Attach the power cable to the power socket on the drive.

10. Attach the SCSI data cable connector to the connector socket on the drive.

11. Attach the terminator to the terminator socket on the drive.

12. Locate the screws that are to be used to secure the drive to the bay.

13. Locate the holes for the screws in the bay and drive.

Sometimes the holes for the screws can be at awkward angles or in tight spaces, making this part of the procedure difficult.

14. Secure the drive to the bay with the screws.

15. Replace the access panel.

16. Secure the access panel by replacing the screws.

TESTING THE SCSI DRIVE INSTALLATION

1. Verify that a mouse, keyboard, and monitor are attached to the server.

2. Plug the power cord into the power supply socket.

3. Verify that the other end of the power cord is plugged into a power source.

4. Power up the server.

5. Listen as each SCSI drive spins up in sequence, and verify that the newly installed drive is "spinning up."

Criteria for Completion

You will have successfully completed this task when you can hear the newly installed SCSI drive spinning up in the server.

Task 1.10: Installing a DVD Drive

As you can see in Tasks 1.6, 1.7, and 1.9, installing different types of drives in a computer requires a very similar process with just a few important differences. Although installing a SCSI drive involves a few different steps compared to installing IDE and SATA drives, in the end you still use the same tools and connect the drive to the motherboard and the power supply.

Installing an IDE DVD drive in a PC involves almost exactly the same steps as installing an IDE hard drive. Most PCs come with some type of optical drive (DVD, DVD-R, DVD-RW), so you won't often be installing the first opticaldrive in a PC. It is more likely that you'll either be upgrading the drive in a computer, adding a second one, or replacing a faulty optical drive Back in the day, a computer might come with separate CD and DVD drives but modern computers come with a DVD or Blu-ray drive installed by default, and these drives are also capable of playing CDs.

Objective

This task covers objective 220-801: 1.5.

Scenario

One of your company's sales representatives has a computer with a failed DVD drive on his Windows XP computer. The failed drive has been removed, and you have just received the replacement unit. You have brought the PC to your workbench and laid out the appropriate tools. Your supervisor has provided you with the IDE DVD drive installation kit and you are ready to install the drive..

Scope of Task

Duration

This task should take about 15 to 30 minutes.

Setup

Ideally, you will have one PC with an IDE controller on the motherboard and one IDE DVD drive installation kit available for this exercise. You will need to verify that the DVD unit is supported on your PC. You can get this information from the store where you purchased the unit or from the manufacturer's website. The kit should contain all of the parts necessary for you to install the DVD drive. As always, take ESD precautions to avoid damaging electrical components in the computer. Although a Windows XP computer was used for this exercise, you will be able to follow the steps using a Windows Vista or Windows 7 computer.

 I continue to mention Windows XP both because it is covered on the A+ exam and because, despite the popularity of Windows 7, it is still a commonly used Windows operating system.

Caveat

Although there is no one set of instructions that will exactly describe how to install a DVD drive in a PC, the steps presented here should be close enough to the computer and DVD drive you are using to be applicable. However, be sure to read any documentation that came with your DVD installation kit before attempting this procedure. Also, since the DVD drive being used is IDE, you will need to be prepared to set jumpers or switches on the drive.

Procedure

In this exercise, you will learn to install a generic DVD drive in a computer.

Equipment Used

You may need a flat-head screwdriver, Phillips screwdriver, or both to open the access panel and attach the DVD drive securely to the drive bay. You will need a pair of needle-nose pliers or tweezers to set the jumpers or switches. You might also need a flat-head screwdriver if you must pry the face off the computer to get at the selected drive bay cover. The task assumes that the drive is installed by removing a front panel on the computer and sliding the drive in the front on a set of rails. To test the installation, you'll need a DVD disc with content on it. You will also need to have a standard monitor, mouse, keyboard, and pair of speakers available for testing.

Details

This lesson will walk you through the process of installing and testing a DVD drive in a computer.

Installing a DVD Drive

OPENING THE COMPUTER AND CONFIGURING THE DVD DRIVE

1. Verify that the computer's power cord is unplugged from the power supply.
2. Use your screwdriver to remove the screws from the access panel.
3. Remove the access panel.
4. Locate the desired drive bay.
5. Locate the desired drive bay cover on the front of the PC.
6. Remove the drive bay cover.
7. Remove the DVD drive from the antistatic bag.
8. Locate the jumpers or switches on the drive.
9. Locate the jumper diagram on the drive.
10. Locate your needle-nose pliers or tweezers.
11. Set the jumpers or switches to the slave position.

Step 11 assumes that the optical drive will be on the same IDE controller as the IDE hard drive. The hard drive jumpers are set to master so the jumpers on the DVD drive are set to slave. The DVD drive will be on the same IDE cable as the hard drive.

INSTALLING THE DVD DRIVE

1. Slide the DVD drive into the drive bay from the front.

The front of the DVD drive should fit flush against the face of the computer.

2. Locate the IDE data ribbon cable that is attached to the first IDE controller on the motherboard and that is also attached to the IDE hard drive.

3. Locate the unoccupied IDE connector on the middle part of the IDE ribbon cable.

4. Carefully match the holes in the ribbon connector to the pins on the IDE connector on the DVD drive.

5. Gently but firmly push the connector in, attaching the ribbon cable connector to the DVD drive (it can only fit one way).

In step 5, since you haven't yet secured the screws to attached the DVD drive to the drive bay, you will need to hold the drive in place with your other hand.

6. Locate a vacant Molex power cable coming from the power supply.

7. Connect the power cable to the power socket on the back of the DVD drive.

8. Verify that all IDE cable connections are firmly in place for the DVD drive, the hard drive, and the IDE motherboard connector, since they could have come loose during this process.

9. Secure the screws to the side of the DVD drive rails to firmly hold it in place..

10. Tuck the cables in the PC case so they are not blocking airflow.

11. Replace the PC access panel and secure it in place.

12. Reattach the power cord to the PC and make sure connections to the monitor, mouse, keyboard, and speakers are secure.

Windows XP, Windows Vista, and Windows 7 all support mpeg decoders and Windows Vista and Windows 7 supply modern codecs. Most modern motherboard chipsets provide hardware mpeg decode acceleration. Also, Windows will most likely provide the drivers for the DVD drive relieving you of the necessity of installing drivers by disc, so installing a DVD drive in an modern computer is extremely easy compared to what it was a number of years ago.

TESTING THE DVD-DRIVE INSTALLATION

1. Locate the test DVD disc.
2. Open the DVD drive.
3. Place the disc in the drive.
4. Close the drive.
5. If Autoplay is engaged, the disc will begin playing automatically.
6. You can also insert a CD music disc to verify that it will play in the drive.

The program used by the DVD drive may prompt you to answer some questions before playing the disc.

You can visit the DVD drive maker's website and download the latest drivers for the drive. Windows Update can also provide the latest drivers.

Criteria for Completion

You will have successfully completed this task when the DVD begins to play and you can hsee and hear the content on the disc.

Task 1.11: Installing a Video Card

Unless you are building a system from scratch, all PCs come with some sort of video capacity—either integrated video, meaning that the motherboard has the capability to output video, a PCIe, or occasionally an accelerated graphics port (AGP) card. Most video expansion cards today are installed in the motherboard's PCIe slot. For information about how to find an available PCIe slot on your computer's motherboard, see Tasks 1.3 and 1.4.

Few modern motherboards come with an AGP slot, but you will likely work with this bus on legacy machines. Also, the A+ exam requires that you be familiar with AGP.

The most common reason for you to install a video card is to upgrade the system to display high-level graphics. Gamers especially need high-end video cards; however, web and graphic designers also require high-quality video displays.

The process is almost identical to that of installing a PCI Express card (see Task 1.4 for details), but there are a few extra steps, especially if you are upgrading a video card.

Objective

This task covers objective 220-801: 1.4.

Scenario

Your company has just hired a new graphic designer. A suitable PC has been located for the new employee but the video card needs to be upgraded to run the design programs the company uses. The PC is already on your workbench, as are the video card and everything else you need to do the upgrade.

Scope of Task

Duration

This task should take about 30 minutes.

Setup

Ideally, you will have a PC with a video card already installed and another video card available so you can use it to replace the original. The driver disc for the new card should be in the installation kit with the video card. As always, before the installation begins, take ESD precautions so you don't damage electrical components in the PC.

Caveat

Make sure to completely read any documentation that comes with the new video card prior to doing this exercise. Your card may require specific procedures that are not included in this set of instructions. Also, for this task it is assumed you are using Windows 7. The exercise also assumes that the original video card is installed in a PCIe slot rather than being integrated into the computer's motherboard. Please read the video card documentation for any additional information about properly installing the new video card.

Procedure

In this exercise, you will learn how to upgrade a video card in a computer and install the video card's drivers.

Equipment Used

You should need only a screwdriver(s) to open the access case, remove the old card, and install the new card in the PCIe slot.

Details

This exercise will take you through the motions of uninstalling an old video card and its drivers and installing a new card.

Uninstalling an Old Video Card

UNINSTALLING THE VIDEO CARD DRIVERS

1. With the system powered up, click Start, right-click Computer, and then click Properties.

 Task 1.23 will show you how to uninstall drivers and other software in Windows 7 using Programs and Features in Control Panel.

2. In the System box on the left-hand menu, click Device Manager.
3. In the Device Manager, expand Display Adapters.
4. Right-click the name of the desired video card and click Properties.
5. In the Properties dialog box for the adapter, click the Driver tab.
6. On the Driver tab, click the Uninstall button.
7. When prompted, select the Delete the Driver Software for This Device check box and then click OK.
8. After the driver is uninstalled, power down the computer.

UNINSTALLING THE OLD VIDEO CARD

1. Unplug the power cable from the power supply.
2. Lay the PC on its side.
3. Locate your screwdriver and remove the screws attaching the access panel to the PC frame.
4. Remove the access panel.
5. Locate the video card.
6. Unscrew the video card from the frame of the computer.
7. Gently pull the old card out of the PCIe socket. (For PCIe x16 and AGP slots, you will need to release an additional locking tab before removing the card).

8. Remove the card and put it in an antistatic bag.

Installing a Video Card

INSTALLING THE NEW VIDEO CARD IN THE PCIE SLOT

1. Locate the new video card.

2. Remove it from the antistatic bag.

3. Line it up with the PCIe slot.

4. Gently but firmly press the card into place.

5. Screw the card onto the PC frame.

WARNING If the video card has an onboard fan, make sure that no cables are at risk of interfering with the fan's operation. Also make sure to follow any special instructions that are required for the proper installation and operation of the fan. High end graphics cards may also require a 6 or 8-pin Molex plug to provide extra power.

6. Replace the access panel.

7. Replace the screws, securing the access panel to the PC frame.

8. Set the PC upright.

9. Plug the power cord into the power supply's socket.

10. Connect the monitor back to the PC and make sure the monitor's power cord is plugged into the power strip or surge protector.

11. Power up the PC.

NOTE If you receive a "New Hardware Found" message, click Cancel and continue to install the video card drivers as described in the video card documentation.

INSTALLING THE NEW VIDEO CARD DRIVERS

1. Locate the disc containing the video card drivers.

2. After the PC powers up, insert the disc into the optical player, launch the disc, and follow the onscreen instructions to install the drivers.

NOTE The onscreen instructions may be slightly different depending on the make and model of card you've installed. You will usually be offered the option of searching for drivers or installing from media like a CD or DVD or Blu-ray. It is usually advisable to download and install the latest drivers from the manufacturer's site, if available.

3. When prompted, remove the driver disc and restart the PC.

4. After the PC reboots, right-click anywhere on the Desktop, and in the menu that appears, click Screen Resolution.

5. In the Screen Resolution dialog box, use the Resolution menu to select the desired screen resolution for your monitor, and then click OK.

WARNING   You can also click Advanced Settings to open the video card's Properties dialog box and configure the adapter and monitor. In most cases, accepting the default settings will work fine.

Criteria for Completion

You will have successfully completed this task when the card and drivers are installed, you have set the display to the desired settings, and the monitor is correctly displaying the desktop.

Task 1.12: Installing a Laptop Keyboard

Swapping out a keyboard on a desktop PC is just a matter of unplugging the keyboard's USB (or rarely its PS/2, or even more rarely its serial) connector from the back of the computer and plugging in the new one. On a laptop, the procedure is quite a bit more involved. New PC techs sometimes shy away from working on laptops because it seems so much more difficult to access the various components. Also, depending on the make and model of laptop, the process of performing repair tasks is highly variable.

All this is true; however, sooner or later you'll have to face laptop repair and maintenance as part of your job. With a bit of practice, you'll become more comfortable working on laptops.

NOTE   Laptops and other mobile devices are rapidly replacing the desktop computer in some work and home environments, so laptop repair skills will be highly useful to the up-and-coming computer tech.

Users can be particularly hard on laptop computers. If a user travels a lot with the laptop, it probably gets a great deal of use and sometimes abuse. Keyboards are vulnerable to having all manner of substances dropped or spilled in and on them. Keys can get stuck and even come off. If the keyboard can't be repaired by a good cleaning, it will need to be removed and a suitable replacement installed.

Objective

This task covers objective 220-801: 3.1.

Scenario

One of the sales associates has just come back from a trip and brings you her laptop. She complains that one of the keys has fallen off and several others are stuck or nonfunctioning. After a careful examination, you explain that the keyboard will need to be replaced. You put in an order to the manufacturer for a replacement keyboard. The sales associate has already uploaded her data to the file server and will be working on her PC at her desk for the next few weeks. She leaves the laptop with you. The keyboard arrives within a few days. You take the laptop and new keyboard to your workbench and prepare to replace the broken keyboard.

Scope of Task

Duration

This task should take from 30 to 45 minutes.

Setup

Ideally, you should have a laptop and replacement laptop keyboard on hand to perform this task. You can also simply remove the keyboard and install it again to perform the same set of actions. Of course, you will absolutely need a laptop of some type to do this exercise. As always, use ESD precautions to avoid damaging electrical components in the laptop.

Caveat

There seem to be as many types of laptops as there are stars in the sky. This translates into as many different ways of replacing a keyboard on a laptop. In this task, an older Dell Inspiron 8200 laptop is used (yes, there are still a few around); however, the actual process of doing the same exercise on your laptop will likely be quite different. Always consult the documentation for your machine or the manufacturer's website for instructions relevant to the laptop you are using.

Procedure

In this exercise, you will learn how to remove and replace a keyboard on a Dell laptop.

Equipment Used

You will need a screwdriver to remove a number of screws on the bottom of the keyboard. You will also need a plastic scribe or similar object to pry the keyboard from the laptop once it's unsecured.

Details

This task will walk you through the steps of removing a laptop keyboard and installing a new one.

Replacing a Laptop Keyboard

PREPARING TO WORK ON THE LAPTOP KEYBOARD

1. Power down the laptop.
2. Unplug the power cord and external mouse cable, if present.
3. Remove any PC cards, if present.
4. Close the display lid.
5. Remove the battery.

On an Inspiron 8200, the battery is usually located on the front edge of the laptop on the right. To remove it, locate the triangular latch on the bottom of the laptop just under the battery. Depress the latch and pull the battery forward. It should just slide out.

The preceding instructions should be followed when you are planning on repairing or replacing any component in a laptop.

REMOVING THE LAPTOP KEYBOARD

1. Turn the laptop upside down and place it so the front is facing you.
2. Locate three screws labeled with a *K* in a circle.
3. Locate one screw labeled with a *K/M* in a circle.
4. Use your screwdriver to remove each of these screws.

The screws in a laptop can be quite long, and it can be somewhat time-consuming to remove them.

5. Turn the laptop right side up with the front facing you.
6. Open the display.
7. Locate your plastic scribe.
8. Locate the blank key on the keyboard.

The blank key is located just above the right-arrow key on the lower-right side of the keyboard on the Inspiron 8200.

9. Place the scribe under the right side of the blank key.

10. Apply pressure from left to right, pushing the keyboard to disengage the tabs on the left side.

11. Gently lift the right side of the keyboard and balance it on its left side on the laptop.

12. Locate the keyboard ribbon cable.

13. Disconnect the cable from the bottom of the keyboard.

WARNING   The keyboard connector in many laptops is extremely fragile, so be very careful when performing this step.

14. Lay the keyboard aside.

INSTALLING THE NEW KEYBOARD

1. Locate the new keyboard.

2. Remove it from the antistatic bag.

3. Rest it on its left side on the laptop.

4. Connect the keyboard ribbon cable to the bottom of the keyboard.

WARNING   The keyboard connector in many laptops is extremely fragile, so be very careful when performing this step.

WARNING   Make sure that the cable does not get crimped when you install the keyboard.

5. Locate the two tabs on the left side of the keyboard.

6. Insert the tabs under the edge of the keyboard housing.

7. Slowly place the keyboard in the housing.

8. Verify that the keyboard is lying flush in the housing.

9. Close the display.

10. Turn the laptop over with the front facing you.

11. Locate the screws removed from the bottom of the laptop.

12. Use your screwdriver to replace the screws.

13. Turn the laptop over so its bottom is on the workbench and the front is facing you.

TESTING THE KEYBOARD INSTALLATION

1. Replace the battery.

   The battery should just slide back in and click into place.

2. Replace the power cord.
3. Lift the display.
4. Power up the laptop.
5. After the laptop has completely booted, open a blank document.
6. Type in the document, verifying that all the keys function properly.
7. Replace any PC cards and other equipment that were attached to the laptop when you received it.

Criteria for Completion

You will have successfully completed this task when the keyboard is installed, the laptop is completely reassembled, and you can use the keyboard normally with all of the keys functioning.

Task 1.13: Installing SO-DIMM in a Laptop

In some ways, installing memory in a laptop is easier than performing the same action in a PC. There seems to be a universal law that says whatever component you need to reach in a PC will be in the most inconvenient and hard-to-reach place. On a laptop, this isn't necessarily so, at least for memory.

The trade-off is that laptop components are smaller and sometimes more delicate (read "easier to break"). SO-DIMM (which stands for "small outline dual-inline memory module") sticks are quite a bit smaller than their desktop counterparts. DRAM (dynamic random access memory) and the clips that hold them into the SO-DIMM sockets are tiny. That's the only real hang-up, though. The actual installation is uncomplicated. You can upgrade a laptop's memory in no time.

Objective

This task covers objective 220-801: 1.5.

Scenario

You have received a trouble ticket stating that one of the testing engineers needs a memory upgrade for his laptop. You receive the specifics regarding the make and model of the laptop and look up the appropriate SO-DIMM module.

WARNING   See Task 1.2, "Installing RAM," to learn how to research which type of memory is right for a particular computer.

You order the appropriate module, and when it arrives, you take it and your tools to the user's cubicle. The user is about to take a break, leaving you free to upgrade his laptop's memory.

Scope of Task

Duration

This task will take about 10 minutes.

Setup

You'll need a laptop and an appropriate stick of SO-DIMM to upgrade its memory. In a pinch, you can simply remove an existing memory module in your laptop and replace it to simulate the task. As always, take ESD precautions to keep from damaging any electronic components.

Caveat

This task is based on upgrading memory in the same Dell Inspiron 8200 laptop used in Task 1.13. The exact method of upgrading memory in your laptop will likely vary. Consult the documentation for your laptop or search the manufacturer's website for specific instructions. The operating system used in this exercise is Windows XP Professional.

Procedure

This exercise will teach you how to upgrade the memory of a laptop.

Equipment Used

You should only need a screwdriver to open the memory module cover on the bottom of the laptop.

Details

In this task, you will learn the procedures necessary to upgrade the memory in a laptop.

Installing SO-DIMM in a Laptop

PREPARING TO WORK ON THE LAPTOP

1. Power down the laptop.

2. Unplug the power cord and external mouse cable, if present.

3. Remove any PC cards, if present.

4. Close the display lid.

5. Remove the battery.

Find the procedure for removing a battery in the section "Preparing to Work on the Laptop Keyboard" in Task 1.12.

UPGRADING SO-DIMM IN THE LAPTOP

1. Turn the laptop over with the front facing you.

2. Locate the memory module cover.

The memory module cover on an Inspiron 8200 is a small panel located on the left side of the laptop (when it is upside down) and attached by a single screw. Consult the documentation for your laptop to locate the module cover on your device.

3. Locate your screwdriver and remove the screw securing the module cover.

4. Release the two metal tabs holding the cover in place.

5. Lift out the cover.

6. Locate an empty SO-DIMM slot.

The Inspiron 8200 typically has two slots. The original SO-DIMM module should be in the slot labeled DIMM A.

7. Locate the slot labeled DIMM B.

8. Locate the SO-DIMM module you brought with you.

9. Remove it from the antistatic bag, holding it by its side edges.

10. Align the module to the slot in the correct direction.

The module is made to fit in the slot in only one direction.

11. Slide the module into the slot.

> The latches on either side will move aside slightly to allow the module to be placed in the slot.

12. Push the module down into the slot until the two latches on either side click into place.

> If the latches don't click and engage, the module may be misaligned. Remove the module and replace it again.

13. Replace the module cover, inserting the side with the metal tabs first.

14. Replace the screw securing the module cover.

15. Place the laptop right side up with the front facing you.

16. Replace the power cord and any other cords and cards you previously removed.

17. Replace the battery.

TESTING THE MEMORY

1. Open the display lid.

2. Power on the laptop.

3. Listen for one beep as the computer boots.

4. Look for a message on the display screen indicating that the amount of memory on the computer has changed.

5. Follow any instructions you see on the screen.

6. Allow the laptop to continue to boot and the operating system to load.

VERIFYING THE MEMORY

1. On the computer's Desktop, click the Start button.

2. Right-click My Computer and select Properties.

3. On the General tab of the System Properties dialog box, locate the amount of SO-DIMM in the laptop.

4. Click Cancel to close the System Properties dialog box.

> Remember, you're working with a Windows XP computer. The process for verifying memory on a Windows 7 machine is outlined in Task 1.2.

Criteria for Completion

You will have successfully completed this task when you have verified that the amount of memory has increased to the correct amount. This amount will vary depending on how much memory the computer originally had and how much you added.

Task 1.14: Installing a Laptop Hard Drive

As you learned in Task 1.6, "Installing an IDE Hard Drive," hard-disk drives periodically fail for a number of reasons. The same can be said for laptop hard drives; however, the procedure to replace a laptop's hard drive is quite a bit different and, in many cases, easier than replacing a drive in a PC.

This task is about as common as replacing an IDE drive in a PC. As always, replacing the drive is easy. Recovering the lost data is harder. Make sure you periodically back up your data.

Since the laptop used for this task is a legacy device, the task involves installing an IDE hard drive. For current laptops, you are more likely to be installing a SATA drive or perhaps an SSD drive.

Objective

This task covers objective 220-801: 1.5.

Scenario

You have received a trouble ticket stating that a marketing associate's hard drive appears to have locked up. You call the associate and she agrees to bring the laptop to the IT department.

When she arrives, she explains that while she was out of town and using her laptop, she started hearing clicking noises coming from the computer. The noises increased in frequency until they abruptly stopped. At that point, she got a blue screen displaying error messages she couldn't understand. She turned off the power by pressing and holding the power button down. When she tried to power the device back up, power was applied but the screen remained blank.

You verify that the problem is the hard drive and , agree to replace it, reload the operating system and application software, and upload her data from the most recent backup on the file server.

You order a new hard drive, and when it arrives you take it and the laptop to your workbench and begin to work.

This task will cover only the physical replacement of the hard drive. Tasks 1.20 and 1.21 cover installing an operating system, and Task 1.22 describes installing Microsoft application software.

Scope of Task

Duration

Physically replacing the drive should take about 15 minutes.

Setup

The ideal setup is to have a laptop and a compatible spare hard-drive unit to use in this task. If a spare unit is not available, you can remove the existing hard drive and then replace it. As always, use ESD precautions to prevent damaging the electrical components in your laptop.

Caveat

As with all laptop tasks, there are many different ways to do this exercise, depending on the make and model of your computer. Read the documentation for your laptop, either the printed copy or online at the vendor's site. In this task, the same legacy Dell Inspiron 8200 used in Tasks 1.12 and 1.13 is used here.

Procedure

This exercise will teach you how to replace a hard drive in a laptop.

Equipment Used

You'll only need a screwdriver to remove the screw securing the hard drive to the laptop.

Details

This lesson will take you through the steps of removing a hard drive from a laptop and replacing it with a new unit.

Replacing a Laptop Hard Drive

PREPARING TO WORK ON THE LAPTOP

1. Power down the laptop.
2. Unplug the power cord and external mouse cable, if present.
3. Remove any PC cards, if present.

4. Close the display lid.

5. Remove the battery.

REMOVING THE LAPTOP HARD DRIVE

1. Locate the hard drive.

Find the procedure for removing a battery in the section "Preparing to Work on the Laptop Keyboard" in Task 1.12.

The hard drive on an Inspiron 8200 is located on the left side of the laptop (when it's upside down) at about the midsection.

2. Locate the screw securing the hard drive.

3. Using your screwdriver, remove the hard drive's restraining screw.

4. Grasp the hard drive and slide it out of its bay.

5. Put the unit aside.

INSTALLING THE LAPTOP HARD DRIVE

1. Locate the new hard drive.

2. Remove it from the antistatic bag.

3. Orient it correctly at the opening of the bay.

4. Slide the hard drive into the bay until it snaps into place.

5. Replace the restraining screw.

6. Turn the laptop right side up with its front facing you.

7. Plug the power cable back in.

8. Replace the battery.

VERIFYING THE INSTALLATION

1. Once the laptop is completely reassembled and connected to a power supply, power it up.

2. Enter the BIOS and verify that the drive is recognized by the computer.

3. When the drive boots, you should receive a message indicating that there is no operating system installed.

The hard drive is now ready to have an OS installed.

Criteria for Completion

You will have successfully completed this task when your laptop successfully boots. In the task scenario, a complete recovery would require the installation of the operating system, applications, and backed-up data.

Task 1.15: Installing a Laptop Optical Drive

The process of installing an optical drive in a laptop is relatively straightforward, largely because laptops typically support one hard drive and one optical drive and the units are modular and have no cables you need to manage.

 NOTE   Since laptops come with a single CD/DVD drive, that drive usually performs the task of reader and writer for CD, DVD, and Blu-ray discs.

The drawbacks are size, capacity, and heat. All of the laptop components are literally on top of each other, so dispelling excess heat remains a problem. However, the process of installing a laptop CD/DVD drive is about the same as that of installing a laptop hard drive (see Task 1.14).

Objective

This task covers objective 220-801: 1.5.

Scenario

You receive a trouble ticket stating that one of the sales reps is complaining that the CD/DVD player on his laptop is broken. You arrange a time to meet the rep at his cubicle. Once there, he explains that he was placing a CD/DVD into the open drive two days ago and he slipped and fell forward, cracking the unit. You examine the drive and confirm that it is damaged.

You take the laptop back to the IT department and place it on your workbench. You locate a suitable replacement unit in the stock room and place it next to the laptop. You lay out your tools and begin your work.

Scope of Task

Duration

This task should take about 15 minutes.

Setup

The setup is virtually identical to the one in Task 1.14. If you don't have a spare optical drive, just remove and replace the existing optical drive on your laptop.

Caveat

As with all laptop tasks, before you begin, check the documentation for your particular laptop and determine if the procedure to perform this exercise differs from the instructions you are reading here. The laptop used in this task is the same Dell Inspiron 8200 used in the previous tasks involving laptop hardware installations.

Procedure

This exercise will show you how to replace the optical drive in a laptop.

Equipment Used

All you should need is a screwdriver to remove the screw holding the optical drive in place. Have a DVD handy for testing purposes.

Details

This lesson will walk you through the steps of removing an optical drive from a laptop and replacing it with another unit.

Replacing a Laptop Optical Drive

PREPARING TO WORK ON THE LAPTOP

1. Power down the laptop.
2. Unplug the power cord and external mouse cable, if present.
3. Remove any PC cards, if present.
4. Close the display lid.
5. Remove the battery.

Find the procedure for removing a battery in the section "Preparing to Work on the Laptop Keyboard" in Task 1.12.

REMOVING THE OPTICAL DRIVE FROM A LAPTOP

1. Locate the optical drive.

On an Inspiron 8200, the optical drive is located on the right side (when the laptop's upside down) of the computer.

2. Locate the drive's restraining screw.

You should find the screw on the bottom of the laptop, directly below the drive. Verify the location of the screw for your laptop in its documentation.

3. Use your screwdriver to remove the restraining screw.
4. Locate the tab on the optical drive.
5. Pull the tab, sliding the drive out of the bay.
6. Put the drive aside.

INSTALLING THE NEW OPTICAL DRIVE IN A LAPTOP

1. Locate the replacement optical drive.
2. Remove it from the antistatic bag.
3. Correctly orient the drive to the bay.
4. Slide the drive into the bay until it clicks into place.
5. Replace the restraining screw.
6. Turn the laptop to its upright position.

TESTING THE OPTICAL DRIVE INSTALLATION

1. Plug the power cable back in.
2. Replace the battery.
3. Lift the display lid.
4. Power on the laptop.
5. After the laptop boots, open the DVD door.
6. Locate your test DVD and place it into the drive.
7. Close the drive door.

You should hear the optical drive spin up as it prepares to play the DVD.

8. If Autoplay is functioning, the DVD's display program will open and the disc will start to play.

In this scenario, the unit that was replaced was identical to the original, so the appropriate drivers and software were already loaded on the laptop.

Criteria for Completion

You will have successfully completed this task when the new optical unit is installed and it correctly plays the test media.

Task 1.16: Installing a KVM Switch

The idea of a keyboard-video-mouse (KVM) switch is that it allows you to use a single keyboard, monitor, and mouse on two or more computers or servers. KVMs are traditionally used to attach several servers so you can switch the use of your keyboard, monitor, and mouse among them. After all, this equipment takes up a lot of space, and space is usually at a premium in a server room. Chances are you don't need to see the display of more than one of your servers at any given time.

 With the current popularity of running numerous virtual machines on a single piece of hardware, KVMs are used less, but you will no doubt still be required to install and maintain such equipment. The current CompTIA A+ exam tests for knowledge about KVM devices.

If you have two computers connected through a KVM device, you can switch to unit A and work on the first server and then switch to unit B and access the second server. Although junior PC techs don't do a large amount of work with server maintenance (the more typical role is in desktop support), occasionally you'll be asked to install a KVM switch and verify that it works.

Objective

This task covers objective 220-801: 1.12.

Scenario

A second server has just been installed at one of your company's branch offices. Both servers have been configured but are currently shut down. You've been assigned to install a KVM switch so that a single keyboard, monitor, and mouse setup in the server room can be used to work with both servers.

The senior tech provides you with a KVM installation kit and explains the setup. You take the kit and your tools and drive to the branch office. You introduce yourself to the supervisor on duty and she takes you to their small server room. You set the KVM unit and toolkit on the table next to the monitor, mouse, and keyboard and start the job.

Scope of Task

Duration

This task should take about 20 minutes.

Setup

You will need to have two PCs, one KVM unit, and one monitor, keyboard, and mouse. Have both PCs powered down before starting this exercise. You will also need the appropriate cabling to connect both computers to the KVM device. Those cables should come with the KVM switch. ESD procedures are not necessary because you won't be coming in direct contact with delicate electrical components.

Caveat

There are a number of different makes and models of KVM switches on the market, so the procedure for installing yours may differ slightly. It is presumed that all keyboard and mouse connections use USB.

Procedure

This lesson will teach you how to connect two computers to a single KVM switch and, using a single monitor, keyboard, and mouse, switch back and forth between the two computers.

Equipment Used

No tools are needed to complete this task besides what is described in the "Scope of Task" section. The only thing you might need is a set of plastic ties for cable management.

Details

You will be guided through the steps necessary to connect two computers to a KVM switch; attach a single monitor, keyboard, and mouse to the switch; and use the switch to toggle back and forth between the two computers.

Installing a Two-Port KVM Switch

CONNECTING THE PERIPHERALS TO THE KVM SWITCH

1. Place the switch in its permanent location in proximity to the servers, monitor, keyboard, and mouse.
2. Verify that both servers have power cords plugged into their power supplies.
3. Verify that both servers are powered down.
4. Locate the output ports for the monitor, keyboard, and mouse on the back of the KVM switch.

5. Attach the monitor connector to the video output port on the switch.

6. Attach the keyboard connector to the keyboard output port on the switch.

7. Attach the mouse connector to the mouse output port on the switch.

CONNECTING COMPUTERS TO THE KVM SWITCH

1. Locate the input ports for the monitor, keyboard, and mouse connections for position A.

2. Locate the input ports for the monitor, keyboard, and mouse connections for position B.

3. Locate the two sets of KVM cables to be used to connect the KVM switch to the two servers.

4. Attach the monitor, keyboard, and mouse connectors on one end of the first cable to the input ports for the monitor, keyboard, and mouse connectors for position A on the switch.

5. Locate the monitor, keyboard, and mouse connectors on the first server.

6. Locate the loose end of the cable you just attached to the switch.

7. Attach the monitor, keyboard, and mouse connectors on the cable to the appropriate ports on the first server.

> Connecting individual cables from the switch to server A and then from the switch to server B will help avoid confusion as to which cable goes with which server.

8. Attach the monitor, keyboard, and mouse connectors on the second cable to the appropriate input ports for position B on the KVM switch.

9. Locate the loose end of the second cable.

10. Attach the monitor, keyboard, and mouse connectors on the cable to the appropriate ports on the back of the second server.

11. Locate the power cord for the KVM switch. A simple USB KVM as described would more likely but unpowered/powered via USB.

> It is likely that a simple KVM would be powered via USB rather than require its own power connector, but this may not be true with the KVM switch you are using.

12. Plug it into the power socket of the switch.

13. Locate a vacant plug on the power strip or UPS unit.

14. Plug the other end of the KVM power cord into the power device.

15. Locate your plastic ties in your toolkit.

16. Organize the different sets of cables and contain each bundle with a set of ties.

WARNING Although you don't need to practice good cable management for the sake of this exercise, in the real world you are expected to be not only technically proficient but also tidy. Nobody wants to deal with a nest of snakes... or cables.

TESTING THE KVM INSTALLATION

1. Power up the KVM device.

2. Power up the first server.

3. Power up the second server.

4. When all devices are fully powered and booted, press the A button.

NOTE You should see the desktop of the first server with the login dialog box. It is assumed that you have login credentials for these servers.

5. Log in to server A.

6. Set the background color or some other obvious visual indicator to a nondefault configuration.

7. Press the B button to switch to the other server.

8. Log in to server B.

9. Repeat switching back and forth between A and B to test the installation.

10. Practice using the keyboard and mouse on both servers to test them.

11. When finished, log off both servers.

Criteria for Completion

You will have successfully completed this task when you are able to freely switch back and forth between both computers and use the monitor, keyboard, and mouse normally on both machines.

Task 1.17: Installing Drivers from a Disc

Long gone are the days when a computer could contain by default all of the hardware drivers necessary to work and play well with every device and component on the market. It's a foregone conclusion that if you install a piece of hardware or a peripheral, you'll also have to install the drivers.

Most of the time, this isn't much of a chore, especially if you are installing a new device and have the driver disc that came with the hardware. Windows makes it pretty easy, but you do have to go through a few steps. Get used to them. As a PC tech, you'll be installing or updating drivers almost all the time.

Objective

This task covers objective 220-802: 1.2.

Scenario

A user has turned in a trouble ticket stating that he is having difficulty playing audio tutorials on his PC. You've investigated and determined that the problem is his sound card. You install a replacement PCIe sound card (see Task 1.4) and now you need to install the drivers. You have the driver disc that came with the sound card and are ready to do the installation.

The sound-card scenario is only an example. You'll end up installing drivers for a wide variety of components.

Scope of Task

Duration

This task should take about 10 minutes.

Setup

Ideally, you will have just installed a new device or component and have the driver disc for the new piece of hardware handy.

Caveat

In this lesson, you'll be using Windows to do the installation, but often the manufacturer's driver disc has its own interface and installation procedure. In the vast majority of cases, you just need to follow the onscreen instructions and the drivers will be successfully installed.

Procedure

This lesson will teach you how to install device drivers from a CD.

Equipment Used

The only thing you'll need after the device is installed is the driver disc.

Details

This task will walk you through the steps of using Windows to install a device driver from a disc.

Installing Device Drivers from a Disc

GETTING READY TO INSTALL DRIVERS FROM THE DISC

1. Locate the driver disc.
2. Locate the driver installation instructions.
3. Verify that the correct procedure is to use Windows to install the drivers.

 For this task, you should have already installed the sound card and powered up the Windows 7 computer.

 Some devices require that you install the drivers before you power up the new equipment. Consult the device's documentation before continuing.

 You may fail to correctly install the device drivers if you don't follow the recommended method of installing them from the driver disc.

INSTALLING FROM THE DEVICE DRIVER DISC USING WINDOWS

1. Sitting at the keyboard, click Start.
2. Right-click Computer.
3. Click Properties.
4. Click Device Manager.
5. Locate the new device in the Device Manager list.

 A yellow exclamation point may appear next to the device, indicating that it is not functional at this time.

6. Expand the Sound Card notation in the list.
7. Right-click the name of the sound card.
8. Click Properties.
9. On the Driver tab, click the Update Drivers button.
10. On the Update Driver Software box, click Browse My Computer for Driver Software.
11. Insert the driver disc in the PC's optical drive.

12. Click Browse and navigate to the optical drive, and then click Next.

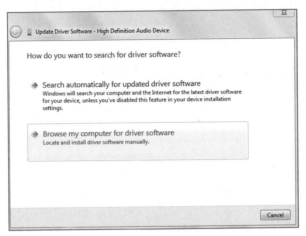

13. When the search of the disk locates the driver, select it and click OK.

 If a dialog box appears saying that the drive isn't digitally signed, this is a serious issue. Windows 7 64-bit requires that drivers be signed. If you want to install drivers that are not signed, you must disable this requirement during boot. Windows 7 32-bit isn't as restrictive regarding unsigned drivers.

14. After the driver installs, click Finish.
15. If prompted, click the Restart button to reboot the PC.
16. Remove the driver disc.

Criteria for Completion

You will have successfully completed this task when the computer reboots and you can use the new device normally.

Task 1.18: Installing Drivers from the Internet

Probably the most difficult task in installing drivers from the Internet is finding them. Although it makes sense to go to the manufacturer's site first, depending on how the company's site is set up it may not be easy to locate the right drivers. Also, if you are looking for drivers for a legacy device, the vendor may have gone out of business. For this task, it is assumed that you've located the right driver page to find the needed driver, downloaded it, and installed it.

Objective

This task covers objective 220-802: 1.2.

Scenario

You are installing an HP All-in-One device as a local printer/fax/scanner on a user's computer. You don't have the driver disc that originally came with the device but can find the drivers online. The computer has an Internet connection and you can go to HP's site and find the drivers page for the product.

Scope of Task

Duration

This task should take about 15 minutes.

Setup

You'll need a computer with an Internet connection and, ideally, a device that's connected to the PC and needs updated drivers. You can also download the drivers for just about any device but not install them.

Caveat

If you wanted to update the drivers of a device already installed on your computer, you could just use the Device Manager to search for drivers online. (Task 1.17 used the Device Manager to install drivers from a disc.) This task focuses on a situation in which you are installing a new device and must locate and download drivers from the Internet. In this example, you are downloading an HP device driver, but this task is applicable for any manufacturer or device.

Procedure

This task will show you how to download and install device drivers from an Internet site.

Equipment Used

You only need a computer with an Internet connection to complete this task.

Details

This task will show you the steps necessary to download and install device drivers from a manufacturer's site.

Downloading and Installing Device Drivers

SELECTING AND DOWNLOADING DRIVERS

1. With the www.hp.com site open in your browser, select Support & Drivers.

2. On the Support page, select Drivers & Software.

3. In the field that appears, enter the name and model number of the device, such as **officejet 6500a plus**.

4. Click the Search button.

5. For Step 1: Select your operating system, use the drop-down menu to select your computer's operating system, such as Microsoft Windows 7 (64-bit), and then click Next.

6. For Step 2: Select a download and, click Driver - Product Installation Software.

7. When additional selections appear, click HP Officejet Full Feature Software and Driver.

8. Make sure to read the Details and Specifications section to verify that this is the correct driver for your product and computer, and then click Download (if necessary, click View Directions for download and installation details).

9. When the popup window appears, navigate to the desired location on your computer's hard drive and then click Save.

When downloading drivers or any file from the Internet, prepare a folder in your directory system ahead of time so you can find the file later. For example, you could create a folder named Drivers on your C drive and download all your drivers to that one folder. This makes it easy to find them later.

The amount of time it takes for the drivers to download depends on your connection speed and the size of the software package.

INSTALLING DEVICE DRIVERS

1. Make sure the printer is not connected to your computer before proceeding.

2. Browse to the folder where you downloaded the driver package.

3. Double-click the driver package.

4. In the installation wizard, accept the default location for the installation.

5.   Click Next to extract the drivers.

This part of the task may take a few minutes. After the drivers are extracted, the process is largely automatic, with the installation software checking your system, preparing for the installation, conducting the installation, and configuring the product.

6.   After the installation is complete, restart the computer.

Depending on the device involved, you may have to complete the configuration wizard before being able to use the device. Follow all of the onscreen instructions and connect the printer to your computer only when prompted; then complete the configuration tasks and test the printer to verify that all of its functions work correctly.

Criteria for Completion

You will have successfully completed the task when the drivers are installed, the device is configured, and you are able to use the device normally.

Task 1.19: Reformatting a Hard Drive Using Windows XP

Reformatting a hard drive is no fun. It usually means that there is something seriously wrong with the computer that cannot be repaired in any other way. Reformatting means erasing everything on the hard drive and then reinstalling the OS, drivers, application software, and data. If possible, back up all of the data on the drive before reformatting.

Reformatting a hard drive will erase everything on it, and all of your data will be lost.

Sometimes a computer will become so overrun with malware that it becomes impossible to recover it through normal means. The solution of last resort is to wipe the drive and reinstall everything. The Windows XP Recovery Console provides an ideal tool for doing this.

Prior to reformatting a hard drive, you should attempt to recover the drive using the Windows XP Recovery Console. Learn more about Recovery Console by going to http://support.microsoft.com/kb/307654 and http://support.microsoft.com/kb/314058.

Objective

This task covers objective 220-802: 1.2.

Scenario

You receive a trouble ticket from a user that his Windows XP laptop seems to go out of control when powered up and connected to the network. You investigate and determine that the laptop has been severely overrun by malware during a business trip taken by the user. Antivirus and antimalware removal solutions have been unsuccessful. Other methods such as System Restore and Last Known Good Configuration have also proved unsuccessful. Your supervisor advises you to reformat the hard drive of the laptop. Fortunately, most of the data on the laptop can be recovered from the last backup, which was made prior to the computer being compromised.

   You take the laptop to your workbench and locate the Windows XP installation disc that you'll need for the reformatting. You know that the file system on the XP machine is NTFS.

Scope of Task

Duration

This task should take about 20 minutes.

Setup

You'll need to have a computer running Windows XP that is able to boot from a CD/DVD drive. You'll also need to have the recovery disc. Most important, the computer must not contain data and software that you will need.

Caveat

Be very sure you have any data you want backed up before proceeding with this task. Once you've finished, any data on the drive will be gone forever. If your computer doesn't check the optical drive before the hard drive when it starts booting, you'll have to change the boot order in the BIOS. Once this process is done, make sure you have all of the application installation discs if you want to reinstall the operating system and all the applications. As you've already read, the operating system used is Windows XP. Formatting a hard drive using other versions of Windows will involve somewhat different steps.

 To reinstall the operating system and all the Microsoft apps, see Task 1.20, "Installing Windows XP Professional as a Fresh Install," and Task 1.23, "Installing Microsoft Applications in Windows XP."

Procedure

This task will show you how to reformat a hard drive using the Recovery Console in Windows XP.

Equipment Used

You won't need any tools for this task, just the Windows XP computer itself and the recovery or installation CD.

Full installation discs are no longer shipped with Windows computers, but you may have received a recovery disc that contains all the XP repair tools when you purchased your Windows XP computer. While I find this very inconvenient, I suppose this is one of the efforts Microsoft is making to curb software piracy.

Computer manufacturers such as HP create a separate directory on the hard drive that contains all of the recovery disc tools. Users are required to create the disc themselves. I highly recommend that you do so as soon as you buy the computer. If you don't, and you subsequently suffer a severe hardware or software failure, you'll most likely be without a method of recovery.

Details

This task will show you all of the information regarding changing the boot order of a computer and using Windows XP Recovery Console to reformat the hard drive.

You'll have the opportunity to use Windows 7 repair tools to diagnose and attempt repairs on a faulty hard drive in Tasks 4.17 and 4.25.

Changing the Boot Order of a Computer

GETTING INTO THE BIOS AND CHANGING THE BOOT ORDER

1. Verify that the laptop is connected to a power source.

2. Open the CD/DVD drive.

3. Insert the recovery disc.

4. Boot the computer.

5. As the boot sequence begins, scan the bottom of the screen for the key or key combination that will let you enter the setup.

6. When the setup screen appears, look for an area or list referencing the boot order.

7. Follow the onscreen notes to enter the boot order menu.

8. View the listing of the boot order.

Different computers have different ways of entering the BIOS setup including pressing F1, F2, F10, F11, or Del.

Exactly how the setup screen is configured varies widely. This task takes you through a basic procedure, but how your BIOS is set up may differ.

9. If necessary, change the boot order to make the CD/DVD drive the first in the list.

10. Press the key that will save your changes and restart the computer.

Reformatting a Hard Disk

USING WINDOWS XP RECOVERY CONSOLE TO REFORMAT THE HARD DISK

1. As the computer boots from the CD, look for the Welcome to Windows Setup screen.

2. Press either the F10 function key or the R (for repair) key.

3. When the Recovery Console opens, select the Windows installation from the list.

Windows will most likely be at the top of the list and be called C:\WINDOWS.

4. Press Enter.

5. At the login screen, use your administrator name and password to log in.

On home Windows systems, the primary user is usually the administrator. In a work setting, admin usernames and passwords are set by the IT department staff. Your supervisor will have provided you with this information.

6. Press Enter.

7. In the command-line emulator, type **map** at the prompt.

Typing **map** will provide a list of drive letters with the associated file system, size, and device name of each drive.

8. Press Enter.

9. Type **format C: /fs:ntfs**.

NOTE   Step 9 assumes that the drive you want to reformat is the primary or C drive. If the drive you are reformatting uses a different drive letter, use that one instead.

10. Press Enter.

11. Type **y** and then press Enter.

12. After the reformatting process finishes, type **exit**.

13. Press Enter to restart the computer.

Criteria for Completion

You will have successfully completed the task when the computer reboots and the hard drive has been reformatted with the operating system, application software, and data deleted.

Task 1.20: Installing Windows XP Professional as a Fresh Install

As you saw in Task 1.19, there are times when even good PCs go bad and there's nothing left to do but reformat the hard drive. Of course, this is only part of the rehabilitative therapy for your ailing computer. To fix the original problem, you had to throw out the good software with the bad. Although you have guaranteed that all viruses and other malware have been removed from the hard drive, you also deleted the operating system, the application software, and all your data.

Hopefully you backed up your data and located software installation discs. You're going to need them if you ever want to use your computer for more than a paperweight. Assuming you took all of the appropriate steps to find your software discs, you'll soon be tapping away at the keyboard and clicking the mouse once again.

Objective

This task covers objective 220-802: 1.2.

Scenario

You have just completed reformatting the hard drive of a laptop that had been corrupted with various forms of malware (see Task 1.19). You have located an authorized Windows XP Professional installation disc and are ready to reinstall the operating system. You will be performing a fresh install, so it will be as if you were installing Windows XP on a brand-new hard drive.

 You can use a Windows XP Home Edition install disk for this task because the installation process is virtually identical.

Scope of Task

Duration

This task should take about 30 to 45 minutes, depending on the capacity of your computer's CPU and memory.

Setup

You'll need a computer with a newly reformatted hard drive. You will also need a genuine Windows XP Professional installation disc and the accompanying product key.

Caveat

This task will take you only as far as the installation of the operating system. Task 1.22 will continue the recovery process by teaching you how to install Microsoft application software. You can complete this task only by reinstalling Windows XP on a reformatted drive.

Procedure

This task will instruct you on how to reinstall Windows XP on the reformatted hard drive of a computer.

Equipment Used

You will need only a computer with a reformatted hard drive and a valid Windows XP installation disc with the accompanying product key.

 Do not use pirated software for this or any other task you perform in this book!

Details

This lesson will walk you step-by-step through the procedure of performing a fresh install of Windows XP on a reformatted hard drive.

Reinstalling Windows XP

REINSTALLING WINDOWS XP ON A REFORMATTED COMPUTER

1. Verify that your computer is hooked up to a power supply.

2. Locate the Windows XP install disc.

3. Insert the disc into the CD or DVD drive of the computer.

4. Reboot the computer.

 In Task 1.19, you made sure that the computer would look to the optical drive first to boot. Watch carefully for the message "Press any key to boot from DVD." It will appear for only a few seconds, so quickly press any key on the keyboard to initiate a boot from the DVD.

You may be asked to activate the product (operating system) at this time or at some point in the installation process. Skip this part of the setup since you will need an Internet connection to complete product activation.

5. When the Welcome to Setup screen appears, press the Enter key to continue with the setup.

 You can also press Enter at this step.

6. The initial Windows Setup window appears.

7. When the Welcome to Setup window appears, press Enter.

8. When the End-User License Agreement appears, press F8 to agree.

```
Windows XP Licensing Agreement

   Microsoft Windows XP Professional

   END-USER LICENSE AGREEMENT

   IMPORTANT-READ CAREFULLY: This End-User
   License Agreement ("EULA") is a legal agreement between you
   (either an individual or a single entity) and Microsoft
   Corporation for the Microsoft software product identified above,
   which includes computer software and may include associated
   media, printed materials, "online" or electronic documentation,
   and Internet-based services ("Product").    An amendment or
   addendum to this EULA may accompany the Product.  YOU AGREE TO BE
   BOUND BY THE TERMS OF THIS EULA BY
   INSTALLING, COPYING, OR OTHERWISE USING THE
   PRODUCT. IF YOU DO NOT AGREE, DO NOT INSTALL
   OR USE THE PRODUCT; YOU MAY RETURN IT TO YOUR
   PLACE OF PURCHASE FOR A FULL REFUND.

   1. GRANT OF LICENSE. Microsoft grants you the following rights
      provided that you comply with all terms and conditions of
      this EULA:

      * Installation and use.  You may install, use, access,
        display and run one copy of the Product on a single
        computer, such as a workstation, terminal or other device
        ("Workstation Computer").  The Product may not be used
        by more than two (2) processors at  any one time on any

 F8=I agree   ESC=I do not agree   PAGE DOWN=Next Page
```

9. When the partition window appears, verify that the desired partition is selected and then press Enter to install Windows XP on that partition.

WARNING   You can also create a new partition by pressing C. To toggle through a list of partitions in the partition window, use the up- and down-arrow keys.

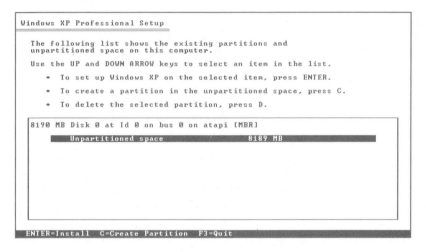

10. When the file system window appears, use the up- and down-arrow keys to select Format the Partition Using the NTFS File System, and then press Enter.

11. Setup will format the partition and then copy files to the Windows installation folders. When it finishes copying files, Windows will reboot.

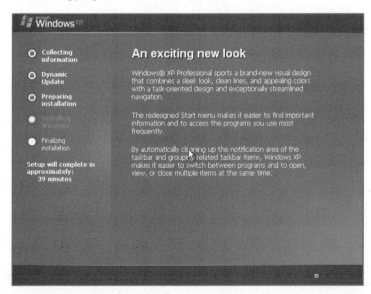

After Windows reboots, the GUI installation screen appears, informing you of the current stage of the installation and about how long it will take. Notice the flashing green lights at the lower right side of the screen. The moving lights indicate that the installation is proceeding.

If those lights stop moving or are moving extremely slowly, it probably indicates a problem with the install. The most common cause is a smudge or dirt on the disc. You will need to stop the installation, remove the disc, and examine it for smudges or damage. If possible, clean the disc and make another attempt to do the installation.

12. When the Regional and Language Options dialog box appears, click Next.

If you live someplace besides the United States, you will want to click the Customize and Details buttons to adjust the Regional and Language Options settings so they are appropriate to your location. After these settings are adjusted, you can click Next to proceed.

13. When the Personalize Your Software dialog box appears, enter your name or the name of the end user in the Name field. You can optionally enter a company name in the Organization field.

14. Click Next.

15. When the Your Product Key dialog box appears, enter the 25-character product key that came with the installation disc.

You can usually find the product key on a label attached to the disc case.

16. After you've entered the key, click Next.

17. When the Computer Name and Administrator Password dialog box appears, type the hostname of the computer in the Computer Name field.

The hostname is can be any name you want to give the computer. It should be a name unique to the network on which the computer will be operating.

18. Type the password for the local computer administrator account in the Administrator Password field, and repeat this step in the Confirm Password field.

This is the password for the administrator account on the local machine, not the domain administrator password.

19. Click Next.

20. When the Date and Time Settings dialog box appears, adjust the Date, Time, and Time Zone settings using the drop-down lists and arrow keys.

Usually, the Date and Time settings are correct and you will only have to adjust the Time Zone setting.

21. If desired, verify that the Automatically Adjust Clock For Daylight Saving Changes check box is checked, and click Next.

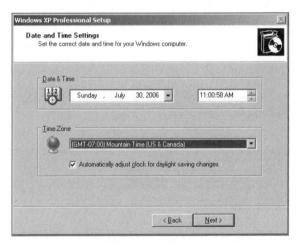

After you click Next in the Date and Time Settings window, you will be returned to the GUI installation window. Allow the installation process to continue until your input is required.

22. When the Networking Settings dialog box appears, select Typical Settings and click Next.

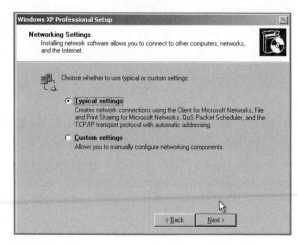

23. When the Workgroup or Computer Domain dialog box appears, select the No, This Computer Is Not on a Network radio button, and accept the default workgroup name of WORKGROUP.

24. Click Next.

If you are installing Windows XP Home edition, the default name of the workgroup is MSHOME.

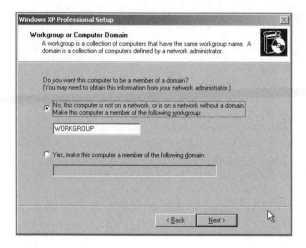

You will join this computer to the domain after the installation is complete. See Task 3.9 for details.

After you click Next in the Workgroup or Computer Domain window, you will be returned to the GUI installation window. The installation will finish after about 30 minutes and the computer will reboot at that time.

25. When the computer reboots and the Display Settings dialog box appears asking to adjust the screen resolution, click OK.

26. When the screen resolution is adjusted, if you can read the message in the Monitor Settings dialog box, click OK.

After you click OK in the Monitor Settings dialog box, Windows XP will load.

CONFIGURING A NEWLY INSTALLED WINDOWS XP PROFESSIONAL COMPUTER

1. When the Welcome to Microsoft Windows screen appears, click Next.

If you have speakers attached to the computer, turn them on and turn up the volume. If the sound card and speakers are operating correctly, you will hear a test song.

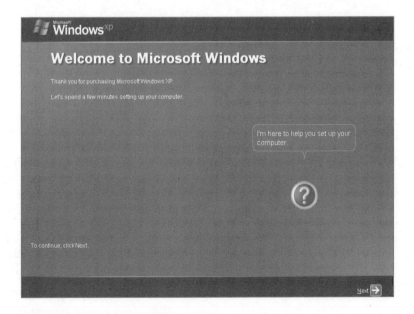

2. When the Help protect your PC screen appears (included with Windows XP SP3), select "Help protect my PC by turning on Automatic Updates now" and then click Next.

3. When the Internet Connection screen appears, select the Yes, This Computer Will Connect Through a Local Area Network or Home Network radio button and click Next.

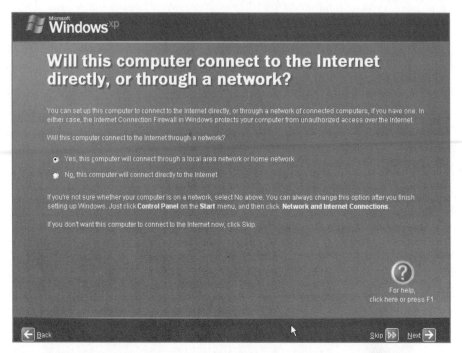

 You also have the option to skip the screen in Step 3 by clicking Skip.

4. When the Ready to Register with Microsoft? screen appears, select the No, Not at This Time radio button and click Next.

5. When the Who Will Use This Computer? screen appears, type the name of the primary user in the Your Name field.

6. If other users need to have their own local computer accounts on this PC, use the additional fields to enter their names.

7. Click Next.

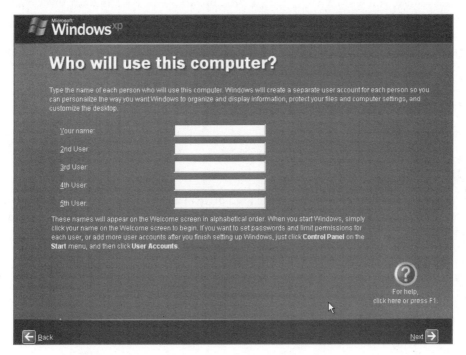

8. When the Thank You! screen appears, indicating that Windows XP Professional has been successfully configured, click Finish.

Criteria for Completion

You will have successfully installed and configured Windows XP on a computer when the operating system loads, and you can use the computer normally.

 Under normal circumstances, your next steps are to activate the onboard firewall, configure the network connection, connect to the Internet, and go to the Windows Update site. You will need to install all the service packs and security patches before you resume any other activity on the computer.

Task 1.21: Installing Windows Vista as a Fresh Install

In this exercise, you will be performing a fresh install but using Windows Vista instead of XP. While Windows XP is still the most widely used version of Windows, with Windows 7 positioning itself to soon take over the lead, there are still many computers running Windows Vista. Windows Vista got a bad rap early on in its career but continues to successfully operate in the world of modern computing.

Objective

This task covers objective 220-802: 1.2.

Scenario

You have just completed reformatting the hard drive of a laptop that had been corrupted with various forms of malware (see Task 1.19). In this scenario, the laptop previously ran Windows Vista rather than Windows XP, and you have been tasked with installing Vista on the notebook device. You have located an authorized Windows Vista DVD and are ready to reinstall the operating system. You will be performing a fresh install, so it will be as if you were installing Windows Vista on a brand-new hard drive.

Scope of Task

Duration

This task should take about 30 to 45 minutes, depending on the capacity of your computer's CPU and memory.

WARNING   To check on the system requirements of the computer you want to use to install Windows Vista, including CPU and memory, visit http://windows .microsoft.com/en-us/windows/help/install-reinstall-uninstall and then click Install Windows Vista.

Setup

You'll need a computer with a newly reformatted hard drive. You will also need a genuine Windows Vista installation DVD and the accompanying product key. The laptop or other computer used for this exercise must be set to boot from the DVD drive.

Caveat

You are most likely aware of the plethora of varieties of Vista available. For the sake of this exercise, the Windows Vista installation will not favor any particular edition of Vista. Since the laptop we are using for this example previously ran Vista adequately, this exercise will not include the steps for checking system requirements or hardware and software compatibility.

Procedure

This task will instruct you on how to reinstall Windows Vista on the reformatted hard drive of a computer using the Windows Vista installation DVD.

Equipment Used

You will need only a computer with a reformatted hard drive and a valid Windows Vista installation DVD with the accompanying product key.

Details

This lesson will walk you step-by-step through the procedure of performing a fresh install of Windows Vista on a reformatted hard drive.

Reinstalling Windows Vista

REINSTALLING WINDOWS VISTA ON A REFORMATTED COMPUTER

1. Verify that your computer is hooked up to a power supply.
2. Locate the Windows Vista install DVD.
3. Insert the disc into the DVD drive of the computer.
4. Reboot the computer.
5. When the GUI setup launches, make whatever regional settings changes you desire and then click Next.

6. When the next screen appears, click Install Now.

7. When the Type Your Product Key for Activation screen appears, enter the product key in the available field and click Next.

 The Automatically Activate Windows When I'm Online check box is selected by default.

8. On the license agreement screen, select the I Accept the License Terms check box and then click Next.

9. On the Which Type of Installation Do You Want? screen, select Custom (Advanced).

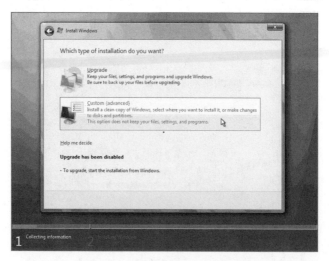

The Upgrade button is disabled because this is a fresh install. This button would only be active if you were installing Vista on a computer that had an operating system present.

10. On the Where Do You Want to Install Windows? screen, click Next.

11. The Installing Windows process will launch, and will take some time to complete, because Windows is performing tasks such as copying files, installing features, and installing updates from the Internet.

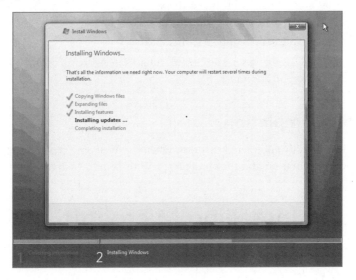

12. After the Windows Vista updates are downloaded and installed from the Internet, Vista will automatically reboot the computer.

13. When it has rebooted, Vista will continue to perform necessary tasks. This may take some time.

14. When the necessary tasks are complete, Vista will reboot the computer again.

SETTING UP WINDOWS VISTA

1. After the computer reboots, the Set Up Windows screen launches. When you are prompted, enter the username and password for the first user on the computer, and then click Next.

You will either need the laptop user's name and password, or you can enter the administrative credentials here and have the user enter their logon information at a later time.

2. On the next screen, enter the hostname for the computer, select the desktop background, and then click Next.

3. On the Help Protect Windows Automatically screen, select the setting that fits your company's security requirements.

WARNING   If you are performing this task on a computer in a home or small lab setting, the best option is to select Use Recommended Settings.

4. On the Review Your Time and Date Settings screen, confirm that the time zone, date, and time settings match your location and then click Next.

5. When the Thank You! screen appears, click Start.

6. The computer will display a series of promotional screens while Windows Vista performs the final configuration tasks.

Criteria for Completion

You will have successfully completed this task when the Welcome center appears showing the Vista version information and the Get Started With Windows area.

Task 1.22: Installing Microsoft Applications in Windows XP

Although most computers you will purchase come with all the necessary application software already installed, you may occasionally have to install some piece of Microsoft application software. Like installing a Microsoft operating system, the process is heavily scripted and doesn't leave much to chance. In the vast majority of cases, you'll need the product key to install the software, and you'll need to activate it within 30 days of the installation.

IT departments tend to keep their software discs, including the product keys, under lock and key, and they keep track of the number of licenses they have available. Before doing an install, always verify the number of licenses your company has for the software. Installing a Microsoft application is as simple as popping the install DVD in the optical drive and following the instructions.

Objective

This task covers objective 220-802: 1.5.

Scenario

You have just finished installing Windows XP on a laptop that had to have its hard drive reformatted (see Tasks 1.19 and 1.20). You have configured a network connection and restored all of the service packs and security updates. Your next step is to install all of the Microsoft application software. You will start by installing Microsoft Office 2007.

 Microsoft Office 2007 is used as an example for this task, but if you're installing Office 2010 or any other Microsoft application software, the process should be similar.

You have located the DVD and product key and are ready to begin.

Scope of Task

Duration

Depending on the software package, this task will take about 15 to 20 minutes.

Setup

You'll need access to a computer and an installation DVD containing a Microsoft application.

Caveat

As you must be aware, Microsoft products are not inexpensive, so you may not want to go out and buy a Microsoft Office suite. In a pinch, you can uninstall and reinstall a Microsoft application on your computer. Make sure you have the appropriate installation discs available before you begin. Also, if you have installed a Microsoft product on one computer and you attempt to install and activate the product on a second computer, this may violate the licensing agreement.

Procedure

This task will show you how to install a piece of Microsoft application software.

Equipment Used

All you'll need is a computer and a Microsoft application installation CD or DVD.

Details

This lesson will guide you through the process of installing a Microsoft application.

Installing a Microsoft Application

1. Verify that the computer is powered up.

2. Log on as Administrator.

3. Locate the Microsoft Office 2007 installation disk.

4. Insert the disc into the computer's optical drive.

 WARNING The disk should Autoplay; if it doesn't, you'll need to open My Computer, right-click the CD/DVD icon, and click Open. Look for a launch or startup file and double-click to execute it. The installation program should launch.

5. When the Product Key screen appears, input the product key that accompanied your installation disc, and when the green check mark appears, click Continue.

 NOTE The product key is usually found on a label attached to the disc case.

6. When the Microsoft Software License Terms box appears, read the content provided, select the I Accept the Terms of This Agreement check box, and then click Continue.

7. On the Choose the Installation You Want screen, click Install Now.

 WARNING If you had chosen Customize, you could have selected only those products in the Office suite to be installed that you desired, such as Word and Excel. You could also have selected a specific path to the location where you wanted Office installed, such as C:\Program Files\Microsoft Office\.

8. Once the installation is complete, you are presented with a dialog box saying the product was successfully installed and offering you the opportunity to visit Microsoft Office Online to get product updates. Click Close on this box.

9. To activate any application in the Microsoft Office 2007 suite, click Start ➢ All Programs ➢ Microsoft Office, and then choose a specific product, such as Microsoft Office Word 2007.

10. When Word launches, the Microsoft Office 2007 configuration screen appears and runs. When it is finished, click Close.

 NOTE If you did not previously enter the 25-character product key, you will be prompted to do so now. If you do not enter the key, Microsoft Office 2007 will not activate. Once you enter the key, click Continue and the configuration dialog box will appear and run.

11. When the Microsoft Office Activation Wizard launches, select I Want to Activate the Software over the Internet (Recommended), and then click Next.

12. Once the activation process has completed, click Close.

13. When the Windows Update dialog box appears, click the Check for Updates button and then download and install all Microsoft Office updates.

Criteria for Completion

You will have successfully completed this task when you can verify that the Microsoft Office 2007 suite has been installed on the computer and you can use all of the applications within the suite.

Task 1.23: Uninstalling Software in Windows XP

Sometimes it's necessary to uninstall software on a computer. Usually you do this when a program is no longer used by the company because it has become obsolete or the firm has decided to go with another vendor for that type of software. Although quite a variety of programs are available, Windows uses the same process to uninstall a program and all its components. It's really a piece of cake.

Objective

This task covers objective 220-802: 1.5.

Scenario

The Payroll department has decided to discontinue the use of its current accounting software and has purchased similar software from a different vendor. You have been assigned to go to the payroll office and uninstall the relevant program from the computers there. It is just past regular business hours, so none of the users will be present. You are free to log on to each PC using your administrator credentials and remove the programs.

Scope of Task

Duration

This task will take 10 to 15 minutes.

Setup

You will need one computer with a program you can uninstall. It can be any sort of software.

Caveat

This is a fairly simple task, so there shouldn't be any particular issues. The computer used for this task is running Windows XP.

Procedure

This task will teach you how to remove a program from a Windows XP computer.

Equipment Used

You will only need a computer and a program on that computer you are willing to remove.

Details

This task will show you the process of removing a program from a Windows XP computer.

Uninstalling a Program

> For this task, it is assumed that you are at a computer that is powered up and you are logged on with an account that has administrator privileges.

1.   Click Start ➤ Control Panel.

> If your Control Panel is currently in Category view, switch it to Classic view.

2.   Double-click the Add or Remove Programs icon.
3.   When the list populates, click the name of the program you want to remove.
4.   Click the Change/Remove button.
5.   When the dialog box opens asking if you are sure you want to remove the program, click Yes.

> You may be asked to remove multiple components. In this event, click Delete All.

Criteria for Completion

You will have successfully completed the task when you return to the Add or Remove Programs list and the program you selected is no longer present.

Task 1.24: Uninstalling an Application Using Windows 7 Programs and Features

If you are familiar with removing software in Windows XP using the Add/Remove Software feature in Control Panel, then uninstalling software on Windows 7 will seem somewhat different. It isn't a particularly difficult task, but it's different enough that an exercise is required to show you how this tool performs.

Objective

This task covers objective 220-802: 1.5.

Scenario

You have a large number of applications installed on your Windows 7 computer that you rarely use and have decided to remove them to recover hard drive space.

Scope of Task

Duration

This task should take about 5 to 10 minutes.

Setup

You will need a Windows 7 computer with at least one application you want to remove. If you don't have any applications on this computer you want to remove, search for open source software for Windows 7, select a small program, and install it. Make sure it is a valid open source product and not a form of freeware that will likely install malware on your computer.

Caveat

Assuming you are going to uninstall a program you can live without, this task is simple and safe. A Windows 7 Profession (64-bit) computer was used in the creation of this task, but any version of Windows 7 should work.

Procedure

This lesson will show you how to uninstall an application in Windows 7.

Equipment Used

All you'll need is a Windows 7 computer and an application you want to uninstall.

Details

This task will walk you through the procedure for uninstalling an application from Windows 7 using the Programs and Features tool.

For the sake of this task, I installed an open source product called paint.net, but you can uninstall any application you desire.

Uninstalling an Application on Windows 7

1. Click Start ➢ Control Panel.

2. Depending on your preference, select Large Icons or Small Icons in the View By menu (you can also select Category view and click Uninstall a program to perform this task).

3. Scroll down in Control Panel and click Programs and Features to launch this tool.

4. Scroll down in the Programs and Features dialog box, and locate and then select the application you want to uninstall.

5. Click Uninstall.

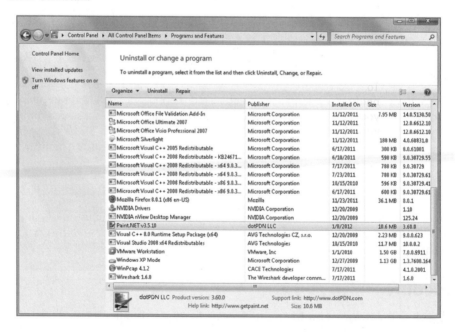

6. When asked if you want to uninstall the application, click Yes.

7. When asked by User Account Control if you want to remove the application, click Yes.

8. When the application is uninstalled, close Programs and Features.

Criteria for Completion

You will have successfully completed this task when the application has been uninstalled from Windows 7.

Task 1.25: Upgrading from Windows XP to Windows 7

While purchasing a brand-new Windows 7 computer to replace an older Windows operating system and older computer hardware is ideal, there are still valid reasons to upgrade an existing computer running Windows XP to Windows 7. Since Windows 7 is known to be rather demanding in its need for resources, an essential task is to determine if the computer running Windows XP is capable of supporting Windows 7.

As with all upgrades, you should back up any data on the computer beforehand, in case the upgrade results in data loss. Also have handy all of the installation discs for your application software. It is also very important to determine if your Windows XP computer is 32-bit or 64-bit, since this affects the version of Windows 7 you will install as well as the type of supporting software.

To find out if your computer is capable of running Windows 7, you will need to download the Windows 7 Upgrade Advisor. The Advisor will scan your PC and analyze any issues with your computer's hardware and software that might cause a problem with the upgrade. Download Windows 7 Upgrade Advisor for free at http://windows.microsoft.com/en-US/windows/downloads/upgrade-advisor.

Before the upgrade procedure, you will also need to move all of your files to external storage, such as a DVD or external USB drive. In addition, you should collect the original installation discs for any software running on the Windows XP machine that you want to run on Windows 7. You can use Windows Easy Transfer to move all of your files to another location. Windows Easy Transfer also provides a report of all of the software running on your computer and enables you to move your files back to the computer once it is upgraded to Windows 7. You can download Windows Easy Transfer for free at http://windows.microsoft.com/en-US/windows7/products/features/windows-easy-transfer. WET is also available on the Windows 7 installation DVD in the D:\support\migwiz folder. To start it, type migsetup.exe in the Search box and press Enter.

Objective

This task covers objective 220-802: 1.2.

Scenario

You've received a request to upgrade the finance manager's PC from Windows XP to Windows 7 as part of a project to upgrade the managerial-staff computers over the next month. You have come in on the weekend so that you'll have free access to the computer, and you have the required administrator logon information for the PC.

You have already logged in to the Windows XP computer and performed a series of pre-installation tasks. These tasks included downloading and running the Windows 7 Upgrade Advisor, correcting the few issues Advisor found on the computer, and then running Advisor again to verify that there were no further issues. You ran the onboard antivirus software and verified that there were no active threats on the computer and then shut down the antivirus program. You connected an external USB drive to the computer and used Windows Easy Transfer to move all of the manager's files to the external drive. Once the upgrade is complete, you will use Windows Easy Transfer again to move the files back to the computer. Additionally, you have made sure you have access to all of the application installation discs so you can reinstall the required programs needed by the user.

> This task focuses on the actual operating system upgrade process. For information on how to use Windows 7 Upgrade Advisor and Windows Easy Transfer, refer to the information provided by the links in the previously supplied tips in this task.

The computer is connected to the Internet so you can get any current installation files from Microsoft during the installation process. You have the Windows 7 upgrade DVD and product key and are ready to proceed.

> You can also purchase and download the Windows 7 installation files from Microsoft over the Internet and then launch the installation from the computer's hard drive by double-clicking the application file. If you downloaded the Windows 7 installation files to a USB drive, you can launch the installation by double-clicking setup.exe, just as you would on a Windows 7 installation DVD.

Scope of Task

Duration

This task should take about an hour to an hour and a half depending on the speed of the PC's CPU, the amount of RAM present, and how much hardware and software Windows 7 must detect during the upgrade.

Setup

You'll need a computer running Windows XP Home or Professional and a Windows 7 installation disc. This exercise does not specify a particular edition of Windows 7 for the upgrade.

Caveat

Before performing the upgrade, it is essential that you go to the Windows Update site and download and install the most current hardware drivers for the computer. The operating system upgrade may fail if you do not perform this task, even though you are directed to update drivers and other software during the upgrade process.

Windows 7 Upgrade Advisor will suggest that you remove any devices and peripherals that are not absolutely necessary for running the computer, including sound cards, printers, and scanners.

Carefully review and perform all of the tasks referred to in the tips and notes provided earlier in this exercise to ensure that the upgrade will not fail. This task assumes that when the installation DVD is inserted in the computer's DVD drive, it will Autorun. The task also assumes you are installing a 32-bit version of Windows 7 on a 32-bit computer. You will need to have the 25-character Windows product key for Windows 7.

Procedure

You will learn how to upgrade a computer's operating system from Windows XP to Windows 7.

Equipment Used

You will need only a computer running Windows XP Home or Professional and a Windows 7 installation DVD.

Details

This task will take you through the steps of upgrading a Windows XP computer to Windows 7.

Upgrading a Windows XP Computer to Windows 7

1. Open the optical drive on the computer, insert the Windows 7 DVD and close the drive.

2. If Autorun does not begin the process, open My Computer, select the DVD drive, browse to the root folder, and double-click setup.exe.

3. When the Windows 7 Setup screen appears, click Install Now.

4. When the Get Important Updates for Installation page appears, install the latest updates for Windows 7 to make sure that the installation goes smoothly, first making sure the computer is connected to the Internet.

5. When the Please Read the License Terms page appears, click I Accept the License Terms and then click Next.

6. When the Which Type of Installation Do You Want? page appears, click Custom.

 There is no direct upgrade path from Windows XP to Windows 7.

7. Select the partition on the hard drive containing Windows XP, which should usually be the C drive, and then click Next.

8. When the Windows.old dialog box appears, click OK.

9. The Windows 7 upgrade will perform necessary tasks, including copying Windows files, gathering files, detecting hardware, installing drivers, and so on. This may take some time.

10. When the necessary tasks are complete, Windows 7 will reboot the computer.

Setting Up Windows 7

1. After the computer reboots, the Set Up Windows screen launches. When you are prompted, enter the username and password for the first user on the computer; then click Next.

 You will need the computer user's username and password, or else you can enter your administrative credentials here and have the user enter their logon information at a later time.

2. On the next screen, enter the unique hostname for the computer, select the desktop background, and then click Next.

3. When prompted, supply the 25-character product key.

4. On the Help Protect Your Computer and Improve Windows Automatically dialog box, configure basic security for Windows 7 by selecting Use Recommended Settings.

5. On the Review Your Time and Date Settings screen, confirm that the time zone, date, and time settings match your location, and then click Next.

6. On the Select Your Computer's Current Location screen, select the option for where you will be using the computer, such as Home Network, Work Network, or Public Network (in the case of this task, choose Home Network).

7. Click Start to begin the configuration, and when prompted, confirm your selection.

8. Once the configuration process is complete, the Windows 7 login page appears, and you can log in to the upgraded Windows 7 computer.

Criteria for Completion

You will have successfully completed this task when Windows 7 loads to the login page.

At this point, you would reinstall the files located on the external USB drive using Windows Easy Transfer and reinstall all required application software. Make sure the antivirus software is installed, updated to the latest version for Windows 7, and updated to the latest virus definitions.

Task 1.26: Shutting Down Background Processes in Windows 7

Every so often, a program in Windows will hang and refuse to close. Worse, it might be a program that has a memory leak, sucking up more and more of your available RAM and giving nothing back. When an average user wants to close Microsoft Word or Internet Explorer, they click the little red box with the white *X* inside in the upper-right corner of the document or window. The vast majority of the time this works quite well, but when it doesn't, a user could wind up both frustrated and unproductive. There is actually a very simple way to shut down a stubborn program.

Objective

This task covers objective 220-802: 1.4.

Scenario

You are walking past the Accounting department when one of the users motions you over to her desk. She has been working extensively in Microsoft Excel for most of the morning but complains that the application has now locked up on her. She asks if you'd mind helping fix the problem. You take a look at the Excel header bar and see the message "Not Responding." You realize this could be a pretty easy fix, and since you have a few minutes, you agree to help her.

In a larger business with an in-house IT department, requesting help for a computer problem requires the end user to call the help desk and file a trouble ticket before a tech is assigned to respond. Smaller businesses are less formal, but if you drop whatever you're doing all the time to help out just because you're handy, you'll never get any of your assigned work finished. Word to the wise...

Scope of Task

Duration

This task should take less than 5 minutes.

Setup

All you'll need is a Windows 7 computer running some application. The easiest way to set up the task is to start a program you'll recognize as it's listed in the Processes tab in Task Manager. You'll easily be able to recognize the program and shut it down.

Sometimes, the offending process is not a normal application like Excel. You may have a rogue process running that was planted there by a virus or other malware. If you don't recognize some of the listings on the Processes tab, you can do an Internet search for the names of the processes to see what results you get. Unfortunately, it is not easy to locate a comprehensive list of all processes that can possibly run on a Windows 7 computer.

Even when you have no application software running (look in Task Manager's Applications tab), the Processes tab will still show numerous programs running. The vast majority of those processes are necessary to provide various services. Occasionally, one is an indication of a problem.

You can view, start, and stop services in Windows 7 in Task Manager by clicking the Services tab. Right-click the desired service and then select from one of the available options. Clicking the Services button on this tab opens the Services dialog box.

Caveat

Every once in a while, closing a program in this manner causes unusual results in the computer. You'll receive a warning dialog box when you attempt to close the program later on in the task. However, it is considered a safe method of shutting down stalled processes.

Procedure

In this task, you'll learn how to shut down stalled processes, including background processes in Windows 7.

This method also works on Windows XP and Windows Vista computers.

Equipment Used

You won't need any equipment to complete this task.

Details

This task will take you through the steps of shutting down a running process in Windows 7.

Shutting Down a Process in Windows 7

1. Using the keyboard, hold down the following three keys: Ctrl+Alt+Delete. From the options that appear select Start Task Manager. Using the mouse, right-click the Taskbar at the bottom of the screen. From the menu that appears, click Start Task Manager (it may be named just Task Manager).

2. When Windows Task Manager opens, click the Processes tab.

3. In the Image Name column, locate excel.exe.

For the purpose of this task, you can choose to stop another program by selecting its name.

4. Select EXCEL.EXE by clicking it.

You may see this displayed as EXCEL.EXE*32, which indicates a 32-bit application running on 64-bit Windows 7.

5. Click the End Process button in the lower-right corner of the Task Manager dialog box.

You'll receive a Task Manager warning stating that "Do you want to end 'ACDSee5.exe*32?' If an open program is associated with this process, it will close and you will lose any unsaved data. If you end a system process, it might result in an unstable system. Are you sure you want to continue?

6. When the Task Manager Warning box appears, click End Process.

You'll be tempted to use the Applications tab in Task Manager to kill Excel, but keep in mind that only application software is listed there. Many other running processes in Windows won't appear in this display, so it's better to use the Processes tab in the vast majority of cases.

Criteria for Completion

You will have successfully completed this task when the selected process disappears from the list in the Processes window. In this example, Excel should close immediately.

 Sometimes applications hang for unknown reasons, and the next time you use them, they work fine. This task is an example of that situation. Keep in mind that there are other circumstances where this symptom could indicate a larger problem that's not so easily solved.

Task 1.27: Installing a Local Printer

In most business settings, users print to one or more network printers. This allows printer resources to be shared among a large number of users, avoiding the need to rely on one user sharing their printer with the rest of the workgroup. A print server performs the queuing and is (hopefully) always available to the network.

There are occasions when one or more users will require a local printer to be attached to their PC. While extremely rare these days, some businesses still use old dot-matrix printers to print multicopy No Carbon Required (NCR) documents such as invoices. Department heads may want to print confidential documents in their offices rather than risk sensitive material being printed on a network printer shared by the rest of the staff. You will occasionally find it necessary to install a local printer on a computer in a business setting. If you support SOHO (small office/home office) customers, this is a very common task.

Objective

This task covers objective 220-801: 4.2.

Scenario

You receive the assignment of installing a local printer on a new sales executive's PC. You are provided with the new printer and installation kit on a cart, and you take the equipment to the appropriate office and get ready to install it.

Duration

This task should take about 15 to 20 minutes at most.

Setup

You'll need a PC, a printer, the USB cable, and the driver disc that came with the printer. If you already have a printer installed, you can uninstall the printer drivers and disconnect the printer from your computer. Then follow the instructions in this task to reinstall the printer. In most cases, you probably don't even need to have the driver disc since Windows 7 contains an extensive list of drivers for common print devices. Of course, having the disc doesn't hurt, just in case the printer is a newer model produced sometime after the Windows 7 computer.

Caveat

Installing a printer on Windows 7 should be a snap. Just make sure you have the right driver disc in the event that Windows doesn't have the drivers on board. Also, some printers require that you use their installation software to do the setup rather than using the Add Printer Wizard. Read the instructions that come with your printer completely before beginning this exercise because the required steps for your printer may vary from the steps presented in this task.

 It is unlikely that you'll use a printer cable for this task, since current printers come almost exclusively with USB cables, but if you are performing this task with an older setup, using a printer cable won't appreciably change the installation process.

Procedure

This task will take you through the process of installing a local printer on a PC.

Equipment Used

The only piece of equipment you might need is a small screwdriver if you are using an older setup requiring a standard printer cable. Even then, some of the connectors are screwed in while others can be tightened by hand. If you are unpacking a brand-new printer from a box, you may need a box cutter to cut through the tape and any other restraints used to secure the printer for shipping.

Details

This exercise shows you the steps necessary to connect a local printer to a PC and verify that it's working.

Installing a Local Printer

CONNECTING THE PRINTER

1. Power up the computer.
2. Log on as the local administrator.
3. Unpack the printer.
4. Place the printer at a desired location near the computer.

5. Verify that all packing equipment and tape have been removed from the printer.

6. Locate the USB cable used to attach the printer to the PC, as well as the printer's power cable.

7. Locate the installation kit, which should include a driver disc, installation manual, and any other equipment or materials that came with the printer.

8. Read the installation manual completely before proceeding.

9. Attach the power cable to the printer and plug the other end into a power socket or surge protector.

10. Attach one end of the USB cable to the printer's USB port and attach the other end to the PC's USB port.

 The connectors at each end of the USB cable will be different. The connector for the printer will be more of a square while the connector for the computer will look like a thin rectangle. Also, some printers require that you install the printer drivers and other software prior to physically connecting the printer to the computer.

11. Following the instructions that came with the printer, open the printer, and find the printer head(s).

12. Locate the printer cartridge(s) that came with the printer.

 If cartridges did not come with the printer, your supervisor should provide you with the appropriate cartridges for this device.

13. Install the cartridge(s) in the printer following the instruction guide.

 There's no standard method of installing printer cartridges, so we won't go into detail on this part of the task.

14. Close the printer.

15. Power up the printer.

 The printer should go through a self-check routine and perform the alignment of the printer head(s) at this point, or it may perform some parts of this process after it is fully installed. There can be a special process associated with printer alignment, depending on the make and model of printer you are installing. Check the printer's documentation for details.

INSTALLING THE PRINTER

1. Click Start ➤ Devices and Printers.

> You can also click Start ➤ Control Panel ➤ Devices and Printers.
>
> If Windows autodetects the printer as a new USB device or the Add Hardware wizard launches, close the wizard and proceed with the instructions in this task.

2. In the upper-left corner of the Devices and Printers page, click Add a Printer.
3. When the Add Printer Wizard launches, select the Add a Local Printer option, and then click Next.
4. On the Choose a Printer Port page, use the drop-down list to select the appropriate port, such as USB001 if the local printer will connect to the computer using a USB cable.

> If you are using an older standard printer cable, select LPT1: (Printer Port).

5. Click Next.
6. On the Install Printer Software page, in the Manufacturer window, scroll down and select the manufacturer of the printer (HP, Brother, etc.).
7. In the Printers window, scroll down and select the specific model of printer you have.

> In the vast majority of cases, your computer manufacturer and model will be included in these lists.

8. Click Next.
9. On the Name Your Printer page, give a name to the printer.

> Use a name that clearly identifies the printer.

10. Click Next.
11. On the Printer Sharing page, verify that the Do Not Share This Printer radio button is selected.
12. Click Next.
13. On the success screen, if you want this printer to be the default printer, select the Set as the default printer" check box, click the "Print a test page" button, and then the "Finished" button.

TESTING THE PRINTER

1. When the Print a Test Page window appears, click Yes.

 A box will appear asking if the test page printed properly. The page should print after a few seconds.

2. When the test page prints, click Close.

3. Once the wizard closes, open the application or applications the user will normally print from.

 The user will probably print from Word and Excel, but find out in advance which applications will be used to print. Occasionally the test page will print fine but a particular application will refuse to share and play well with the printer.

4. Systematically open each application, create a small document, and then print it.

5. When you have successfully printed from each application, close it.

6. When the test is completed, verify that all application software is closed.

7. Log off the PC.

8. Make sure that the user has plenty of printer paper and extra print cartridges.

Criteria for Completion

You will have successfully completed this task when you have printed a test page from the Add Printer Wizard and from each application you will be printing from.

Task 1.28: Installing Printer Drivers

You may think this task is a subset of Task 1.28. Although the steps are similar, the situation is different. Besides, there's more than one way to install printer drivers.

Occasionally drivers (or any kind of software) will become corrupted or newer drivers will become available. Sometimes the print device begins to act strangely, and the solution is to update or reinstall the drivers. In any event, there are various reasons why you will be asked to perform this task.

Objective

This task covers objective 220-801: 4.2.

Scenario

One of the marketing executive's local printers has started printing "garbage." Your supervisor believes the printer drivers have been corrupted and provides you with the driver disc appropriate for the user's device. You have been assigned to reinstall the printer drivers and correct the problem.

Duration

This task should take about 10 minutes.

Setup

You will need a driver disc for your local print device.

Caveat

You can also attempt to install drivers from Windows Update if they are available or from the printer manufacturer's website.

Procedure

You will learn the steps necessary to install printer drivers on a computer.

Equipment Used

You will need no special equipment to complete this task besides the driver disc and a Windows 7 computer.

Details

This task will walk you through the procedure of installing new printer drivers on a computer from a disc.

Installing Printer Drivers

INSTALLING PRINTER DRIVERS USING THE ADD A PRINTER DRIVER WIZARD

1. Click Start ➢ Devices and Printers.

 You can also click Start ➢ Control Panel ➢ Devices and Printers.

2. Right-click the desired printer.
3. Click Printer Properties, and if necessary, select the desired printer name.
4. Click the Advanced tab.

5. Click the New Driver button.

6. Click Next to launch the Add Printer Driver wizard.

7. In the Printer Driver Selection page, in the Manufacturer window, scroll down and select the manufacturer of your printer.

8. In the Printers window, scroll down and select the specific model of your printer.

9. Click the Have Disk button.

10. Insert the driver disc in the computer's optical drive.

11. In the Install from Disk dialog box, use the drop-down list to select the drive letter of the optical drive.

WARNING   Instead of using the drop-down list to select a drive letter, you can click the Browse button and use *Locate File* dialog to browse to the correct drive.

12. Click OK.

13. Click Next.

14. When the Completing the Add Printer Driver Wizard page appears, click Finish.

15. Click OK (to close the Printer Properties dialog).

NOTE   The drivers should install at this point of the process.

TESTING THE PRINTER DRIVER INSTALLATION

1. In the Devices and Printers dialog box, right-click the printer.

2. Click Printer Properties.

3. On the General tab, click Print Test Page.

NOTE   After you click Print Test Page, a box will appear asking if the test page printed properly. The page should print after a few seconds.

4. When the test page prints, click Close.

WARNING   If the test page doesn't print or if it doesn't print properly, instead of clicking OK in Step 4, click Get Help with Printing. The Help and Support page will open, and you can work your way through a wizard process to diagnose the problem. You can also consult either the printed documentation for the printer or the printer's documentation on the manufacturer's website.

5. Click OK to close the Printer Properties dialog box.

6. Open the applications the user will use to print.

7. Create a test document in each application and print it.

8. When you have finished, close all applications.

Criteria for Completion

You will have successfully completed this task when you have installed the drivers and the printer operates normally.

Task 1.29: Installing a Bluetooth Printer on Windows 7

As you likely know, Bluetooth is a wireless protocol used to connect devices over a very short distance to construct wireless personal area networks, or PANs. A Bluetooth device can be almost anything, such as a keyboard, mouse, or printer. As of 2005, versions of Bluetooth and Wifi use methods such as Adaptive Frequency Hopping to avoid interfering with each other.

As a support technician, you won't need to know a great amount of detail about the specifications associated with Bluetooth, but you will need to know how to install various Bluetooth devices on a PC. This task will show you how to install a Bluetooth printer on a Windows 7 computer.

Objective

This task covers objective 220-801: 4.2.

Scenario

The chief operations officer at your company wants a Bluetooth printer installed for his Windows 7 computer. He has just left for lunch and expects the printer to be up and running when he gets back.

There is a built-in Bluetooth adapter on the computer, so all you have to do is physically install the device and set it up.

 You can also add a Bluetooth adapter to a computer by plugging the appropriate adapter in a USB port on the PC.

You have been provided with the Bluetooth printer and cable. You have been shown how to turn on the Bluetooth device and make it discoverable.

Duration

This task should take about 10 to 15 minutes.

Setup

You will need a Bluetooth device, cable, and, if your computer does not have a built-in Bluetooth adapter, an external adapter that will plug into a USB port. You can use any Bluetooth device, but it is ideal if you have a Bluetooth printer to install. Also, it is common to use a passkey with Bluetooth devices to protect your data from other devices that are in range of your computer. Except for the Bluetooth-specific steps, this task is the same as adding a local printer to a Windows 7 computer, as you saw in Task 1.27.

 A passkey, or passcode, is a number used to associate a Bluetooth device with a computer. Passkeys are used to provide security so that your device cannot be accessed using another computer. Low-security devices such as keyboards and mice typically don't use passkeys.

Caveat

The process of activating the Bluetooth device and making it discoverable will vary depending on the device, so consult the device's documentation for details. You will also need to refer to the device's documentation if you will be installing it from the device's control panel rather than using Windows 7.

Procedure

You will learn the steps needed to install a Bluetooth printer on a Windows 7 computer.

Equipment Used

You will need the Bluetooth printer and possibly a Bluetooth adapter, unless the computer has a built-in adapter. The adapter plugs into any USB port, so installation is straightforward. You will also need the driver disc that comes with the printer.

Details

This exercise will show you how to install a Bluetooth printer.

Installing a Bluetooth Printer

SETTING UP THE BLUETOOTH PRINTER

1. Make sure you are logged on to the computer with an account that has administrator privileges.

2. Make sure the Bluetooth printer is plugged into a power source such as a surge protector.

3. Turn on the Bluetooth printer.

4. Make the Bluetooth device discoverable (consult the printer's documentation for the specific steps).

SETTING UP A BLUETOOTH PRINTER IN WINDOWS 7

1. Click the Windows 7 Start button.

2. Click Start ➤ Devices and Printers.

3. On the Devices and Printers screen, click Add a Printer.

4. On the Add Printer screen, select Add a Network, Wireless or Bluetooth Printer.

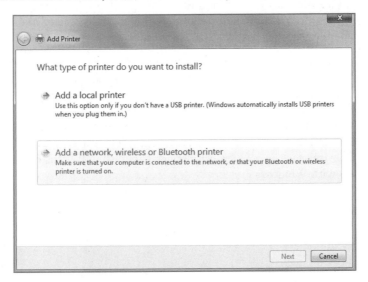

5. In the list of available printers that appears, select the Bluetooth printer and then click Next.

6. When prompted, click Install Driver.

7. Then complete the steps in the "Installing the Printer" section of Task 1.27, starting at Step 11.

8. After the printer is installed, follow the steps for testing the printer as outlined in Task 1.27.

Criteria for Completion

You will have successfully completed this exercise when the Bluetooth printer is installed and is able to print as expected.

Task 1.30: Installing a Bluetooth Device for Pairing with Windows 7

Just because you physically connect a Bluetooth device to your Windows 7 computer, it doesn't mean that Windows will be able to see and interact with the device. You may have to pair the device with Windows 7. *Pairing*, in Bluetooth, means that two devices, either two Bluetooth devices or a Bluetooth device and a Bluetooth-enabled computer, are able to communicate with each other over an established connection. This task will show you how to install a Bluetooth device, such as a phone, to Windows 7 and enable pairing so the phone and Windows 7 can communicate with each other. You will likely need the passkey for the phone and to input that passkey during the pairing process if prompted.

Refer to Task 1.29 for more information on Bluetooth passkeys.

In Task 1.29, you installed a Bluetooth printer, but the process of installing other Bluetooth devices and making sure they can communicate with Windows 7 is not the same for other devices such as a Bluetooth phone. This task will focus on pairing a Bluetooth phone with Windows 7.

Objective

This task covers objective 220-802 3.2.

Scenario

You have just purchased a Bluetooth phone for personal use, and you want to be able to connect it to your Windows 7 Professional computer and have the two devices be able to communicate with each other. You have all of the ancillary materials and documentation that came with the phone, and you have Windows Update enabled to automatically connect to Microsoft so it can download and install updates on your computer.

There is a built-in Bluetooth adapter on the computer, so all you have to do is physically connect the phone to your computer and install the device.

Duration

This task should take about 10 to 15 minutes.

Setup

You will need a Bluetooth device such as a phone, a cable, and, if your computer does not have a built-in Bluetooth adapter, an external adapter that will plug into a USB port. You will also need the passkey for the device because you may be prompted to provide it during the pairing operation.

Caveat

The process of activating the Bluetooth device and making it discoverable will vary depending on the device, so consult the device's documentation for details. You will also need to refer to the device's documentation if you will be installing it from the device's control panel rather than using Windows 7.

Procedure

You will learn the steps needed to install and pair a Bluetooth phone on a Windows 7 computer.

Equipment Used

You will need the Bluetooth phone and possibly a Bluetooth adapter, unless the computer has a built-in adapter. The adapter plugs into any USB port, so installation is straightforward. You will also need a cable to connect the device to your computer and the device's passkey.

Details

This exercise will show you how to install a Bluetooth phone.

Installing and Pairing a Bluetooth Phone

SETTING UP WINDOWS 7 FOR PAIRING WITH A BLUETOOTH PHONE

1. Connect the Bluetooth device to a USB port on the computer and then turn on the Bluetooth device.
2. Turn on the Bluetooth phone and make the device discoverable (consult the documentation for the device and follow the appropriate steps).
3. Click the Start button and then click Devices and Printers.
4. On the Devices and Printers screen, click Add a device.
5. On the Add a Device screen, select the Bluetooth device, and then click Next.
6. If prompted for the phone's passkey, enter the passkey in the available box and then click Next.

 Consult the phone's documentation for the default passkey. The default passkey for many Bluetooth devices is 0000.

7. Verify that Windows begins to install drivers for the device (Windows will download them from Windows Update if necessary).

8. When the This Device Has Been Successfully Added to Your Computer screen appears, click Close.

Criteria for Completion

You will have successfully completed this exercise when the Bluetooth phone is installed and is able to communicate with your Windows 7 PC.

Task 1.31: Syncing a Mobile Device with Media Player in Windows 7

You may have several mobile devices that you want to sync with Windows 7. This means that the mobile device and an application in Windows share the same files. However, when the files change on the mobile device or in Windows, the numbers and types of files are no longer synchronized and do not match.

In the case of audio files, such as music you play on an MP3 player, you may want to sync those files with music stored on your Windows 7 computer. You can set up your Windows 7 computer so those files are synced using Windows Media Player. Once the device is set to sync, you can then have it sync automatically with Media Player, so the music files on your MP3 player and on Windows are identical. Media Player also can convert any file formats on the remote device to formats it supports during the syncing process.

    Remote devices are seen by Windows 7 as removable storage devices. They can include MP3 players and mobile phones and be set up to sync with Windows applications such as Media Player or Outlook. However, some mobile devices, such as an Apple iPod, may not work with Media Player.

Objective

This task covers objective 220-802 3.2.

Scenario

You work for a company that provides desktop computer and network support for small office and home office users. One of your customers just bought a new MP3 player and wants you to set it up to sync with his music files on his Windows 7 PC using Windows Media Player.

All you have to do is connect the MP3 layer to the computer and install the device.

Duration

This task should take about 10 to 15 minutes.

Setup

You will need an MP3 player and a Windows 7 computer. You should also have some music files on your computer to use to initiate the sync process.

Caveat

As previously mentioned, not all MP3 players will work with Windows Media Player. Media Player particularly doesn't work well with Apple's iPod product, which is the most popular MP3 player on the planet.

After setting up the MP3 device to sync with Media Player, if the device's storage capacity is greater than 4GB and your entire music library will fit on the device, automatic device syncing is already configured at this point. However, you may want to have automatic syncing available but not sync every file on your computer with your MP3 player. The second set of steps on this task will show you how to do this.

If your MP3 player has less than 4GB of storage or your entire music library will not fit on the device, you will have to set up manual syncing. This task assumes that your entire library will fit on your MP3 device, and the procedure for setting up a manual sync is not covered.

Procedure

You will learn the steps needed to set up syncing between an MP3 device and Windows Media Player on a Windows 7 machine and then set up the device to sync automatically.

There is also a process for manual syncing that will not be covered in this task.

Equipment Used

You will need an MP3 player that is compatible with Windows Media Player, as well as the device's instructions and a cable to connect it with your computer. You will also need a Windows 7 computer on which to perform the sync process using Windows Media Player.

Details

This exercise will show you how to set up syncing between an MP3 device and Windows Media Player and then how to configure them for automatic syncing. This involves two sets of steps: first setting up basic syncing between the device and your computer, and then setting up automatic syncing.

Configuring Syncing and Then Setting Up Automatic Syncing

SETTING UP AN MP3 DEVICE FOR SYNCING WITH WINDOWS MEDIA PLAYER

1. Attach the MP3 device to the computer and then turn on the device.

2. Turn on the MP3 player and make the device discoverable (consult the documentation for the player and follow the appropriate steps).

3. If required, configure the MP3 device to use a specific syncing option such as Sync Music (consult the device's documentation for details).

4. On Windows 7, click Start, and in the Search box, type **Windows Media Player**.

5. Under Programs (1), click Windows Media Player to open the program.

6. On the Device Setup screen, either accept the default name Windows gives to the device or create one of your own. Under to Tools ➢ Options tab.

7. Allow Windows to automatically select the optimal sync method for the connected device.

   Your entire music library on your computer will automatically sync with your MP3 player and will do so every time your MP3 player is connected with your computer. You will need to continue to the next set of steps to select which music files on your computer you want to auto-sync with your MP3 player.

CONFIGURING AUTOMATIC SYNCING BETWEEN AN MP3 DEVICE AND WINDOWS MEDIA PLAYER

1. Connect your MP3 player to your Windows 7 computer and turn on the MP3 device.

2. If necessary, select the appropriate syncing options such as Sync Music.

3. On Windows 7, click Start, and in the Search box, type **Windows Media Player**.

4. Under Programs (1), click Windows Media Player to open the program.

5. To display the sync screen, click the Sync button.

6. Click the Sync Options button and then click Set Up Sync.

7. When the Device Setup page appears, select the Sync This Device Automatically check box if necessary.

8. Under available playlists, click Sync Playlists and select a playlist you want to configure for automatic syncing, such as All Music.

9. To add a particular playlist that isn't selected for syncing, click the list and then click Add.

10. To remove a playlist that is selected for syncing, click the list and then click Remove.

11. To change the priority of a playlist, click the list and then click either the Up Priority or Down Priority button.

12. To start an automatic sync with your new selections, click Finish.

Criteria for Completion

You will have successfully completed this exercise when your MP3 player automatically syncs with the desired playlists in your Windows 7 computer's Windows Media Player application.

Phase 2

Maintaining and Documenting Computer Systems

A large part of your day-to-day duties as a PC tech will involve maintaining computer and server systems and documenting your work. In this Phase, you will build on the basic skills you learned in Phase 1, "Installing Hardware and Software." You will discover how to leverage those elementary tasks and learn how to perform regular maintenance tasks on computers.

Among other tasks, you'll learn how to identify a motherboard, how to clean and oil cooling fans, how to flash BIOS, and how to roll back device drivers. So take the book over to your lab computer and get ready for the next step.

Task 2.1: Identifying a Motherboard

On occasion, you may have to replace a computer's motherboard. Most of the time the type of motherboard is easily identified by the documentation that came with the computer. Sometimes, though, you won't be able to locate any relevant information about the motherboard. In this case, you can use one of a number of handy (and free) utilities that have the ability to extract that information from the system BIOS and other sources on the device.

Objective

This task covers objective 220:801:1.2.

Scenario

You have been assigned to replace the motherboard of an older server that has been providing print services to one of your company's branch offices. You attempt to locate the computer's documentation but it can't be found. You open up the server's case and examine the motherboard but can't determine the make and model. You close the server, power it up, and log on. Then you open up a web browser to begin the process of identifying the motherboard.

Scope of Task

Duration

This task should take about 10 to 15 minutes, including download and installation time.

Setup

You'll need a computer with an Internet connection. This task also requires that you download and install software that can query your computer and gather relevant information.

Caveat

This method isn't practical if you are trying to identify the motherboard of a computer that is nonfunctional. Also, this task was performed on a Windows 7 Professional 64-bit computer but is applicable to other Windows PCs.

Procedure

This task will teach you the steps to take in identifying a motherboard.

Equipment Used

You won't need any special equipment for this task, but you will have to download and install a piece of software on your computer to query the motherboard's BIOS and other resources.

Details

This task will take you through the process of searching for a motherboard's make and model.

Download, Install, and Run Belarc Advisor

1. At a computer with an Internet connection, open a web browser.

2. Type in the following URL: `www.belarc.com/free_download.html`.

NOTE   I found the site mentioned in Step 2 by using the search string "finding the motherboard model in Windows 7." Since the Internet is very changeable, if the URL is not available when you attempt this task, use the same string in any search engine and locate a site with the same or a similar tool. Please keep this suggestion in mind for any other URL you encounter in this book.

3. Read all of the instructions on the belarc.com website when it loads, and then click the Click Here to Download Your Free Copy of the Belarc Advisor button.

4. When the Save As window appears, navigate to the location on your computer where you want to save the `advisorinstaller.exe` file and then click Save.

5. Navigate to the location where you saved `advisorinstaller.exe` and double-click the file to launch it.

6. When prompted to allow the Belarc executable access to your computer, click Yes.

7. When the Belarc Advisor license agreement box appears, click I Agree.

8. When the Belarc Advisor Installation box appears, click Install.

9. When the Belarc Analysis—Check for New Definitions box appears, click No (the latest definition will not be necessary for this task). You can optionally select the Remember This Choice and Don't Ask Me Again check box if desired.

10. After the Belarc Advisor runs and the results are displayed, locate the section for Main Circuit Board and document the information found there.

Main Circuit Board [b]
Board: Dell Inc. 0XPDFK A01
Serial Number: .CN708219B630SL.
Bus Clock: 4800 megahertz
BIOS: Dell Inc. A03 09/09/2009

The output of the Belarc Advisor provides a great deal of useful information about your computer, including details about the operating system, system model, processor, any hosted virtual machines present, memory modules, drive volumes, and so forth. In addition, it provides information on security benchmarks for the computer as well as assessing virus-protection software and how up to date Microsoft security updates are for the Windows computer.

Criteria for Completion

You will have successfully completed this assignment when you have located all of the information to identify your computer's motherboard.

Task 2.2: Identifying a Power Supply

While the utility used in Task 2.1 has the ability to present a report on almost every system that makes up your PC, it can't do everything. One device it does not identify is the power supply attached to the computer. As you might imagine, if you should ever need to replace the power supply on the PC, you would need to know the make and model required by your computer.

You can also refer to the motherboard manual for the computer noting its requirements for wattage, correct ATX connector, correct peripheral connectors such as Molex, SATA, and so on, then when you are looking for a replacement power supply unit, verify that it meets all of the computer's specified requirements.

Objective

This task covers objective 220:801:1.8.

Scenario

You have recently replaced the motherboard on a computer that functions as a print server for one of your company's branch offices. You receive another trouble ticket for the same device stating that the PC is subject to intermittent reboots. You investigate and determine that the power supply may be failing. You will still need to test the power supply to be sure, but you want to identify the proper replacement unit, should it become necessary.

   You are unable to locate any documentation identifying the power supply, and there are no identifying markings in the unit itself. You will need to determine the correct power supply to use as a replacement based on the make and model of the computer.

Scope of Task

Duration

This task should take about 10 minutes.

Setup

All you'll need is a computer with an Internet connection. You will only be identifying the correct power supply to be used for your computer.

Task 2.3 will show you how to test a potentially failing power supply and how to replace the unit in a computer.

Caveat

All you will need to know is the manufacturer, make, and model number of the computer that may require the new power supply. This task is as easy as knowing how to use a search engine.

Procedure

This task will teach you how to determine the correct power supply required by your computer.

Equipment Used

You will need no special equipment for this task.

Details

This task will take you through the process of searching for the correct power supply for a computer.

Locating the Correct Power Supply for Your PC

1. Verify that you have the specifications for your computer available.

2. Open a web browser and use a search engine to enter a search string such as "power supply for dell precision t3500."

 You must enter the specific make and model for the computer for which you want to find the correct power supply.

3. On the search results page, locate one or more links that provide specific information regarding the correct power supply type for your computer and click a suitable link, or click the Shopping Results link for the power supply to see locations where you might purchase the appropriate device.

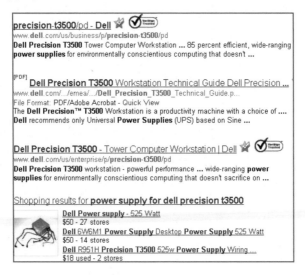

4. If you desire to do so, select a link where you can purchase the correct power supply, and proceed through the online purchasing process.

Criteria for Completion

You will have successfully completed this task when you have identified the power supply most suited to your computer and determined its pricing and availability.

Task 2.3: Performing a Quick Test and Replacing a Power Supply

Now that you have determined the correct model of power supply required for your computer, you will need to know how to verify that the power supply is actually failing and, if it is, how to replace it.

 See Task 2.2 for more details on the current scenario.

While you are reasonably convinced that the power supply of the computer is failing, you will need to test it to be sure, prior to purchasing and installing a replacement unit. Although you can perform an extensive test on the power supply using a multimeter, there is a quick test that will almost always determine if a power supply is bad, and it takes only a few minutes.

Objective

This task covers objectives 220:801:1.8 and 220:802:4.1.

Scenario

You previously received a trouble ticket (Task 2.2) stating that the computer used for print services at one of your company's branch offices has been spontaneously rebooting. This is a likely symptom of a failing power supply. You have determined the type of power supply required if the unit needs replacing. You have a replacement unit in your department's inventory, so you take the replacement unit, along with your tools, to the branch office to test and, if necessary, to replace the power supply.

Scope of Task

Duration

This task should take 30 minutes, which includes performing the quick test and replacing the power supply unit.

Setup

To test the power supply, all you'll need is a paper clip or other short length of conductive metal. This is a good test if you don't want to remove the power supply from the computer until you are sure it is bad. For this task, you probably won't want to remove and replace your lab computer's power supply, but you can do so for the full effect.

Caveat

When you insert the paper clip into the 20/24-pin motherboard connector from the power supply, do not touch the paper clip while you are applying electrical power to the power supply. It will impart a rather nasty shock if you do. Make sure you follow all instructions for this task carefully for your own safety and the safety of your computer.

While the process of removing and replacing a power supply isn't complex, it can be cumbersome. Also, the power supply is the largest and heaviest single component in a computer's case. Proceed slowly and carefully with all the steps in this task.

This task assumes you will be testing a power supply for an ATX motherboard, rather than an AT motherboard, which is an obsolete form factor not covered in the CompTIA A+ exams. The paper clip test works with all ATX power supplies.

Procedure

Equipment Used

You will need to have a paper clip, which you will unfold and bend into a "u" shape. You will also need to have the type or types of screwdrivers needed to remove the screws attaching the access panel to your PC's case and to remove the attachment screws holding the power supply in place.

Details

This task shows you how to test a potentially failing power supply and then how to replace the power supply with a new unit.

Testing and Replacing a Power Supply

TESTING A POWER SUPPLY WITH A PAPER CLIP

1. Arrange your tools and take a common paper clip, unfold it, and bend it into a general "u" shape.
2. Power down the computer and unplug the power cable from the back of the power supply.
3. Use ESD precautions before opening the PC case.
4. Remove the screws attaching the access panel to the PC case.
5. Remove the access panel and set it aside.
6. Locate all of the wires that connect the power supply to the various computer components including the motherboard, and disconnect them carefully.

 Make sure you note which wires go to which component connections so you can replace the power leads after the test is complete.

7. Locate the 20- or 24-pin motherboard connector that supplies power to the motherboard.

8. Locate the green wire (the power-on wire) which is attached to pin 16 on a 24 pin connector and pin 14 on a 20 pin connector.

9. Insert one end of the paper clip into the pin opening for the green wire, making sure the paper clip end is making firm contact.

10. Insert the other end of the paper clip to the pin opening for any black wire (black wires are ground wires).

11. Release the paper clip and verify that both ends have a firm contact inside their pin openings.

12. Plug the power cable back into the power supply, and look to see if the fan spins up.

If the fan fails to spin, the power supply is bad and must be replaced.

13. Unplug the power cable from the back of the power supply.

14. Remove the paper clip from the motherboard connector pin openings.

Since you have determined that the power supply is bad, according to the scenario, your next step is to remove the power supply and replace it with a known-good unit. If you don't want to remove the power supply in your test computer only to put it back again, you can just replace all of the connections and end the task. Otherwise, continue to follow the subsequent steps. See Task 1.5 for further details.

REPLACING A POWER SUPPLY IN A COMPUTER

1. Remove the power cable from the power supply at the back of the PC case.

2. Locate the screwdriver that is appropriate for removing the screws attaching the power supply to the PC case (most likely a Phillips screwdriver).

3. Remove the screws holding the power supply to the PC case, while supporting the power supply inside the case with your other hand.

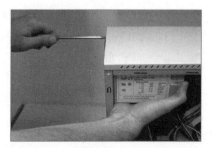

4. Once the power-supply screws have been removed, use the hand supporting the unit to slide it forward, toward the front of the PC case, until the power supply comes completely free.

5. Remove the power supply from the PC case and set it aside.

6. Remove the new power supply from its packaging.

7. Verify that all packaging and other unnecessary items are removed from the power-supply unit and all its connectors.

 The paper clip test is also a quick and easy way to verify that a new power supply is good. Occasionally, electronic components can be faulty, even when they come straight from the retailer.

8. Continuing to observe ESD precautions, carefully insert the power supply in the case, holding it toward the top of the case.

9. Slide the unit toward the back of the case until the screw mounts match those on the PC case and the power-supply electrical socket matches the aperture in the case.

10. Supporting the unit with one hand, replace the mounting screws on the back of the PC case.

11. Once the power supply is securely mounted, replace all of the internal connections between the power supply and the drive units, motherboard, and other components, making sure that each connector is correctly oriented and fitted securely.

 Unless the power-supply unit and all of the connectors are exactly identical to the old unit, you may want to consult with the documentation for the replacement power supply to verify how the connections are correctly made.

12. Arrange the internal connector cables, including any unused cables, so that they don't impede airflow on the inside of the PC case.

 Some power supplies use a modular system that lets you remove any unused cables from the unit.

13. Reconnect the power cable to the power supply at the back of the PC case.

14. Before reattaching the PC-case access panel, power up the computer.

15. Watch the monitor for any error messages and listen for any beep signals.

16. Once you've verified that the computer boots and runs normally, replace the PC-case access panel and secure it with the panel's screws.

Criteria for Completion

You will have successfully completed this task when you have replaced the power-supply unit and verified that the computer boots and operates normally. If the original symptom was a periodically rebooting computer, you may have to remain near the computer for 30 minutes or so to make sure the computer runs consistently. Notify the staff at the branch office to monitor the computer after you leave so you can make sure that it continues to run normally.

Task 2.4: Searching for Windows Vista Drivers

Historically, Windows Vista has had a reputation for not supporting various devices. This was expected when it was first released, but after the first service pack was issued, it continued to be a problem. Although device support in Vista today isn't the issue it was in the past, you may still have some difficulty in locating Vista-compatible drivers. This task will make that job a lot easier.

Objective

This task covers objective 220:802:1.2.

Scenario

You have received a trouble ticket stating that the HR manager is unable to print from her laser printer. You know that she has just had an older Windows Vista computer installed in her office. You receive instructions from your supervisor to search for and install the drivers that will allow her to print. The instructions include the URL www.radarsync.com/vista/. You proceed to the HR manager's office to respond to her request.

Scope of Task

Duration

This task should take at most about 15 minutes, which includes searching for and downloading the drivers.

Setup

There's no special setup for this task beyond Internet access and having a Windows Vista computer.

Caveat

If you are trying this task from a computer with an operating system other than Vista, you can select another operating system version, including 32-bit or 64-bit support, on the site. However, since you won't need to actually install the drivers, this won't pose a problem.

Procedure

This task will show you how to locate and download device drivers for Windows Vista computers.

Equipment Used

No special equipment is required.

Details

This task will show you the steps required to locate and download device drivers compatible with a Windows Vista computer.

Locating Device Drivers for a Windows Vista PC

1. At the Windows Vista computer, log in with an account that has administrative privileges.
2. Open a web browser and go to www.radarsync.com/vista/.
3. Scroll down the page until you locate the manufacturer for the device you are seeking (by default, the page lists only 20 items in the search results, so not all possible devices are listed).
4. If the device you are looking for isn't immediately visible, under Limit to Category, click the name of a manufacturer and then look through the available results, or use the Search box to search for a specific device.
5. Locate the name of the required device, and then click on its name.
6. Click the Download the Latest Version button.

Criteria for Completion

You will have successfully completed this task when you have located and downloaded the Vista-compatible drivers for the desired device.

Task 2.5: Listing All of the Drivers Installed on a Windows 7 PC

You may think that using the Device Manager is the only way to find out what drivers are installed on a Windows computer, but Windows XP, Windows Vista, and Windows 7 offer another solution. You can use the DriverQuery command-line utility to show you a comprehensive list.

Most people, except for actual Windows system administrators, don't associate administering Windows with the command line. However, the command line is a powerful tool for performing a large number of helpful tasks. This task shows you only one small sample. If you go on to administer Windows systems, you will be required to learn a great deal more.

Objective

This task covers objective 220:802:1.2.

Scenario

You have recently installed drivers for a laser printer on the HR manager's Windows 7 computer. The printer now works flawlessly, but the HR manager is concerned about what her new PC does and doesn't support in terms of drivers. Your supervisor has directed you to generate a printable list of the drivers currently installed on her computer using the DriverQuery command-line utility. The other requirements for this assignment are that the list be verbose, showing the filename and the size of each driver, along with being "human-readable." You proceed to the HR manager's office to fulfill the request.

Scope of Task

Duration

This task should just take a few minutes.

Setup

There's no special setup for this task. You can perform this task on Windows XP, Windows Vista, and Windows 7 computers.

Caveat

While the task is straightforward, as with many command-line tools, a number of arguments or switches are available to tailor the output of the command. To find out more, go to http://technet.microsoft.com/en-us/library/bb490896.aspx.

Procedure

This task will show you how to generate a printable list of drivers installed on a Windows Vista computer.

Equipment Used

No special equipment is required.

Details

This task will show you the steps required to use the command line to create a drivers list.

Listing All of the Drivers on a Windows Vista Computer

1. Log in to the Windows 7 computer.
2. Click the Windows Start button.
3. Click Search, type **cmd** in the Run box, and then press Enter to open a command-line window.
4. At the prompt, type **driverquery /v /fo list >drivers.txt** and then press Enter.
5. At the command prompt, type **drivers.txt** and then press Enter.
6. After the text document opens, if you want to print the document, click File ➢ Print. Otherwise, save it to a shared folder on the network or at a location where your supervisor instructed you to store the file.

This document can be very long, so don't print it unless you absolutely need to have a hard copy.

The driverquery /si command can be used to check which drivers on the computer hare signed.

Criteria for Completion

You will have successfully completed this task when you have generated a text file containing a list of all the drivers installed on the Windows 7 computer.

Task 2.6: Cleaning Fans

Dust usually enters a computer case through the cooling and power-supply fans. These fans can also become dusty and eventually will start to spin more slowly, losing effectiveness. You must regularly clean the fans in order to make sure that cooling efficiency inside the computer case remains at optimal levels.

Objective

This task covers objective 220:801:1.6.

Scenario

As part of the process of maintaining the computers in your company, you have been assigned to clean and maintain the cooling fans. You are starting by cleaning the fans in your desktop computer in the IT department.

Scope of Task

Duration

This task should take about 10 minutes or so.

Setup

There is no special setup for this task.

Caveat

Due to the amount of dust that can accumulate inside a PC case, it is recommended that you do the task in an area where you don't mind making a mess. Also, wear clothing that you don't mind getting dirty. Before cleaning out the fans, you may want to use your can of compressed air to blow off all of the random dust that has collected inside the computer case.

Procedure

This task will show you how to clean the dust out of a computer's cooling fan.

Equipment Used

You'll need a can of compressed air, which can be purchased at any computer repair or supply store, and a small brush such as one used for painting watercolors or for cleaning delicate equipment. You can probably find such a brush at any art store or hardware outlet.

Details

This task will show you the steps necessary to clean the cooling fans in a computer.

Cleaning the Computer Fans Using Compressed Air and Brushes

 For this task, it is assumed your computer is powered down and the case is already open.

1. Locate the can of compressed air.

 Remember to take ESD precautions before touching the inside of the computer case.

2. Direct the long nozzle on the compressed-air can toward the cooling fan.

Using compressed air to clean computer fans in Step 2 may or may not be difficult, depending on the design of your computer case and how components are placed. Also, extended cleaning of fans with compressed air is not advised because it is possible for the fans to be damaged. Limit the amount of time you spray the compressed air onto fans to just a few seconds.

3. Depress the trigger on the can and direct air at and around the cooling fan.

4. Direct air at and around the chassis of the power supply.

5. From outside the case, spray all visible fans, making sure to clear off as much dust as possible.

6. Check inside the case and see if any additional dust was dislodged.

7. Use the compressed air to clear out any additional dust.

8. Put down the air can and pick up the brush.

9. Reach inside the case and gently brush the fan, including the blades and other components.

10. Repeat Step 9 on the outsides of the fans, including the power-supply fan.

11. Check one last time to see if any more dust has been dislodged inside the case.

12. Clean out any dust you find with compressed air.

This task shows you how to clean a computer that has a separate external cooling fan; however, some computers do not have this feature.

13. Replace the access panel.

14. Replace the screws holding the access panel in place.

Criteria for Completion

You will have successfully completed this task when the computer's fans are clear of built-up dust.

Task 2.7: Oiling Fans

Along with cleaning fans, you occasionally have to oil them. Fans in a computer have lubrication around their bearings, but eventually that runs dry. When this happens, the noise from the fan becomes louder and quite annoying; this is a sign that the fan bearings are starting to wear out. If you let this go on, the fan will become slower and slower and eventually will stop spinning altogether. That usually means disaster for your power supply and CPU.

Oiling the power supply fan from the outside of the unit is a fairly routine task however, you should never open a power supply. Even with the computer completely powered down, touching the inside of a power supply can be extremely hazardous.

Objective

This task covers objective 220:801:1.6.

Scenario

As part of your regular maintenance duties, you have been assigned to periodically oil the fans in the company's computers. Right now, you are about to perform this task on your own PC in the IT department.

This task picks up where Task 2.6 left off.

Scope of Task

Duration

This task should take about 15 or 20 minutes.

Setup

There is no special setup for this task.

Caveat

Although you can use this procedure to oil all the fans in your computer, this task will focus on oiling the bearing in the power-supply fan. Be careful not to use too much oil.

Procedure

This task will teach you how to oil the bearings of fans in a computer.

Equipment Used

You'll need a small can of oil and a screwdriver. Either three-in-one oil (the mineral-based version is better than the vegetable-based product) or sewing-machine oil is acceptable. You will need to keep a paper or cloth towel available to soak up excess oil.

Do not use WD-40 for this task. WD-40 and products like it are not lubricants. They are made mainly of kerosene with only a little oil. The kerosene will quickly evaporate and the tiny amount of oil that's left won't last long in rapidly spinning fan bearings.

Details

This task takes you through each of the steps necessary to oil the power supply fan bearings.

Oiling a Power-Supply Fan

ACCESSING THE FAN BEARINGS

1. Locate the power-supply fan at the back of your computer.
2. Locate your screwdriver.
3. Remove the screws holding the finger guard in place over the fan.

There are all kinds of ways the guard can be secured over the power-supply fan. Step 3 refers to only one method. Your computer may be built differently.

4. Remove the finger guard.

The screws also hold the fan in place, but it's unlikely that it will fall out given the lack of space in the fan casing.

5. Locate the adhesive sticker over the center of the fan.
6. Gently pull the sticker aside.

If you accidentally pull the sticker off or rip it, when you have finished oiling the bearings, just put a large piece of tape over the area that was covered by the sticker.

7. If there is a rubber or plastic cap covering the bearings, remove it.

Smaller fans typically cover the bearings with just the sticker, but larger fans will likely have the cap as well. When you open the cap (if it has one), you'll see either ball bearings or sleeve bearings inside.

8. Locate the can of oil.

9. Carefully put oil inside the bearing case, but do not overfill.

  Excess oil can leak out of the bearing case, no matter what you seal it with.

10. Let the computer sit in position for a few minutes to let the oil permeate the bearings.
11. Soak up any excess oil.

  If the back of the fan has any excess oil on it, the sticker will fail to adhere.

12. If the fan came with a cap, replace it.
13. Replace the sticker.
14. Replace the finger guard.
15. Replace the screws holding the guard and the fan in place.
16. Wash your hands.

  Chances are you got some oil on your hands during this procedure, and you don't want to get oil all over your keyboard and mouse.

VERIFYING THAT THE FAN FUNCTIONS

1. Power up your computer.
2. Listen to the power-supply fan as the computer powers up.
3. Verify that the fan is spinning smoothly and quietly.

Criteria for Completion

You will have successfully completed this task when you have oiled the bearings and verified that the fan is spinning normally.

Task 2.8: Defragging a Hard Drive

Information stored on hard drives using the Windows file systems FAT 32 and NTFS are prone to file fragmentation. As data is added to the drive, it is written sequentially on the drive platters; as information is accessed and edited, however, parts of the files are moved out of sequence. This means that the read/write heads in the drive must zip to and fro locating the different pieces of a single file. Defragmenting the drive improves read performance. This is a regular maintenance task. Desktops should be defragged once every couple of weeks to once a month, depending on how heavily they are used. Servers should be defragged on a weekly basis.

> Occasionally, you'll hear the question "Can defragging too frequently damage a hard drive?" While it's true that defragging a drive does involve a certain amount of wear on the drive, it is the general consensus among hardware gurus that allowing your drive to go too long without being defragged is far more damaging than the defrag process.

Objective

This task covers objective 220:802:1.7.

Scenario

You have been assigned to defragment the hard drive of a Windows XP machine being used as a print server for a small branch office. You are working after regular business hours, so the end users won't need to access print services while you're performing the defrag.

Scope of Task

Duration

Depending on the size of your hard drive, how much data is on board, how badly fragmented the data is, and how full the drive is, this process could take several hours.

Setup

No special setup is required for this task. The example uses Windows XP Professional. Defragging is slightly different on a Windows Vista or Windows 7 computer.

Caveat

This is a pretty straightforward task with very few "gotchas." It just takes some time.

Procedure

This task shows you the steps to take in defragmenting a Windows XP computer.

> The steps are the same or substantially similar but not identical for other Windows operating systems.

Equipment Used

No equipment is required for this task.

Details

This task will take you through the steps to defragment a hard drive/disk running Windows XP.

Performing a Disk Defrag on a Windows Computer

1. Sitting at the keyboard of the computer, click Start and then click My Computer.
2. Right-click the drive you want to defrag, which will most likely be the C drive.
3. Select Properties.
4. The Local Disk (C:) Properties box will open. Click the Tools tab.
5. Under Defragmentation, click the Defragment Now button.

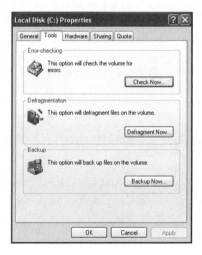

6. Click Analyze.

 NOTE When the analysis dialog box opens, click Defragment. The defragmentation process will begin. The defragmentation process could take a long time. All you can do is periodically check on its progress until it finishes.

7. A dialog box will open telling you that the process has completed. Click Close.
8. Close the disk-defragmentation utility.
9. Close the Disk Properties box.
10. Close the My Computer box.
11. Log off the computer.

Criteria for Completion

You will have successfully completed this task when the disk-defragmentation utility reports the disk has been defragmented.

Task 2.9: Scheduling Automatic Defragging in Windows 7

One of the things that always bugged me about the Windows XP defragging utility is that there wasn't an option to schedule the tool to run automatically. After all, defragging is a task that just begs to be done at two in the morning when you're asleep. I can't believe that Microsoft waited until Windows Vista to implement this option. Fortunately, they finally got around to it and then continued to make this option available in Windows 7.

Objective

This task covers objective 220:802:1.7.

Scenario

You have received a trouble ticket directing you to report to the Support department for your company and schedule each of their Windows 7 computers to automatically run the defragmentation utility every Tuesday starting at 2 a.m. This specific day and time are required since the help desk staff's regular hours are from 6 a.m. to 8 p.m. seven days a week and the other automatic tasks are scheduled to be performed on most of the other available days and times when the help desk is not open.

Scope of Task

Duration

This task should take only a few minutes.

Setup

No special setup is needed for this task, but you will need to have a computer running Windows 7 available. You can also perform this task on a Windows Vista computer.

Although the scenario requires that you perform this task on numerous computers in a support department, to successfully complete the task you need only to set the defragmentation schedule on one Windows 7 computer.

Caveat

While the good news is that the Windows defragmenter utility has the ability to be scheduled, there are a few points of bad news. The first point isn't bad news as such but could potentially pose a problem. By default, the Windows 7 defrag utility is enabled and scheduled to run every Wednesday, starting at 1 a.m. If you are unaware of this fact, you may have other automatic tasks set to run at the same time. It's best to have all of your after-hours tasks running at different days and times to prevent any sort of conflict.

Another downside to the Windows 7 defragger is that it runs in the background, providing no visual representation of the defragmentation process. You are not presented with a graphic illustration of the state of the hard drive's fragmentation before and after the utility runs.

Procedure

This task will instruct you on how to schedule the Windows 7 defragmentation tool to run automatically at a specific time and day of the week.

Equipment Used

No special equipment is needed to complete this task.

Details

This task will show you how to set up the Windows 7 defragger to run automatically on a regular schedule.

Scheduling the Windows Windows 7 Defragmentation Tool to Run Automatically

1. Click the Windows Start button and, in the menu that appears, click Control Panel.

2. Click Performance Information and Tools, and then click Advanced Tools.

3. On the Advanced Tools page, click Open Disk Defragmenter.

4. Click Configure Schedule.

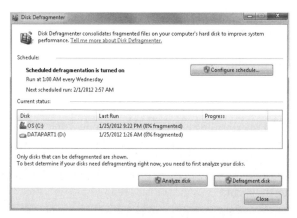

5. When the Disk Defragmenter: Modify Schedule dialog box appears, next to the Frequency menu, select Weekly.

6. Next to the Day, select Tuesday.

7. Next to the Time, select 2:00 AM.

8. Click Select Disks and in the Select Disks for Schedule box, select the disk or disks you want to be defragmented on this schedule.

9. Click OK in the dialog box and then click OK again to close the utility.

The defragmentation utility is now scheduled to start the tool every Tuesday at 2 a.m.

Criteria for Completion

You will have successfully completed this task when you have set the defragmentation tool to run each Tuesday at 2 a.m. and have closed the utility.

Task 2.10: Defragmenting a Single File

As you are likely aware, it can take quite some time to defragment an entire hard drive, depending on the extent of the drive's file fragmentation and the system load on the computer. There may be times when you want to quickly optimize a single file that, due to heavy computer use, has been fragmented extensively across the hard drive. Both Windows Vista and Windows 7 offer the option of defragmenting an individual file on the computer's hard drive, but not natively.

This scenario requires that you download and install a utility called Contig, which is free from Microsoft. The utility is ideal for defragging a large, often-used file such as a virtual machine image. While downloading and installing Contig is outside the scope of this task, the process is very easy to do. Go to http://technet.microsoft.com/en-us/sysinternals/bb897428.aspx and follow the instructions to install the tool on your Windows computer.

Objective

This task covers objective 220:802:1.7.

Scenario

You have been tasked with performing a defragmentation on a virtual machine in a file called vsrv01.vmx on a test machine in your IT department. The machine is running Windows 7 and has the Contig utility installed and available. You have been given the instructions for using Contig to complete your task. You are in the server room at the keyboard of the Windows 7 computer and are ready to begin.

Scope of Task

Duration

This task should take no more than a few minutes, depending on your degree of comfort in using the command-line utility and the size of the file you choose to defragment.

Setup

No special setup is needed for this task. You can perform this task on either Windows Vista or Windows 7. A Windows 7 machine was used for the purpose of this task.

Caveat

As previously mentioned, the Contig tool requires that you use the command line. One big downer is that you must run Contig from the folder where the `Contig.exe` file is located. You cannot open the command prompt, navigate to the location of the desired file, and then execute the `contig` command, even if you run the command prompt as administrator. If you do, you will get an error message stating that `contig` is not recognized as an internal or external command. However, you could put the file anywhere on the PATH such as `C"\Windows\System32` so that you could use the Contig tool anywhere.

Procedure

This task will tell you how to use the Contig utility to defrag a single file on a Windows 7 computer.

Equipment Used

No special equipment is required, but you will need to be working at a Windows Vista or Windows 7 computer that has Contig installed.

Details

This task will take you through the process of defragmenting a single file on a Windows 7 computer using Contig.

Installing Contig on Windows 7

1. On a Windows 7 machine, open a web browser and go to `http://technet.microsoft.com/en-us/sysinternals/bb897428.aspx`.

2. On the Windows Sysinternals Contig page, click Download Contig.

3. Use Windows Explorer to navigate to where you saved `Contig.zip`, right-click the zip file, and then click Extract All.

4. Open the extracted `Contig` folder and then double-click `Contig.exe` to launch the installer.

5. When prompted by the Security Warning dialog box, click Run.

6. When the License Agreement box opens, click Agree.

7. In Windows Explorer, navigate to the location of the Contig folder.

8. Press and hold the Shift key, and then right-click the Contig folder.

9. When the menu appears, select Open Command Window Here.

10. To test Contig, at the command prompt, type **contig -a** and press Enter.

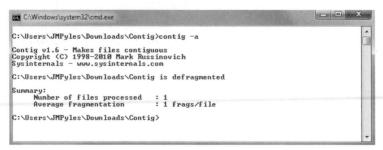

Executing contig -a returns information about how fragmented the files are in the current directory by analyzing the fragmentation.

Using Contig to Defragment a Single File on a Windows 7 Computer

1. Log in to the computer using an account with administrator privileges.

2. Use Windows Explorer to navigate to the folder where you installed Contig.

3. Press and hold the Shift key, and then right-click the folder where you installed Contig.

4. When the menu appears, select Open Command Prompt Here.

> You must press and hold the Shift key in order for the Open Command Prompt Here option to be available. Also, you must click on the folder in the right or main Explorer pane and not in the left menu pane.

5. At the command prompt, type **Contig <filename>**, where <filename> is the path to the file you want to defragment.

> The full path to the file will look something like C:\Users\JMPyles\ Virtual_Machines\vsrv01.vmx.

6. Press Enter to begin the defragmentation of the file.

To run Contig and see a printout in the command-prompt window of the defrag process, use the -v switch after specifying the path, such as C:\Users\JMPyles\Virtual_Machines\ vsrv01.vmx -v.

Criteria for Completion

You will have successfully completed the task when you have executed the command and the file has been defragmented.

Task 2.11: Updating Security Patches

While Windows computers can be set to automatically check for Windows updates occasionally, you may want to perform this process manually, particularly in the event that a computer has not been online for quite some time or has been manually configured to not check for updates. A Windows computer that is online but not updated is a problem looking for a place to happen.

Objective

This task covers objective 220:802:1.7.

Scenario

You have received a trouble ticket stating that one of the managers in your office has been on a sabbatical for several months and not been available to use her computer. She is returning to the office next week and wants her Windows 7 PC serviced and updated before she returns. You have also been told that she had previously set her computer to not automatically check for updates and you have been directed to change this setting on the computer so it will check for Windows updates but still allow the manager to choose whether to download and install them.

You arrive at her office, power up, and log in to her computer as domain administrator. You want to manually update her computer so that it has the latest Windows hotfixes and updates available.

NOTE Normally once a Windows computer is powered up and connects to the Internet, it should automatically check for updates, but this computer is not configured to perform that task.

Scope of Task

Duration

This task should take about 10 minutes or so.

Setup

No special setup is required beyond having a Windows 7 computer that is connected to the Internet.

Caveat

This should be a relatively straightforward task.

Procedure

This task will show you how to manually run Windows Update.

Equipment Used

You won't need any special equipment.

Details

This task will take you through the steps to run Windows Update manually and then change the update settings to let the computer automatically check for Windows updates.

Manually Checking Windows Updates on a Windows 7 Computer

1. Click the Windows Start button and then click Control Panel.
2. In Control Panel, click Windows Update.
3. In the left-hand panel, click Check for Updates.
4. Once the list of available updates has been returned, select the link for the updates.
5. On the Select the Update you want to Install screen, select all of the required updates and then click OK.
6. Click Install Updates.

Changing the Settings in Windows 7 for Checking Windows Updates

1. Once the computer has rebooted, click the Windows Start button and then click Control Panel.
2. In Control Panel, click Windows Update.
3. In the left-hand panel, click Change Settings.
4. Use the Important Updates menu to change the selection from Never Check for Updates (Not Recommended) to Check for Updates but Let Me Choose Whether to Download and Install Them.
5. Click OK.

Criteria for Completion

You will have successfully completed the task when the computer has downloaded and installed all of the latest updates from Microsoft and you have configured the computer to automatically check for Windows updates.

Task 2.12: Checking Internal Connectors

There are quite a number of internal connectors inside a computer, and any connector inside a computer occasionally can work its way loose. Sometimes you have to do a general inspection of the connectors in a PC's case to make sure they are all linked firmly. Even in a PC that hasn't been moved lately, subtle motions of the box may have caused a connection to separate just enough to cause a problem.

Objective

This task covers objective 220:801:1.11.

Scenario

A user in the reception area reports that her PC won't start. She's made sure it's plugged in and that the surge protector is turned on, but when she pushes the power button on the PC, nothing happens. You investigate and can find no external cause. You decide to open the case and see if there is a reason for the problem inside.

Scope of Task

Duration

This task should take about 10 minutes.

Setup

No special setup is required to complete this task.

Caveat

Make sure to take ESD precautions before putting your hands inside the box.

Procedure

This task will show you how to verify that internal connectors inside a PC's case are firmly connected.

Equipment Used

You should need only a screwdriver to successfully complete this task.

Details

This task will walk you through the steps of checking internal connectors in a PC to make sure they are all securely fitted.

Checking Internal Connectors

VERIFYING THAT ALL INTERNAL CONNECTORS IN THE COMPUTER ARE FIRMLY SEATED

1. Unplug the computer's power cord from the surge protector.

2. Locate a screwdriver and remove the screws holding the access panel in place.

3. Remove the access panel.

 Make sure you use ESD precautions before putting your hands inside the computer.

4. Locate the connectors between the power supply and the motherboard.

5. Disconnect the connectors.

6. Firmly reseat the connectors.

7. Locate the hard-drive cable connector on the motherboard.

8. Pull the connector away from the hard-drive controller connector.

9. Carefully reseat the connector to the hard-drive controller.

10. Repeat Steps 8 through 10 for the CD/DVD drive.

11. Repeat Steps 8 through 10 for any other drive if one is present.

12. Locate the CPU and heatsink.

13. Remove the heatsink assembly from the CPU.

14. Locate the lever that will release the CPU from its slot.

 If necessary, check online documentation for your computer's CPU because it may release from your computer's motherboard using a different method.

15. Pull the lever up to release the CPU.

 It should not be necessary to remove the CPU fan or thermal paste. You should check the CPU fan's connector, though.

16. Reseat the CPU in its slot.

17. Replace the lever to its original position, securing the CPU in place.

18. Replace the heatsink assembly.

19. Make a general visual survey of the interior of the PC to verify that you didn't miss any connectors.

20. When finished, replace the access panel.

21. Replace the screws holding the panel in place.

22. Plug the PC's power cord back into the surge protector.

VERIFYING THAT THE PC FUNCTIONS NORMALLY

1. Power up the PC.

2. When the PC loads the OS, log on as Administrator.

3. Open various applications and services to verify that the PC is operating normally.

Criteria for Completion

You will have successfully completed this task when you can power up the computer and it behaves normally.

If there were no loose connections in your computer, this task will not change its performance.

Task 2.13: Backing Up with Acronis True Image Home

Although Windows 7 comes with an excellent built-in Backup and Restore application, it may not have all of the features you desire or offer sufficient ease of use. Acronis True Image can be installed on a Windows 7 computer and provide backup and restore protection for all of your valuable data. Acronis can back up the entire contents of the disk or disks on the computer or only selected directories on a drive.

Objective

This task covers objective 220:802:1.7.

Scenario

You want a quick and easy backup and restore utility for your Windows 7 computer, and you have chosen Acronis True Image Home (Full Version) as the third-party solution that meets your requirements. You have downloaded and installed the application on your computer and are ready to create your first backup.

Scope of Task

Duration

This task should take about 20 to 30 minutes.

Setup

It would be ideal if you had a Windows 7 Professional Desktop to work with, but if not, a Windows XP or Windows Vista computer should do as well. You will need to purchase this software or use the free 30-day trial version from www.acronis.com.

Caveat

For the purpose of this task, only back up something small, unless you really do want to back up all of your data. You do not need to back up applications and you certainly shouldn't back up your operating system. If your computer is compromised and those programs are damaged, you should have the original installation or recovery discs.

Acronis True Image Home 2011 was used for this task. The steps may be different if you are using a different version of this product or a different third-party backup utility.

Procedure

This task will teach you how to back up a specific folder on a schedule using Acronis True Image Home 2011.

Equipment Used

As previously mentioned, you will have to have Acronis True Image Home 2011 installed on your computer. You will also need a destination drive, such as a second drive in your PC or an external USB drive, for the backed-up data.

Details

This task will take you through the process of selecting a directory or directories to back up, determining a destination for the data to be backed up, and setting a schedule for when backups are to occur.

Scheduling Regular Backups on Windows 7 with Acronis True Image Home

1. Click the Windows Start button and then click All Programs.
2. Click Acronis, click Acronis True Image Home, and then click Acronis True Image Home.
3. When prompted, click Yes to allow Acronis access to Windows 7.

4. On the Welcome screen, click Use Backup Assistant.

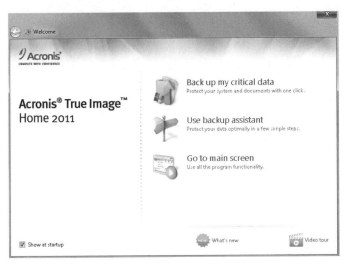

5. On the What Do You Want to Back Up? screen, click Files and Folders, and then click Next.

6. On the How Do You Want to Protect Your Data? screen, click Back Up on a Schedule, and then click Start Backup Configuring.

7. On the Configure File Backup Process screen, under Categories, click a directory such as the name of your user directory.

8. In the Name column, select a specific directory or library you want to back up, such as My Documents.

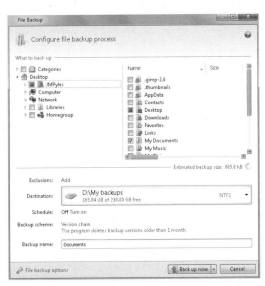

9. Next to Destination, use the drop-down menu to select a destination directory, such as D:\My backups.

10. Next to Schedule, click Turn On.

11. When the Schedule Your Operation screen opens in a separate window, select Weekly; under Weekly, select a day such as Wednesday, and use the Start At menu to select a start time for the backup; then click OK.

12. Accept the default selection of Version Chain for Backup Scheme, which will delete any backup versions older than one month.

13. Create a name for the backup in the Backup Name field, such as **Documents**.

14. Click the arrow to the left of the Back Up Now button, and select Later.

15. On the Acronis True Image Home screen under My Backups, verify that your backup settings are correct.

16. To test the backup process, click Back Up Now.

17. Once the backup is complete, verify that you can see a success message.

18. Close the Acronis screen.

Criteria for Completion

You will have successfully completed this task when the selected file or directory is saved in the My Backups directory as a .tib file. This file cannot be accessed directly and is used only if you need to restore the data.

Task 2.14: Flashing the BIOS

I suppose "flashing" could be taken the wrong way, but this is actually a method of enhancing a computer's basic functioning. BIOS, or basic input/output system, is a very old element in PC engineering. The BIOS is software on a special chip on the motherboard that dictates the boot process, initializes essential hardware, and determines the abilities and capacities of the computer (such as how big a hard drive it can use).

In the "bad old days," you were stuck with whatever BIOS your motherboard came with. If newer versions of the BIOS supported larger hard drives and faster CPUs or fixed particular bugs, you needed to get either a new motherboard or a new computer. More modern computer systems make it possible to upgrade the BIOS and keep the motherboard; however, it's not the same process as updating a program living on your hard drive.

Flashing the BIOS on older computers requires special software tools, and if you make a mistake and damage or destroy the BIOS, you will turn your PC into nothing more than a really big paperweight (short of replacing the BIOS chip). For modern computers, updating the BIOS is as simple as downloading the .exe file from the website of the PC manufacturer, running the file, and rebooting the computer. Let's take a look at the process.

Objective

This task covers objective 220:801:1.1.

Scenario

A BIOS update has been issued that fixes several bugs and allows your computer to use a faster CPU. You have the computer powered up and connected to the Internet. You are ready to proceed.

Scope of Task

Duration

This task should take anywhere from 15 to 30 minutes, including prep time.

Setup

You will need to identify the current BIOS for your Windows 7 computer and check the website for the company that made your computer for BIOS updates.

Caveat

As previously mentioned, in the "bad old days" if this process went wrong, your computer probably wouldn't even boot. For current computers, the process is quite streamlined and relatively safe, as long as you make sure you are installing the correct BIOS update for your computer.

You will need to make sure all applications are closed before you update the BIOS.

The PC manufacturer's website usually asks you to choose the BIOS type by make and model of the computer, so as long as you know that information, you should be okay. Also, some BIOS updates will detect if you are using the wrong update for your computer's hardware.

Procedure

This task will teach you how to flash (update) the BIOS chip on a computer's motherboard.

Equipment Used

All you need is the computer itself and an Internet connection.

Details

This task will take you step-by-step through the process of downloading and installing a BIOS update for a computer's motherboard.

Downloading a BIOS Upgrade and Flashing the BIOS

IDENTIFYING THE CURRENT BIOS ON THE COMPUTER

1. Click Start, and in the Search box, type **msinfo32** and then press Enter.

2. When the System Information screen opens, find the entry in the list for BIOS Version/ Date and write this information down.

3. When finished, close the screen.

LOCATING AND DOWNLOADING THE LATEST BIOS

1. Go to the computer manufacturer's site and search for the make and model of your computer.

2. Select the search result that takes you to the page where you can update the BIOS for your computer.

3. On the downloads page for the BIOS, confirm that it is the correct BIOS type and that the date for the BIOS is later than what is currently installed on your computer.

WARNING   While there are many benefits to updating your BIOS, the possibility of a bad flash always exists. Only flash your BIOS to fix a bug you are actually experiencing or to add a feature you require.

Read any installation instructions available on the computer vendor's website regarding how to install the BIOS. There may be steps you need to take that are different than those listed in this task.

4. Click the Download button, and if prompted, select a download method such as For Single File Download via Browser.

NOTE   Some BIOS updaters require that they be written to a boot disk (floppy/ CD/DVD/USB) and then used to boot the computer into a receptive state for BIOS flashing.

5. If prompted, select a specific directory where you want the .exe file to be downloaded onto your computer.

INSTALLING THE BIOS UPDATE

1. Navigate to the location of the .exe file and double-click it to start the BIOS update.

2. When the BIOS Flash window appears, click Continue.

3. When the message stating that pressing OK will close down all applications, shut down the Windows OS, and flash the BIOS appears, and then to reboot, click OK.

4. After the BIOS update completes and the computer reboots, log in to Windows, and in the Search box type **msinfo32**.

5. When the System Information screen appears, verify that the BIOS has been updated by noting that the date has changed to match the date of the BIOS you just installed.

Criteria for Completion

You will have successfully completed this task when you flash the BIOS, reboot the computer, and note on the BIOS screen that the changes show the current BIOS version. You can also enter the CMOS setup itself to verify this and make sure all the configuration settings are correct.

Task 2.15: Changing the CMOS Battery to Correct a Slow PC Clock

The CMOS battery is usually a small lithium manganese dioxide battery similar to the ones that power wristwatches. It is located on your motherboard and provides electricity to hold certain configuration settings, including system time, even when the computer is completely powered down. The lifetime of this battery is roughly 10 years, but how long it actually lasts usually depends on how heavily the computer is used.

Most computers in a corporate environment receive their time from a local or Internet time server. This doesn't mean that the local system time is unimportant. If the CMOS battery dies, not only will the system time be lost but so will other configuration settings your computer depends on, such as video display type, initial boot drive selection, and so on. A slow system clock is just the first sign of a dying CMOS battery.

Objective

This task covers objective 220:801:1.2.

Scenario

The Shipping department on the main loading dock uses a Windows XP Professional computer as a file and print server for its local computers. It is usually powered down on the weekends and powered up again Monday morning. You have received a trouble ticket from Shipping saying that the computer prompts them to press the F10 key every time the computer is powered up in order to set the date and time. This is the classic sign of a dying CMOS battery. You look up the system information for this computer and find the correct replacement battery in inventory. You take the battery and your tools and report to the main loading dock.

Scope of Task

Duration

This task should take about 30 minutes or less.

Setup

There is no special setup for this task.

Caveat

When you remove the CMOS battery, the BIOS chip will lose power and the information will be lost. Make sure you record all of your configuration information prior to removing the battery. Also, make sure you have the correct replacement battery for your motherboard.

The easiest way to perform this task is to simply remove and immediately replace the same battery.

Procedure

This task will teach you the proper method of replacing a dying CMOS battery.

Equipment Used

You will need a Phillips-head screwdriver to open the access panel and a flat-head screwdriver to remove the CMOS battery. You also will need your ESD equipment so you can reach into the computer case safely.

Details

This task takes you through the process of recording your BIOS settings, replacing a CMOS battery, and restoring computer settings.

Replacing a CMOS Battery

RECORDING THE BIOS SETTINGS

1. Sitting at the keyboard, reboot the computer.
2. When the computer begins to boot, press the correct key to enter into Setup.

The key to enter Setup can be Esc, F1, F12, or some other key or key combination, depending on the BIOS.

3. Use the Tab and Enter keys to navigate to the different screens in the BIOS Setup.

4. Write down all of the configuration information contained on all of the screens.

5. When finished, press the correct key combination to save and exit the BIOS.

Make sure you didn't miss any areas of the setup. You will need this information after you replace the battery.

REPLACING THE CMOS BATTERY

1. Power down the computer.

2. Disconnect the power cable from the power supply.

3. Locate your Phillips-head screwdriver.

Make sure to take ESD precautions before opening the computer case.

4. Remove the screws holding the access panel in place.

5. Remove the access panel.

6. Position the computer so the motherboard is lying flat.

7. Locate the CMOS battery on the motherboard.

8. Locate your flat-head screwdriver.

9. Gently pry the battery up out of the socket on the motherboard.

Be extremely careful when you are performing these steps. You could accidentally puncture the motherboard or battery slot. Also, some CMOS batteries are held in place by small clips. Make sure to move them aside prior to removing the battery.

10. Locate the replacement battery.

11. Gently but firmly insert it in the socket on the motherboard.

12. Verify that it is securely in place.

13. Verify that you did not inadvertently loosen any connections or components while working inside the computer.

14. Put the computer back in its original position.

15. Replace the access panel.

16. Replace the access-panel screws.

17. Plug the power cord back into the power supply.

RESTORING THE BIOS SETTINGS

1. Boot the computer.

2. Using the correct key or key combination, enter the BIOS Setup.

3. Using the Tab and Enter keys, access each page in the BIOS and restore the settings, using the information you wrote down in the section "Recording the BIOS Settings" earlier in this task.

4. Press the correct key combination to save the settings and exit the BIOS.

5. Allow the computer to continue to boot.

6. Instruct the loading-dock staff to periodically monitor the system time to verify that it is accurate.

Criteria for Completion

You will have successfully completed this task when you have replaced the battery and restored the BIOS settings and the computer boots and operates correctly.

Task 2.16: Resetting Passwords

This is one of the most common tasks you will perform as a PC support tech. It seems like end users have a great deal of difficulty remembering their passwords. One reason for this may be that the "strong" passwords typically required in a corporate setting are not always easy to remember.

A strong password is one that is not easily guessed by an intruder or discovered by a dictionary attack. It is usually a combination of letters and numbers but can also contain special characters such as $ and #.

In a large, corporate environment, it is common to reset the passwords for domain users. However, this task would require that you set up a domain controller in your test environment. For this task, you will change the password for a user in a small office or home office setting where the password is managed on the PC directly and not in an Active Directory domain.

Objective

This task covers objective 220:802:2.1.

Scenario

You receive a call from one of your home office customers stating that he believes his computer's password was acquired by a hacker and he doesn't know how to change it. The computer is currently on and the user is logged in. You had the customer scheduled for a routine maintenance visit for today and when you are at his office, you will perform the task of changing the computer's password.

Scope of Task

Duration

This task should take about 10 minutes at most.

Setup

This task was created using a Windows 7 computer.

Procedure

This task will show you how to change a user's password on a Windows 7 computer.

Equipment Used

You will need no special equipment to complete this task.

Details

This task will take you through the necessary steps to change a user's password on a Windows 7 computer.

Changing a User's Password

ACCESSING THE DOMAIN USER'S ACCOUNT ON A DOMAIN CONTROLLER

1. Verify that the user is logged into the computer.
2. Click Start and then click Control Panel.
3. Click User Accounts.
4. On the User Accounts screen, click Change your password.
5. On the Change your password screen. have the user type his old password in the Current password field.

6. Have the user type his new password in the New password field and then type the same password again in the Confirm password field.

7. Have the user type a hint in the Type a password hint field that will help him remember what his password is should he ever forget.

8. Click Change password.

9. Close the User Accounts screen.

VERIFYING THAT THE PASSWORD HAS BEEN CHANGED

1. Log off the computer.

2. Have the user login to the computer with the new password and verify that he is successful.

Criteria for Completion

You will have successfully completed this task when you have changed the computer user's password and he is able to login with the new password.

Task 2.17: Creating a New Local User in Windows Vista

Multiple Local Group Policy Objects (MLGPO) is a feature that is included by default in Windows Vista Business, Enterprise, and Ultimate editions. It improves upon the Local Group Policy settings used in Windows XP and allows administrators to apply different Local Group Policy levels to local users on stand-alone computers. While such Group Policy settings are applied by domain controllers (DCs) for computers that are domain members, MLGPO is ideally used for computers used in stand-alone settings, such as in publicly accessible Internet kiosks or other shared computer environments like schools and libraries.

This task will show you only how to create a nonadministrative user account on a Windows Vista computer that would be appropriate for one of these settings. For more information on MLGPO, perform a search for this data at http://technet.microsoft .com/en-us/.

Objective

This task covers objective 220-802:1.4.

Scenario

A Windows Vista computer has been installed in the Internet kiosk in the lobby of your company's main office. You have been assigned to create a nonadministrative user on that computer, so guests in the lobby can use it for accessing the Web without compromising security on the corporate network. It is after business hours, and you are at the keyboard of the computer in the lobby and ready to get to work.

Scope of Task

Duration

The task will take just a few minutes.

Setup

No special setup is required for the task beyond having a Windows Vista Business, Enterprise, or Ultimate edition computer.

Caveat

There are no particular caveats associated with this task; however, you must have the name you want to use for the new user in this task prepared before proceeding, such as "internet01." Don't forget to record the password you use for this user's account.

Procedure

This task will show you how to create a nonadministrative user for a Windows Vista local computer.

Equipment Used

No special equipment is required.

Details

This task will take you through the steps required to create a nonadministrative user for a local Windows Vista computer.

Creating a Nonadministrative User Account on a Windows Vista Computer

1. Log in to the Windows Vista computer with an account that has administrative privileges.
2. Click the Windows Vista button.
3. In the menu that appears, right-click Computer and then click Manage. (If a UAC screen appears, click 'Yes'.)
4. Click the arrow next to Local Users and Groups.
5. Right-click Users, and then click New User.
6. In the Username field, type the name of the user, such as **internet01**.
7. In the Full Name field, type the name of the user, such as **internet01**.

8. In the Password field, type the password to be used with this user account.

9. In the Confirm Password field, type the same password that you used in the Password field.

10. Clear the User Must Change Password at Next Logon check box.

11. Select the Password Never Expires check box.

12. Select the User Cannot Change Password check box.

13. Click Create, and then click Close.

14. Click File, and then click Exit to close the dialog box.

Criteria for Completion

You will have successfully completed this task when you have created the new, nonadministrative local user on the Windows Vista machine. You can test the new user account by logging out of your administrative account and logging in as the new user.

Task 2.18: Testing Ports with an Online Scanner

Testing the effectiveness or ineffectiveness of your firewall and other security procedures is vital in order to keep the network safe from outside attack. As an entry-level PC support tech, you will not be expected to configure or monitor network security measures. Depending on the size of your organization, that task will be performed by either a senior staff member or a security specialist.

However, you may occasionally be asked to test an individual computer or server's security with an online port scanner. This is a utility provided for free by various security organizations, and it can be very effective in detecting which ports of a computer are vulnerable from the Internet.

Objective

This task covers objective 220-802:2.6.

Scenario

A new test server has been set up and you have been asked to use an online port scanner to verify the vulnerability of the port settings on the device and record the results. You are told that the test server has deliberately been left with some vulnerabilities to determine how quickly an attack occurs from the outside.

Scope of Task

Duration

The task will take about 10 to 15 minutes depending on the length of the scan and the speed of your Internet connection.

Setup

No special setup is required for this task.

Caveat

You may be shocked at just how vulnerable your computer is after the scan results are displayed.

Procedure

This task will show you how to use an online port scanner to check a computer's vulnerability.

Equipment Used

No special equipment is required.

Details

This task will take you through the steps required to use an online scanner to scan the security of various ports on a computer or server.

Locating and Using an Online Port Scanner

1. At the computer you intend to scan, open a web browser.
2. Use your favorite search engine to search for "online port scanner" or a similar word string.
3. When the results come in, select ShieldsUP!.

 NOTE   In Step 3, you could select any number of other services, but ShieldsUP! is the tool used in this task.

4. When the initial page loads, scroll down and click Proceed.
5. When the next page loads, scroll down if necessary, until you see the ShieldsUP! Services box.
6. Click the Common Ports button.
7. The scan will begin.

8.   Scroll down and review the results when the scan is concluded.

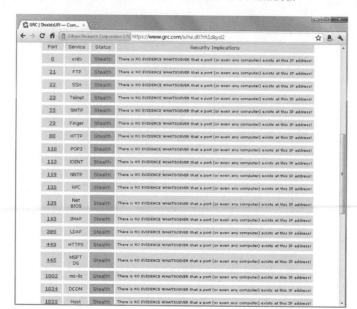

9.   Scroll down and click Text Summary.

10. Review the summary and compare the results to what the IT staff expected.

 This was only a simple port scan. ShieldsUP! and other third-party port scanners are capable of running more detailed tests on your online security.

Criteria for Completion

You will have successfully completed this task when you can view the results of the port scan. You can perform other specialized scans on this site and obtain a text summary of the results that you can then print.

Task 2.19: Changing Printer Toner

This is another extremely common task you will be performing as a PC tech. It isn't a particularly difficult task, but you could find yourself doing it on an almost daily basis, if you support a large number of printers. The procedure differs somewhat depending on the make, model, and size of the printer. (Some large and specialized printers use separate and rather large cartridges for the colors black, blue, green, yellow, and red.)

Objective

This task covers objective 220-801:4.3.

Scenario

You receive a trouble ticket stating that the toner is low in the printer used by the Software Development department. You look up in your records the type and model of printer they use, locate the correct replacement cartridge in inventory, and report to the department.

Scope of Task

Duration

This task should take about 5 to 10 minutes at most.

Setup

No special setup is required for this task, outside of access to a printer and the correct toner cartridges.

Caveat

There are a number of different printer types and models in existence as well as different types of printer cartridges and procedures for changing them. The steps in this task may not quite match the ones you'll need to take to change your printer cartridge.

Procedure

This task will show you how to change the toner cartridge in a printer type that is typically used in a business environment.

Equipment Used

In addition to having access to a printer, you will need an appropriate toner cartridge to use in this task. For this example, it is advisable to have a drop cloth or two handy to put the cartridges on and to wipe up any toner mess. The simplest way for you to complete this task is to remove the toner cartridge in your printer and then replace it.

Details

This task walks you through the steps necessary to remove an empty printer cartridge and replace it with a fresh unit.

Changing a Printer's Toner Cartridge

OPENING THE PRINTER

1. When you arrive at the printer, put the box containing the new cartridge aside.

2. Look at the printer readout and verify the error message indicating it is low on toner.

 This display will vary depending on the make and model of the printer.

3. Locate the latch securing the main access panel of the printer.

4. Pull the latch, releasing the panel.

5. Open the panel.

REPLACING THE CARTRIDGE

1. Locate the cloth you brought with you.

2. Spread the cloth on the floor below the open access panel.

3. Verify that there is sufficient room on the cloth to hold two toner cartridges and protect the floor from spills.

4. Open the box containing the new cartridge.

5. Remove the cartridge and place it on the cloth.

6. Locate the old cartridge inside the printer.

7. Locate the cartridge-release latch.

8. Pull the latch to release the old cartridge.

9. Carefully pull the cartridge toward you, out of the printer.

10. Place the old cartridge on the cloth to contain any toner spills.

11. Locate the new cartridge and remove any tape or seals covering toner access.

 You may have to shake the cartridge prior to Step 11 to ensure that the toner is distributed evenly inside the cartridge.

12. Correctly orient the new cartridge and push it in its container inside the printer.

13. Verify that it is firmly in place.

14. Close the latch securing the cartridge.

15. Close the printer's access door.

16. Close the latch and secure the door.

CLEANING UP AND CONDUCTING A TEST PRINT

1. Put the old cartridge in the box the new cartridge came in.

2. Note any toner spills on the cloth.

If you used the drop cloth correctly, there should be no spills on the floor.

3. If you have toner on your hands, wipe them thoroughly on a clean section of the cloth.

4. Carefully fold the cloth so all of the spilled toner is inside and cannot spill out.

5. Place the cloth inside the box with the old toner cartridge.

6. Access the printer controls and print a test page.

The procedure for accessing the printer controls in Step 6 is highly variable and no one method can be presented. Alternatively, you could have an end user print a test page from a computer.

7. When the test page prints correctly, remove the box containing the spent cartridge and cloth and dispose of it appropriately.

There are programs available that will recycle spent print cartridges. Your IT department supervisor will be aware of the procedure used in your department.

Criteria for Completion

You will have successfully completed this task when the toner cartridge has been replaced and the printer is printing normally.

Task 2.20: Scanning a Document Using Windows 7

Scanning documents and images is a task that users need to perform, sometimes frequently, depending on their job duties, but it isn't always apparent how to perform this task. For instance, using an HP All-in-One product, should the user perform the scan using an HP utility or from Windows? You may occasionally have to train a user in which option is best, which usually translates into which option is the easiest to perform.

An HP OfficeJet 6500A All-in-One printer was used to create this task. The task scenarios should work the same way for other imaging devices, but expect there to be some differences.

Objective

This task covers objective 220-801:4.3.

Scenario

The chief operations officer (COO) for your company has had a Windows 7 computer installed in his office but complains that he is unable to scan documents from Windows 7 using his HP All-in-One device. You have been assigned the task of instructing the COO as to the method he can use to perform this task.

Scope of Task

Duration

It should take about 10 minutes or so to progress through the steps.

Setup

The only setup that's required is for an imaging device to be directly attached to a Windows 7 machine, the correct drivers to be installed, and for both machines to be powered up and running. Since scanning documents does not require printing, the document imaging device does not require adequate ink in its print cartridges, but it's always good to keep a printing machine in good operating order. An original document to scan must be on hand.

Caveat

The steps in these tasks should work with all HP All-in-One imaging devices, but the results cannot be guaranteed for other HP devices for non-HP devices.

Procedure

This task will teach you two simple methods to scan a document using an HP All-in-One imaging device with Windows 7.

Equipment Used

As previously stated, a computer running Windows 7 and an HP All-in-One printer with scanning abilities are required to get the most out of this set of tasks.

Details

This task will walk you through the various workaround methods for scanning a document from Windows 7 using an HP All-in-One device.

Scanning a Document from an HP All-in-One Device Using Windows 7

LOADING THE ORIGINAL DOCUMENT

 You will use this same method for loading an original document in the HP imaging device, regardless of the following scanning methods you select.

1. Make sure that both the Windows 7 PC and the HP All-in-One device are connected, powered up, and ready.
2. Raise the top cover of the imaging device.
3. Place the original document, print side down, onto the glass, using the guides around the glass to line up the document.
4. Close the lid.

SCANNING A DOCUMENT USING WINDOWS 7

1. Click the Windows Start button and then click Devices and Printers.
2. Right-click the image of the HP All-in-One device, and then select Start Scan.
3. In the New Scan screen, leave the Profile selection at Photo (Default) and the Source as Flatbed.
4. For Color format, select Grayscale.
5. For File type, select PNG (PNG image).
6. Click Preview and then wait for the preview to appear.
7. If the preview image is acceptable, click Scan.
8. When the Import Pictures and Videos box appears, you can add an optional tag to the image.
9. Click Import Settings.
10. In the Import Settings box, click the Browse button next to Import To and select a destination directory on your computer for the scanned file.
11. Click OK.
12. In the Import Pictures and Videos box, click Import.
13. When the scanned image appears in the Imported Pictures and Videos screen, close the screen.
14. Navigate to the directory where you had the scanned image saved and verify that it is there and can be opened by right-clicking the image and selecting Preview.
15. Close all open screens and windows.

SCANNING A DOCUMENT USING PAINT

1. Click the Windows button.

2. In the menu that appears, click All Programs.

3. Click Accessories.

4. Click Paint.

5. When the program opens in a separate window, click the File icon button, and then click From Scanner or Camera.

6. Click Scan.

7. On the What Do You Want to Scan? screen, select Flatbed as Paper Source.

8. Select the type of picture you want to scan, such as Grayscale Picture.

9. Click Preview, and then wait for the preview to appear in the screen.

10. If the preview image is acceptable, click Scan.

11. Once the image is scanned into Paint, save the image to the desired directory.

Criteria for Completion

You will have successfully completed this task when you have scanned a document using both methods. Remember, though, that your results may not be the same if you are using an imaging device different from the HP All-in-One series used to create this scenario.

Task 2.21: Managing Windows Startup and Recovery Behavior in Windows XP

By default, when Windows XP suffers from an extreme failure such as the dreaded Blue Screen of Death (BSOD), it automatically reboots. Unfortunately, there may be valuable information contained in the BSOD that you will not be able to read before the PC restarts. Of course, Windows XP is much more stable than previous versions of Windows, so the BSOD appearance is rare, but it's still not completely a thing of the past. You can take control of the reboot process so that it's not automatic, which will allow you to read valuable troubleshooting messages should the BSOD happen to you.

Objective

This task covers objective 220-802:4.2.

Scenario

You have been assigned to diagnose a Windows XP computer that has suffered a BSOD. The user reports that she started her computer on Monday morning as usual and, after the operating system had fully loaded, double-clicked her web-browser icon in the System Tray. The browser didn't launch, so she double-clicked again and the system seemed to freeze. The BSOD appeared, but the computer rebooted before she could read any of the information that appeared.

   The system seems responsive now and you'd like to try to duplicate the error but be able to read the BSOD message. For that, you will need to disable the automatic reboot under Startup and Recovery.

Scope of Task

Duration

Disabling the automatic reboot feature will just take a few minutes.

Setup

No special setup is required.

Caveat

There are no special issues associated with this task, and you do not need a computer that is malfunctioning to successfully change this setting. A Windows XP Professional computer was used to create this scenario, but the steps are identical for Windows XP Home.

Procedure

This task will teach you how to disable the automatic reboot feature under Startup and Recovery.

Equipment Used

No special equipment is required. This task should work the same on both versions of Windows XP.

Details

This task will walk you through the procedure of disabling the automatic reboot feature under Startup and Recovery.

Disabling Automatic Reboot Under Startup and Recovery

1. Click Start.
2. In the menu that appears, right-click My Computer.
3. Click Properties.
4. Click the Advanced tab.
5. Under Startup and Recovery, click Settings.
6. Clear the check box next to Automatically Restart.
7. Click OK.
8. Click OK to close the System Properties box.

Criteria for Completion

You will have successfully completed this task when you have cleared the Automatically Restart check box and saved your changes by clicking OK. This task does not require that your computer suffer a BSOD event or that you solve such an error.

Task 2.22: Turning Windows 7 Features On or Off

There are a large number of services and features in Windows 7 that most people are unaware of. As a computer technician, you must be familiar with these features, what they do, and how to turn them on and off as needed. Windows 7 features are turned on or off by default, but you can enable or disable these features manually in the Control Panel.

Objective

This task covers objective 220-802:1.5.

Scenario

You work for a small city IT department and receive a trouble ticket from a customer stating that she may have turned off the Windows Search feature on her Windows 7 computer. You report to her work area and speak with her. She says she was exploring the Control Panel in her computer and discovered the ability to turn features on and off under Programs and Features. You are aware of how this works in Windows 7 and agree to investigate and restore Windows Search on her computer.

Scope of Task

Duration

This should only take a few minutes.

Setup

No special setup is required. You only need access to a Windows 7 computer. In order to create this scenario, I first turned off the Windows Search feature on my Windows 7 computer and then rebooted. Read through this task to see the entire process; then turn off Windows Search, reboot, work through the task, and turn Windows Search back on.

Caveat

The only real issue here is that turning off one or more features in Windows 7 may affect how it performs in a variety of areas. If you want, you can extend the scope of this task and practice turning on and off different features in Windows 7, but depending on what features you enable or disable, you may experience unanticipated behaviors from your computer.

If you explore the Windows features box, you'll see that some Windows features are organized together in folders and some of the folders contain subfolders that give you access to additional features. If you see a check box that appears only partly checked or appears dark, this means some of the items inside the folder are turned on and others are turned off.

Procedure

This task will teach you how to turn Windows features in Windows 7 on and off.

Equipment Used

No special equipment is needed.

Details

This task will walk you through the process of turning on the Windows Search feature in Windows 7, which has previously been disabled.

Turning On the Windows Search Feature in Windows 7

1. Click the Windows Start button and then click Control Panel.

2. In Control Panel, in Large Icons or Small Icon view, double-click Programs and Features.

3. In the Programs and Features dialog box, in the left-hand pane, click Turn Windows Features On or Off.

4. After the Windows Features dialog box appears and loads, scroll down to Windows Search and select the Windows Search check box.

5. Click OK and then wait for your selection to take effect.

6. When prompted, click the Restart Now button. The restart sequence may take longer than normal because of the configuration changes that are required.

Criteria for Completion

Once the computer has rebooted, Windows Search will be turned back on. You will have successfully completed this task when the computer has rebooted.

Task 2.23: Controlling AutoPlay Settings in Windows 7

AutoPlay is the feature in a Windows computer that automatically responds to an optical disc placed in the disc player using some predetermined action. For an audio disc, for example, placing the disc in the CD/DVD player may result in the disc being automatically opened using Windows Media Player and the music beginning to play.

There are a large number of AutoPlay options available in Windows 7 that can be configured. Most of them have default settings, but you can override the defaults and select customized behaviors depending on your requirements.

Objective

This task covers objective 220-802:1.5.

Scenario

You have a customer who plays a large number of audio and video files on CDs, DVDs, and other sources. These files are sent to her for review and editing from a number of different artists, and she wants to be presented with a menu of possible actions when she puts a piece of removable media in her optical drive or insert removable storage in a USB port. She wants this behavior to occur when she accesses video files, audio files, mixed content, DVD movies, and DVD audio discs.

You access her computer and prepare to configure the AutoPlay feature to her specifications.

Scope of Task

Duration

This task should only take a few minutes.

Setup

No special setup is required besides having access to a Windows 7 computer.

Caveat

This task will require that you change the default behavior of the AutoPlay feature. You can return the settings you change to their defaults after the task is over if you desire.

You cannot choose to reset just one selection to its default. In order to set all selections to their defaults, in the lower left area of the AutoPlay dialog box, click the Reset All Defaults button and then click Save.

Procedure

This task will show you how to configure the AutoPlay feature in Windows 7.

Equipment Used

No special equipment is required.

Details

This task will walk you through the steps of changing the default settings for a number of disc and file types in AutoPlay.

Configuring AutoPlay in Windows 7

1. Click the Windows Start button and then click Control Panel.

2. In Control Panel in Large Icon or Small Icon view, double-click AutoPlay.

3. In the AutoPlay dialog box, click the drop-down menu next to DVD Movie and select Ask Me Every Time.

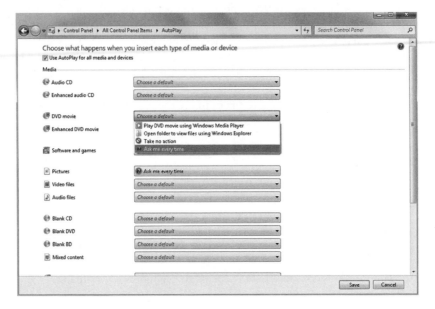

4. Click the drop-down menu next to Video Files and make the same selection.

5. Perform the same action on the drop-down menus next to Audio Files, Mixed Content, and DVD Audio.

6. Click Save.

7. To test your changes, insert a DVD movie into the computer's DVD player and verify that you are prompted as to how to open the DVD.

8. When finished, eject the DVD.

Criteria for Completion

You will have successfully completed this task when you have configured and tested your AutoPlay settings changes.

Task 2.24: Setting Up Advanced File Sharing in Windows 7

A Windows 7 Workgroup is configured to use specific sharing settings by default, but you can manually configure advanced file sharing features in Control Panel. This allows you to override the default sharing settings for your Workgroup or for public sharing and increase or decrease the level of security.

Objective

This task covers objective 220-802:1.5.

Scenario

You work for a small city IT department and have been assigned to change the sharing configuration settings on the Windows 7 computer used by the manager of the city's Accounting office. Specifically, you are to prevent network discovery for the Workgroup so this computer cannot be seen over the network, disable file and print sharing, and disable public folder sharing.

Scope of Task

Duration

This task should take just a few minutes.

Setup

In order to test the effectiveness of your configuration changes, your Windows 7 computer must be connected to a local network, be part of a Workgroup, and there should be another Windows computer that is also connected to the network and part of the Workgroup. The Windows 7 computer should have one or more folders shared, and it would be a bonus if the Windows 7 computer had a directly connected printer that it is sharing on the network.

Caveat

If you change the settings on your Windows 7 computer to a configuration you don't use in its day-to-day operation, make sure to return the settings to their previous values after you are finished with this task. If necessary, write down the settings you normally use before making the changes recommended in this task.

Procedure

This task will teach you how to change the advanced file-sharing settings in a Windows 7 computer.

Equipment Used

No special equipment is required.

Details

This task will show you the procedure for changing advanced file- and print-sharing settings in Windows 7.

Changing Advanced Sharing Settings in Windows 7

1. Click the Windows Start button and then click Control Panel.
2. In Control Panel in Large Icon or Small Icon view, click Network and Sharing Center.
3. On the Network and Sharing Center screen, in the upper- left pane, click Change Advanced Sharing Settings.
4. On the Advanced Sharing Settings screen, expand Home or Work.
5. Under Network Discovery, click Turn Off Network Discovery.
6. Under File and Printer Sharing, click Turn Off File and Printer Sharing.
7. Under Public Folder Sharing, click Turn Off Public Folder Sharing.
8. Click Save Changes.
9. Go to another computer on the same network, and in the Share or Run box attempt to connect to the Windows 7 computer you have just configured, verifying that you cannot discover the computer over the network.

To do this, depending on the type of Windows computer you are using to connect to the Windows 7 test PC, in the Search or Run box, enter *computername* (using the actual hostname for the Windows 7 PC) or *computerIPaddress* (using the actual IPv4 address for the Windows PC) and then press Enter. You should not be able to connect to the computer. If the Windows 7 computer has been sharing a printer on the network, you will not be able to use the printer from the remote computer.

Criteria for Completion

You will have successfully completed this task when you have completed the advanced sharing configuration changes and are unable to connect to the Windows 7 computer from another Windows PC on the same network. If you need to have the Windows 7 computer and its shared files and folders available on your local network, reverse the sharing setting you configured during this task.

Task 2.25: Installing Windows Live Mail

Windows Live Mail is a Microsoft product that can be used on Windows 7 instead of Microsoft Office Outlook. In the original release of Windows Vista, users needed three separate products—Windows Mail, Windows Calendar, and Windows Contacts—to perform all of the functions offered by Windows Live Mail on Windows 7. Windows Live Mail is a free desktop utility that is part of Windows Live Essentials. To use Windows Live Mail, you must first use Live Essentials to download and install Windows Live programs.

Objective

This task covers objective 220-802:1.5.

Scenario

You have a client who has just purchased a Windows 7 computer but would like a low- or no-cost alternative to using Microsoft Windows Outlook for an email client, to organize contacts, and to use a calendar. You suggest Windows Live Mail, and she agrees that it would be a good option. You are then commissioned to download and configure Live Mail for her use.

Scope of Task

Duration

This task should take about 15 minutes, depending on the speed of your Internet connection.

Setup

You will need a Windows 7 computer and Internet access for this task.

Caveat

You may not want to use Windows Live Mail on your lab computer, but after installing it, you can uninstall it to save space. However, Task 2.27 is dependent on the current task, so don't remove Live Mail until after completing Task 2.27.

Procedure

This task will show you how to download and install Windows Live Mail.

Equipment Used

No special equipment is needed.

Details

This task will outline the steps to take in order to use Windows Live Essentials to download and install Windows Live Mail.

Downloading and Installing Windows Live Mail

1. Click the Windows Start button and then click All Programs.

2. Click Accessories and then click Getting Started.

3. On the Getting Started screen, click Go Online to Get Windows Live Essentials.

4. Click the Go Online to Get Windows Live Essentials link.

5. When the Windows Live Essentials web page opens, if you are unsure if your computer meets the system requirements, click the View System Requirements link and review the information there.

6. When you are ready, click Download Now.

7. When the File Download - Security Warning dialog box appears, click Run.

8. If prompted, click Run again.

9. When the What Do You Want to Install? screen appears, click Choose the Programs You Want to Install.

10. When the Select Programs to Install screen appears, click Mail and then click Install (the installation process may take some time).

11. When prompted, restart the computer.

12. After the computer restarts, log in, click the Windows Start button, and then click Windows Live Mail.

13. After Windows Live Mail launches, close the program.

Criteria for Completion

You will have successfully completed this assignment when you have installed Windows Live Mail and can open the program on your Windows 7 computer.

Task 2.26: Configuring Mail Accounts in Windows Live

Once you have installed Windows Live Mail (see Task 2.25) you can configure Live Mail with one or more email accounts, setting up Live Mail to use the POP3, IMAP4, and SMTP servers of your choice. The first task you must perform before you can use Windows Live Mail is to add the first email account. If you have ever set up an email account in Outlook, this process is quite similar.

Objective

This task covers objective 220-802:1.5.

Scenario

You have just installed Windows Live Mail on a client's Windows 7 computer and are now ready to create an email account for her. She has provided you with all of the information necessary to create the email account.

Scope of Task

Duration

This task should take about 15 minutes to set up your first email account.

Setup

You will need a Windows 7 computer and to have Windows Live Mail installed. You will also need to have all of the required information including data on any POP3, IMAP4, and SMTP servers involved. You may also want to connect Live Mail to an online service such as Gmail or Hotmail.

Caveat

You will need to contact your ISP for all of the required email server information in order to complete this task. If this information is missing or inaccurate, you can complete the steps to create an email account, but your email account will not be able to send or receive email. You can use a Yahoo! or Gmail account and, in most cases, Live Mail will automatically configure the server data for the email account once you enter a valid email address and password.

Procedure

This task will show you how to configure a new email account in Windows Live Mail.

Equipment Used

No special equipment is needed.

Details

This task will take you through the steps required to set up an email account in Windows Live Mail.

Creating an Email Account in Windows Live Mail

1. Click the Windows Start button and then click All Programs.
2. Click Windows Live Mail.
3. When Live Mail opens, click Accounts and then click Email.
4. In the Email address field, enter the desired email address (you can click Get a Windows Live Email Address if you want to use Hotmail or Live.com).
5. In the Password field, enter the desired password and, if you desire, select the Remember This Password check box.
6. In the Display Name for Your Sent Messages field, enter the name you want displayed for this email account.
7. Click Next.
8. On the Configure Server Settings screen, under Incoming Server Information, use the Server Type drop-down menu to select the appropriate server such as POP, IMAP, or Hotmail.
9. In the Server Address field enter the IP address or URL of the desired server (you will need to get his information from your ISP) and enter the appropriate port number for the server type (select the Requires a Secure Connection (SSL) check box if necessary).
10. Use the Authenticate Using drop-down menu to select the authentication type, such as Clear Text, Secure Password Authentication, or Authenticated POP (APOP).
11. Under Outgoing Server Information, in the Server Address field, enter the address of the SMTP server and, if necessary, select the Requires a Secure Connection (SSL) and/ or Requires Authentication check boxes.
12. Click Next.
13. When the Your Email Account Was Added screen appears, click Finish.

14. In Live Mail, click the Windows Live Mail button, click New, and then click Email Message.

15. When the New Message window appears, if necessary, select the correct account in the From menu.

16. Address the message to an email account you can check.

17. Add a subject line and some content, and then click Send.

18. After a few moments, check the email account to which you sent the test message to make sure it arrived.

19. From that email account, send a test message to the email account you configured in Windows Live Mail and verify that the message was received.

20. When you have finished, close Windows Live Mail.

Criteria for Completion

You will have successfully completed this assignment when you have created a new email account in Windows Live Mail and can send and receive emails using this account.

Task 2.27: Rolling Back Device Drivers

Generally, it's a good idea to keep the device drivers for all devices installed on a computer up to date, but occasionally, after updating a device driver, a problem can occur. This can include the device no longer functioning properly or even resulting in the computer not being able to boot.

For device driver problems that are severe and that prevent your computer from booting, you'll need to restore to options such as Last Known Good Configuration or Safe Mode. However, for device driver problems that allow your computer to boot, you can always roll back the device driver to the previous version. This assumes that you know it was a device driver update that caused the problem on the computer.

Objective

This task covers objective 220-802:4.6.

Scenario

You have just updated a device driver for the sound card on your Windows 7 computer, rebooted the PC, and immediately noticed that the sound card no longer works. You open a web browser and search for any issues involving the sound card's device driver and discover that this is a known issue and the manufacturer recommends rolling the device driver back to the previous version.

Scope of Task

Duration

This task should take about 15 minutes or less.

Setup

This task was performed on a Windows 7 computer but it should work almost the same using Windows Vista or Windows XP. You will need an Internet connection if you want to update the drivers of a device on your computer, but you will only need the computer and to select an appropriate device in order to roll back the driver.

Caveat

It is almost always recommended that you keep the drivers for the devices on your computer updated to the latest version, so rolling back the driver for any device on your computer may have unintended consequences, such as the device no longer functioning. It is recommended that you update the driver for the device you intend to use for this task, such as a sound card, to the latest version (if necessary), and then roll the driver back to a prior version. Once you have finished this task, update the driver for the device to the current version again.

Procedure

This task will show you how to roll back the driver for a device on your PC.

Equipment Used

No special equipment is needed.

Details

This task will take you through the steps you will need to perform to roll back the driver for a device installed on your Windows 7 computer.

Rolling Back a Device Driver

1. Click the Windows Start button and then click Control Panel.
2. On the Control Panel screen in Large or Small Icon view, click System.
3. In the left pane of the System screen, click Device Manager.
4. On the Device Manager screen, expand the device category in the list, such as Display Adapters, right-click the desired device, and then click Properties.
5. On the Device Properties box, click the Driver tab.

6. If the Roll Back Driver button on the Properties box is inactive, click the Update Driver button; otherwise, proceed to Step 10.

7. When prompted, select Search Automatically for Updated Driver Software, and then allow the driver software to download and then to install.

8. When the Success message box appears, click Close.

9. Once the driver is updated, repeat the steps necessary to arrive at the Driver tab on the device's Properties box.

10. Click Roll Back Driver.

11. When prompted, click Yes (it may take several moments before the rollback is complete).

12. After the rollback is complete, click Update Driver again and allow the driver software to be downloaded and then to install.

13. When the Success message box appears, click Close.

14. Close the device's Properties box, close Device Manager, and then close Control Panel.

Criteria for Completion

You will have successfully completed this assignment when you have rolled back the device driver for a device on your computer and then restored the current device driver.

Task 2.28: Disabling and Removing Hardware Devices

Chances are you use a lot of portable storage devices with your desktop PC, including digital cameras, external USB drives, MP3 players, and mobile phones. These devices can attach to your computer via eSATA, FireWire, and USB interfaces. They are devices that are meant to be portable and easily detachable from your computer, but that doesn't mean it's always safe just to "pull the plug." You'll need to follow a set of recommended steps in order to make sure any attached storage device is properly removed.

You may also want to disable an internal device on the computer without physically removing it. There are times when a device, or more likely its drivers, is causing a problem on your computer. You can disable the device in Device Manager, which will prevent the device's drivers from being loaded.

Objective

This task covers objective 220-802:4.7.

Scenario

You have an external USB drive and a smartphone attached to your Windows 7 computer and you would like to safely remove them. You also are having problems with the DVD drive on your computer and want to disable the device without physically removing it.

Scope of Task

Duration

This task should take about 15 to 20 minutes.

Setup

You'll need to have a Windows 7 computer, a USB flash drive, and a smartphone. The external devices must be already attached to the computer. You must also select an internal device, such as the computer's DVD drive, to disable.

Caveat

Although people often just remove an attached device such as a USB thumb drive without taking steps in the software to disable the device first, it isn't recommended to do so. Although the devices themselves may not be harmed, the data integrity can be compromised. When in doubt, always play by the rules.

Procedure

This task will show you how to safely disable and remove portable and internal hardware devices.

Equipment Used

No special equipment is needed besides the equipment already described in the "Setup" section for this task.

Details

This task will take you through the steps for removing a portable device from a Windows 7 computer and disabling an internal device.

Disabling or Removing a Portable Storage Device and Internal Devices

REMOVING PORTABLE STORAGE DEVICES

1. Close all web browsers, screens, dialog boxes, files, and windows on your computer.
2. Click the Windows Start button and then click Computer.

3.   In the Devices with Removable Storage section of the Windows screen, right-click a removable disk and click Eject.

4.   After the Success message appears, remove the storage device.

5.   To remove a device such as a smartphone, use the smartphone's software or recommended procedure before removing the device, rather than disconnecting it in Windows.

6.   Remove the smartphone's cable from the computer when the phone's software indicates it is safe.

The procedure to remove a smartphone using its own software varies widely depending on the make and model of the device. Refer to the smartphone's documentation for the correct set of steps. You can also use Windows to disconnect the smartphone by right-clicking the Safely Remove Hardware icon in the System Tray notification area.

7.   Close the Computer screen when finished.

DISABLING AN INTERNAL DEVICE WITHOUT REMOVING IT

1.   Click the Windows Start button, right-click Computer, and then click Properties.

2.   On the System screen in the left pane, click Device Manager.

3.   Expand an item in the Device Manager list such as DVD/CD-ROM drives.

4.   Right-click the desired device and click Disable.

5.   When prompted by the Warning box, click Yes.

When a device is disabled, a black down arrow appears next to the device.

6.   Right-click the device in the list again and verify that instead of the Disable option, the Enable option is available.

7.   If you so desire, click the Enable option to reenable the device.

8.   When you have finished, close Device Manager and then close the System screen.

Criteria for Completion

You will have successfully completed this task when you have safely removed the portable USB drive and smartphone and when you have disabled the internal DVD drive on the computer.

Phase

3

Networking Computer Systems

You may be asking yourself what a PC desktop-support tech is doing performing any sort of networking function. Although trade schools, universities, and certification vendors may segregate IT operations into distinct and separate categories, real life is rarely so neat. Desktop support isn't all hard drives and RAM sticks. There are quite a number of elementary networking tasks you will perform in the course of your duties.

Task 3.1: Mapping Drives

Mapping a network drive is a handy way to give end users access to various file shares by making a share appear as if it were a separate drive on their computer. You can set up a share so that it uses a particular drive letter, and that letter is the one all your users will use to access that share. After it's set up, all the user has to do is open My Computer or Computer, depending on which version of Windows you're using, and open the drive. The information on the share will appear as if it were on a partition on the user's local hard drive.

Objective

This task covers objective 220:802:1.6.

Scenario

A new employee in Accounting needs to get access to the Accounting department's share on one of the servers. You've been assigned to map a network drive on her computer to that share and then test to make sure it works.

Scope of Task

Duration

This task should take 5 or 10 minutes at most.

Setup

You will need two computers that are networked together. One will act as the server with a shared folder and the other as the client machine. If you are unsure how to create a shared folder on a computer, see Task 3.2, "Creating File Shares."

Caveat

In a real production environment, be careful which directories you make available for sharing. Make sure that the directory doesn't contain any information that shouldn't be accessed by unauthorized personnel. Also, be careful which drive letters you use. Some devices that you may want to connect to a computer come hard-coded with a particular drive letter. If you use that letter for a share and then try to connect the device, you will be unable to access the device.

Procedure

This task will teach you what you need to know to map a network drive to a server share on a client computer.

Equipment Used

No special equipment will be needed.

Details

This task will take you through the steps needed to map a network drive.

> This task was written using Windows 7, but the steps should work just as well if you are using another version of Windows.

Mapping a Network Drive

ACCESSING AND MAPPING THE DRIVE FROM A CLIENT PC

1. At the client machine, click the Start button and then right-click Computer.
2. Click Map Network Drive.
3. When the Map Network Drive dialog box appears, use the Drive drop-down menu to select a drive letter.
4. In the Folder field, type the path of the share or use the Browse button to navigate to the desired directory.

> The share path you enter in step 4 is usually the server name followed by the share name and expressed as *server_name**share_name*.

5. Check the Reconnect at Logon box.

6. Click Finish.

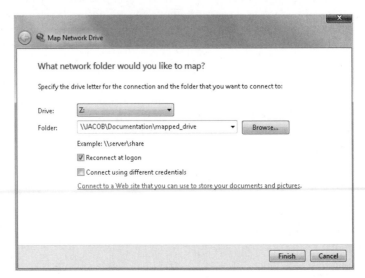

 After you click Finish, Windows will attempt to locate and open the share.

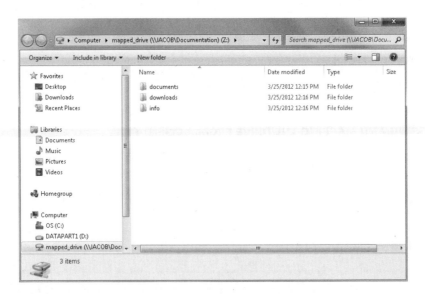

7. Close the window.

TESTING THE MAPPED DRIVE

1. Open Computer to see if the mapped drive appears under Network Location.

2. Double-click the Z drive (or whatever drive letter you assigned to the mapped drive) to open it.

3. Close Computer.

Criteria for Completion

You will have successfully completed this task when you have verified that you have mapped the correct drive letter to the server share.

Task 3.2: Creating File Shares

As you saw in Task 3.1, very often users need to access file shares on a file and print server in order to locate documents, forms, and other tools of their trade. Rather than have the users download copies of a shared folder's contents to their local drives, it is very common for users to access their tools across the network in a shared folder. (Never share the root of your hard drive; instead, share only those folders on the network that other users must access.) Of course, before the users can locate their tools in the appropriate directory, the directory has to be shared to the network. Here's how to do that.

Objective

This task covers objective 220:802:1.2.

Scenario

A folder named Research on the Research team's server needs to be shared with the Engineers group so the engineers can use it to save and access work for a new project. The file and data already exist. You have been assigned to create the network share of the folder on the Engineering server.

Scope of Task

Duration

This task should take about 5 to 10 minutes.

Setup

There is no special setup for this task.

Caveat

As was mentioned in Task 3.1, be careful of what you share and with whom. Verify with your supervisor the specific directory to be shared and whatever permissions need to be configured.

Procedure

This task will show you how to set up a simple shared folder on the network.

Equipment Used

No special equipment will be needed for this task.

Details

This task will take you through the steps necessary to locate and share a folder on a server to the network.

This task was written using Windows XP Professional. This computer is a domain member and the shared folder is on an NTFS partition. You should be able to perform this task reasonably well with Windows Vista and Windows 7, but there will be some differences depending on the exact version of the operating system and partition type (FAT vs. NTFS) as well as the file-sharing type (Simple File Sharing vs. access control lists).

Creating a File Share

1. Sitting at the server's keyboard, right-click the Start button.

2. Click Computer.

3. Navigate to the location of the folder you want to share and select it.

4. Right-click the desired folder.

5. Click Sharing and Security.

6. Click the Share This Folder radio button.

7. Verify that the name of the share is correct in the Share Name field.

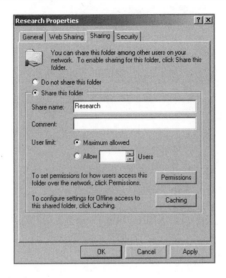

8. Click the Permissions button.

9. On the Share Permissions tab in the Permissions box, click Add.

 By default 'Everyone' has read permission. It is good security practice to remove this permission.

10. In the Select Users, Computers, or Groups dialog box, scroll down and select the Engineers group.

 Make sure you select the correct domain in the Look In drop-down menu of the Select Users, Computers, or Groups dialog box.

11. Click Add.

12. Click OK.

The Engineers group will be added to the Share Permissions box after you click OK in step 14.

13. Under Permissions, check the boxes of the permissions you want this group to have.

14. Click OK.

15. Back on the Research Properties dialog box under User Limit, click the Maximum Allowed radio button.

16. Click OK.

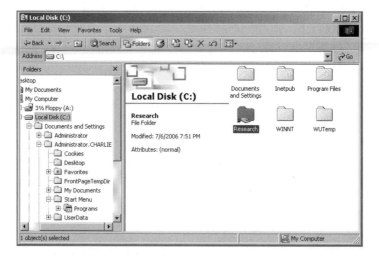

If you were using Simple File Sharing, no Security tab would be present.

Notice in the Local Disk (C:) dialog box that after you click OK in step 16, the Research folder is shared.

17. Close any other open dialog boxes.

Criteria for Completion

You will have successfully completed this task when you have shared the folder on the network. You can further test this by attempting to access the share from another computer on the same network segment.

Task 3.3: Configuring PCs to Use Dynamic Addressing

Each computer on the network requires a unique Internet Protocol address along with the subnet mask used by the network and the IP address of the the default gateway that allows the computer to have access to other networks including the Internet. The computer will also need the IP address of a Domain Name System (DNS) server for name to address resolution.

In a small workgroup environment, you can manually configure these address settings for a limited number of computers. In a corporate environment, manually setting IP addresses for hundreds of computers would be impractical and a real pain in the neck.

Fortunately, with the use of a Dynamic Host Configuration Protocol (DHCP) server on the network, addressing information can be automatically assigned to a computer when it is first powered up. In order to use dynamic addressing, the computer must be configured to request and accept this information.

While IPv6 is far from being ubiquitous, it is becoming more apparent in networking environments. However, the current A+ exam only requires that you perform networking tasks using IPv4.

Objective

This task covers objective 220:802:1.6.

Scenario

You are setting up a PC for a newly hired member of the Accounts Receivable department. One of the tasks you must perform is verifying that the computer is configured to accept dynamic IP addressing. The PC is powered up, and you are logged in and ready to proceed.

Scope of Task

Duration

This task should take no more than 5 or 10 minutes.

Setup

To verify that the configuration is correct, you must have a DHCP server available on your lab network. Most DSL and cable modems come equipped with a built-in DHCP server, so this service should be readily available to most people. You can perform this task for an Ethernet or Wi-Fi network as long as your lab computer is configured to use either of those network types.

Caveat

The DHCP server should be directly connected to the network segment it is serving so that dynamic addressing requests and offers do not have to cross a router. Also, the server must be configured to provide the correct addressing information for the network segment and have sufficient DHCP leases to provide addresses for all of the computers on the segment.

Configuring a DHCP server typically is not one of the tasks a beginning PC support tech is assigned. Instructions for configuring a DHCP server are not included in this book. See *CompTIA Network+ Lab Manual* by Toby Skandier (Sybex, 2012) for more information.

Procedure

This task will show you how to configure a Windows 7 computer to accept dynamic addressing information.

Equipment Used

You will not need any special equipment to complete this task.

Details

This task will take you through the necessary steps to set up a computer to accept dynamic IP addressing from a local DHCP server.

Configuring a Computer to Accept Dynamic Addressing

SETTING THE LOCAL AREA CONNECTION ON A PC TO ACCEPT DYNAMIC ADDRESSING

1. Sitting in front of the computer, click Start ➢ Control Panel.

2. In Control Panel using Large or Small Icon view, click Network and Sharing Center.

3. In the left sidebar of the Network and Sharing Center dialog box, click Change Adapter Settings.

4. In the Network Connections dialog box, right-click Local Area Connection and then click Properties.

5. In the Local Area Connection Properties dialog box, select Internet Protocol Version 4 (TCP/IPv4) and then click Properties.

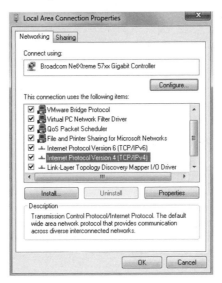

 The Internet Protocol Version 4 (TCP/IPv4) check box in the Local Area Connection Properties dialog box should be checked by default. Also notice that the Internet Protocol Version 6 (TCP/IPv6) option is available in the same list.

6. In the Internet Protocol Version 4 (TCP/IPv4) Properties dialog box, select the Obtain an IP Address Automatically radio button.

7. Select the Obtain DNS Server Address Automatically radio button.

8. Click OK.

9. Click OK to close the Local Area Connection Properties dialog box and all other open dialog boxes.

VERIFYING THAT THE PC IS RECEIVING DYNAMIC ADDRESS INFORMATION

1. Click Start, in the Search box type **cmd,** and then press Enter.

2. When the command-line emulator opens, at the prompt type **ipconfig/all**.

3. Press Enter.

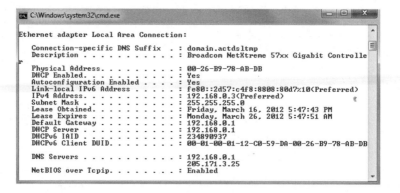

After you press Enter in step 3, the IP addressing information should display in the command-prompt window under Ethernet Adapter Local Area Connection.

If an IP address in the 169.254.x.x range (169.254.0.1–192.168.255.254) should be displayed, this indicates that a DHCP server was not available and the address was assigned by Automatic Private IP Addressing (APIPA). The computer will not be able to connect to the rest of the network with this address.

4. At the command prompt, type **exit** and press Enter to close the command-prompt window.

Criteria for Completion

You will have successfully completed this task when your computer receives automatic IP addressing information from your local DHCP server and is able to communicate with other computers on the network.

Task 3.4: Releasing and Renewing a Dynamic Address Assignment

This task is somewhat similar to the previous one in that you need to have a computer that dynamically received an IP address assignment from a DHCP server. This time, you will need to understand how to perform a release and renew of a dynamically assigned IP address on a Windows XP, Windows Vista, or Windows 7 computer. It's a relatively simple task, but one that you will commonly perform as part of troubleshooting a computer that has lost its connection to the network.

Renewing a DHCP address is also useful when APIPA has previously assigned an address to a client computer, due to a DHCP server being unavailable. Once a DHCP server is available, use the ipconfig/renew command to request a DHCP address for the client.

Objective

This task covers objectives 220-801:2.3 and 220-802:1.3.

Scenario

You receive a trouble ticket on Monday morning stating that one of the marketing staff cannot connect to the LAN or the Internet. On Friday, he left his computer logged in but locked his desktop, and at that time he had a network connection. You respond to the ticket, go to the marketing person's cubicle, and begin diagnosing the problem. He allows you access to his keyboard and is still logged in to the computer.

Scope of Task

Duration

This task will take about 5 minutes.

Setup

There is no special setup for this task, and it can be performed on a Windows XP, Windows Vista, or Windows 7 computer.

Caveat

The computer will need to receive a dynamic IP address assignment from a DHCP server. See Task 3.3 for more information on configuring a computer to receive dynamic IP addressing.

Procedure

This task will teach you how to renew a dynamic IP address assignment.

Equipment Used

No special equipment is necessary.

Details

This task will show you how to release and renew a dynamic IP address on a Windows computer.

Releasing and Renewing a Dynamic Address Assignment

1. Open a command-prompt window and verify that the computer has an assigned IP address.

The section "Verifying That the PC Is Receiving Dynamic Address Information" in Task 3.3 shows you how to open the command-prompt window and issue the ipconfig/all command, which will tell you if DHCP is enabled and if an IP address is assigned to the computer. Even if an address is apparently assigned, the computer may still not be connected to the network, and renewing the address assignment may still be required.

2. At the command prompt, type **ipconfig/release**, press Enter, and wait for the prompt to return.

3. At the prompt, type **ipconfig/renew** and press Enter.

4. After you have received the message stating that the address has been renewed, test the connection by typing the ip address of the DHCP server and then pressing Enter.

> While Google currently responds to echo requests, this may not be so indefinitely. Firewall settings at either the requestor's or receiver's end may refuse the echo request, even though there is a connection.

5. After the successful ping test, type **exit** at the prompt and press Enter to close the emulator.

Criteria for Completion

You will have successfully completed this task when you have installed, released, and renewed the IP address for the computer and it has acquired a valid IP address for your network.

Task 3.5: Installing a Network Printer

Although it is common to have a print server control the printing processes of several networked printers in a business environment, you can also install printers that have a print server built in. Instead of the printer connecting to a server or computer with a printer or USB cable, it connects directly to the network with its own network interface card (NIC). As a PC support technician, you occasionally may be asked to install and configure a new network printer on a network segment.

Objective

This task covers objective 220-801:4.2.

Scenario

The Research department has hired several new engineers over the past few months, and it needs another network printer installed in its area. You have been assigned to install the network printer and make it available on the Research network segment. You have been given all the information you need, including the printer's static IP address, subnet mask, and DNS hostname. Another tech has already added the printer's IP address information to the DNS server. All you need to do is install the printer itself.

Scope of Task

Duration

This task will take about 30 to 45 minutes.

Setup

Ideally, you will need a printer with a NIC and built-in print server. There are models available for the home and small-office user; however, it is still more popular for this class of user to have a printer connected to a PC with either a printer cable or a USB cable. You will also need a small network switch, since testing your setup will require that a PC on the network be able to print from the network printer. Both the network printer and the PC will be connected through the switch. The PC should already be connected to the switch. You will connect the network printer to the switch during the exercise.

I continue to mention printer cables, just in case you're working with older equipment, but most printers connected to PCs these days use USB.

Caveat

There is no single procedure for installing a network printer, so for this task I will present a generic set of steps. Most of the installation is done using the printer's configuration buttons and display, but navigating printer menus is as much art as it is technology. If you have a network printer, make sure the instruction manual and any installation discs are handy.

Procedure

This task will teach you how to install a network printer.

Equipment Used

No special equipment is necessary except for a patch cable to connect the printer to the network and whatever manuals and installation software came with the printer.

A patch cable is an Ethernet cable typically used to directly connect one network device to another.

Details

This task will walk you step-by-step through the process of installing a network printer so that it can be accessed by computers on the same network segment.

Installing a Network Printer

ACCESSING THE CONTROLS TO CONFIGURE A NETWORK PRINTER

1. Power up the print device.
2. Locate the Ethernet patch cable.

3. Connect one end of the cable to the printer's NIC.

4. Connect the other end to an Ethernet port on the network switch.

5. Once the power-on and self-test are finished on the printer, locate the control buttons.

6. Locate the display window.

7. Click Menu.

8. Click Configure Device Menu.

9. When the menu appears, use the down-arrow to navigate to Configure Device and select it.

10. When the Configure Device menu appears, use the down-arrow to navigate to Manual and select it.

11. When the hostname appears, use the letter and number buttons on the printer to input the printer's DNS hostname (or if it's available, you can enter the static IP address).

In this scenario, your supervisor will provide you with the appropriate DNS hostname or IP address, subnet mask, default gateway, and TCP connection time-out information.

12. Click Next.

13. When either the Secure Web or Web Options menu item appears, use the down arrow to navigate to HTTP and select it.

14. Click Next.

15. When the IP Address field appears, use the number keys to input the printer's IP address.

16. Click Next.

17. When the Subnet Mask field appears, use the number keys to input the subnet mask.

18. Click Next.

19. When the Default Gateway IP Address field appears, use the number keys to input the gateway's IP address.

20. Click Next.

21. When the Time-Out field appears, use the number keys to set the TCP connection time-out in seconds.

22. Click Next.

23. Click Save.

24. Click Online.

25. Click Exit.

CONFIRMING THE CONFIGURATION SETTINGS ON A NETWORK PRINTER

1. Click Menu.

2. Click Information Menu.

3. Click Network Cfg.

4. Click Print.

After you click Print, the network-configuration page will print with all the network information you configured on the printer, including IP address, subnet mask, and so on.

5. Verify that the information on the page is correct.

VERIFYING THE PRINTER'S NETWORK CONNECTION

1. Go to a computer on the same network segment as the new network printer.

2. Click Start.

3. In the Search box, type **cmd**.

4. Press Enter.

5. When the command-prompt window opens, at the prompt, type **ping 192.168.0.4** (or whatever IP address is assigned to the network printer).

6. Press Enter.

7. Observe the output of the ping command to confirm the network connection.

```
Command Prompt                                                        □ X

Microsoft Windows [Version 6.1.7601]
Copyright (c) 2009 Microsoft Corporation.  All rights reserved.

C:\Users\JMPyles>ping 192.168.0.4

Pinging 192.168.0.4 with 32 bytes of data:
Reply from 192.168.0.4: bytes=32 time=258ms TTL=64
Reply from 192.168.0.4: bytes=32 time=69ms TTL=64
Reply from 192.168.0.4: bytes=32 time=2ms TTL=64
Reply from 192.168.0.4: bytes=32 time=121ms TTL=64

Ping statistics for 192.168.0.4:
    Packets: Sent = 4, Received = 4, Lost = 0 (0% loss),
Approximate round trip times in milli-seconds:
    Minimum = 2ms, Maximum = 258ms, Average = 112ms

C:\Users\JMPyles>
```

The final test would be to connect a PC on the network segment to the network printer and print a test page. This will be covered in Task 3.14.

Criteria for Completion

You will have successfully completed this task when you have installed and configured the network printer and pinged the printer from a computer.

Task 3.6: Making a Straight-Through Cable

One of the less glamorous jobs you will be assigned is making network cables. Although it is true that an IT department may keep a supply of patch cables handy, sometimes cables of a specific length that aren't easily purchased are needed. You will need to become familiar with the tools necessary to make a network cable and how to pin out different types of cable.

A straight-through cable is one that connects two unlike devices, such as a PC to a switch or a switch to a router. See Task 3.7, "Making a Crossover Cable," to see how to make a cable to connect two like devices.

 Newer network devices may have autosensing Ethernet ports that can detect the cable type and adjust to be able to use the cable.

Objective

This task covers objectives 220-801:2.2 and 2.3.

Scenario

Several new servers are going to be installed in the server room, and your supervisor has assigned you to make the straight-through patch cables that will connect the servers to the patch panel.

 Typically, servers and computers are not directly connected to a switch. Instead, they are connected to a patch panel and then other patch cables connect the specific patch-panel ports to the switch ports.

Scope of Task

Duration

Making a single straight-through cable can take about 10 to 15 minutes; however, if you are not practiced in this task, making a cable successfully the first time can take much longer.

Setup

You will need a supply of Category 5 (Cat 5), Cat 5e, or Cat 6 cable and a number of RJ-45 network connectors (get more than you think you'll need).

Caveat

Some people learn to make network cables very easily, but it can be a difficult chore for others. Don't be disappointed if the first few cables don't work. It takes practice to become proficient with this task.

Procedure

This task will show you how to successfully make a network straight-through cable.

Equipment Used

You will need the following pieces of equipment to complete this task:

- A wire stripper
- A wire cutter
- A crimp tool
- A cable tester

The cable tester is optional for this task because you can also test whether the cable works by connecting one end to a PC's NIC and the other end to a switch and then attempting to ping another computer on the network. Also, some wire strippers and cutters come as a single tool.

You should be able to find everything you need, including RJ-45 connectors and Ethernet cable, at your local computer-supply store or a large hardware store.

An optional bonus tool would be a desk lamp with a built-in magnifying lens. This will help you see the individual pairs of wires as they emerge from the cable jacket.

Details

This task will take you through the process of constructing and testing a straight-through patch cable.

Constructing a Straight-Through Patch Cable

PREPARING TO CONSTRUCT THE CABLE

1. Locate your tools.
2. Arrange your tools on your workbench.
3. Locate the RJ-45 connectors.
4. Arrange two connectors on the workbench.
5. Locate a length of Cat 5, Cat 5e, or Cat 6 cable.

In a medium to large IT department, cable will be purchased in spools rather than lengths. You will need to pull out the appropriate length of cable (actually, pull out more than you need) and cut it away from the spooled cable using the wire cutters.

6. Arrange a light so you can see the cable end clearly (an optional magnifying lens comes in very handy about now).

7. Locate a pin-out diagram for a straight-through cable connection.

Four pairs of wires are bound inside the cable jacket. When you untwist the pairs, you'll see that each wire is differently colored. Those wires must be inserted into the RJ-45 connector in the correct color-coded order for the cable to work correctly.

You can use your favorite search engine to locate a pin-out diagram for a straight-through cable, such as the one displayed in the following illustration.

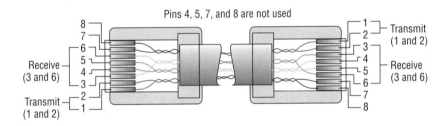

Pin number	Wire Color	Straight-Through		Pin number	Wire Color
		Wire	Becomes		
Pin 1 →	Orange/White	1 →	1	Pin 1 →	Orange/White
Pin 2 →	Orange	2 →	2	Pin 2 →	Orange
Pin 3 →	Green/White	3 →	3	Pin 3 →	Green/White
Pin 4 →	Blue	6 →	6	Pin 4 →	Blue
Pin 5 →	Blue/White			Pin 5 →	Blue/White
Pin 6 →	Green			Pin 6 →	Green
Pin 7 →	Brown/White			Pin 7 →	Brown/White
Pin 8 →	Brown			Pin 8 →	Brown

MAKING THE CABLE ENDS

1. Locate the wire stripper.

2. Hold out one end of the cable.

3. Use the wire stripper to strip off a length of the cable jacket, leaving the pairs of twisted wires inside intact.

It is very important to strip off the correct length of the cable jacket. You must expose just enough of the wires so that they'll be able to be completely inserted into the RJ-45 connector and so that a small length of the cable jacket also fits in the connector.

If you strip off too much of the cable jacket, when you crimp the RJ-45 onto the cable, the tiny wires will extend outside the connector, making them vulnerable to breakage. If you strip off too little of the cable jacket, the wires won't be long enough to make a firm connection to the pins inside the RJ-45.

4. Untwist the exposed twisted pairs.

5. Refer to your pin-out diagram to order the colors of the wires correctly.

TIP Even after you untwist the wires, they have a tendency to shift position between your fingers. You will have to press your finger and thumb together securely to keep them in the right order.

6. Trim the wires straight across about half an inch from the wire jacket.

7. Locate an RJ-45 connector.

8. Locate pin 1 in the connector.

TIP Look in the open end of the RJ-45 connector. Orient the connector so that the broad end of the opening is up and the narrow end (with the clip) is down. You will see eight copper connectors inside. They are ordered 1 through 8, left to right.

9. Refer again to the pin-out diagram and orient the correctly colored wires to their pin numbers as follows:

   - Orange/White to Pin 1
   - Orange to Pin 2
   - Green/White to Pin 3
   - Blue to Pin 4
   - White/Blue to Pin 5
   - Green to Pin 6
   - White/Brown to Pin 7
   - Brown to Pin 8

NOTE The pin-out in this task represents the ANSI/TIA/EIA 568B standard. You could also use pin-outs based on the 568A standard as long as both ends of the cable use the same standard.

10. Insert the wires into the open end of the RJ-45 connector, making sure the wires are straight across about half an inch from the wire jacket.

11. Locate the crimp tool.

12. Insert the RJ-45 connector into the crimp tool.

 NOTE Step 12 is the most difficult part of the process. You have to hold the wires in the RJ-45 connector in the correct order, making sure the connection remains firm while you hold the connector in the crimp tool and use the grips of the tool to clamp down on the connector.

13. Press the handles of the crimp tool firmly together and hold with the RJ-45 inside the tool.

14. Release the pressure on the handles and remove the connector.

15. Look closely at the RJ-45 connector and verify that the wires are in the correct order and that the pin connectors are making good contact with the wires.

 NOTE The connectors are usually clear plastic so you can see through them.

16. Locate the other end of the cable and repeat steps 1 through 15 with that end.

 NOTE The pin-out order on both ends of a straight-through cable is identical.

TESTING THE NEWLY MADE CABLE

1. Locate the new cable.

2. Connect one end to the NIC port of a PC.

3. Connect the other end to an active switch.

4. Verify that there is at least one other computer connected to the switch.

 TIP Both computers will have to be configured with IP addresses that are on the same subnet. If you are using a DHCP server on the network, see Task 3.3, "Configuring PCs to Use Dynamic Addressing." Otherwise, you'll need to configure the IP addresses of both PCs manually.

5. Open a command-prompt window on one of the computers.

6. Ping the IP address of the other computer.

NOTE   See Task 3.5, "Installing a Network Printer," and review steps 1 through 7 in the section "Verifying the Printer's Network Connection" if you aren't sure how to ping another computer.

Criteria for Completion

You will have successfully made a straight-through cable when you have gone through steps 1 through 6 in the section "Testing the Newly Made Cable" and successfully pinged one computer from the other.

NOTE   See Task 3.8, "Testing Network Cables," for more information.

If the cable you made does not work, the most likely cause is that either the order of wires in one or both connectors is wrong or some of the wires in the connector are not in contact with their corresponding pins. In either event, the way to proceed is to cut off both RJ-45 connectors and repeat the task until you have successfully built a cable. I recommend that you establish a track record of successfully building a number of cables to firmly establish that you have acquired this skill.

Task 3.7: Making a Crossover Cable

To make a crossover cable, you use the same skills you use to make a straight-through cable (see Task 3.6). However, the purpose of a crossover cable is different. Whereas you use a straight-through cable to connect dissimilar devices in a network directly together, you use a crossover cable to connect two like devices. The simplest form of networking is connecting two PCs together using a crossover cable. As long as both computers have IP addresses on the same subnet, they'll be able to communicate. You won't often have to make a crossover cable as a PC tech, but the occasion does sometimes come up. As mentioned in the previous task, newer networking devices can autosense the cable type and adjust to allow a connection.

Objective

This task covers objectives 220-801:2.2 and 2.3.

Scenario

The folks in the IT department have been trying to connect a new high-speed cable modem to a server using a straight-through cable but they aren't getting a link light. After consulting the documentation for the modem, they discover that the device acts like a server and they'll need to use a crossover cable to make the connection between both devices and begin testing. You have been assigned the task of making the crossover cable.

Scope of Task

Duration

This task should take about 10 to 15 minutes, especially if you've been practicing Task 3.6 sufficiently.

Setup

You can use the same setup you used for Task 3.6.

Caveat

The caveat for this task is the same as for Task 3.6.

Procedure

This task will show you the process of making a crossover cable.

Equipment Used

See Task 3.6. You will need exactly the same equipment to complete this task.

Details

This task will take you through the steps necessary to make and test a crossover patch cable.

Constructing a Crossover Cable

PREPARING TO MAKE THE CROSSOVER CABLE

1. Locate your tools.
2. Arrange your tools on your workbench.
3. Locate the RJ-45 connectors.
4. Arrange two RJ-45 connectors on your workbench.
5. Locate a length of Cat 5 or Cat 5e cable.
6. If you're using a spool of cable, cut away a length of cable from the spool using the wire-cutting tool.

 The pin-outs for each end of the cable are different. See the subsequent diagram for details.

7. Locate a diagram of the pin-out for a crossover cable.

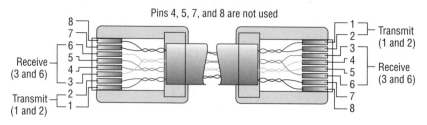

Pins 4, 5, 7, and 8 are not used

Pin number	Wire Color	Crossed-Over		Pin number	Wire Color
		Wire	Becomes		
Pin 1 →	Orange/White			Pin 1 →	Green/White
Pin 2 →	Orange	1 →	3	Pin 2 →	Green
Pin 3 →	Green/White	2 →	6	Pin 3 →	Orange/White
Pin 4 →	Blue	3 →	1	Pin 4 →	Blue
Pin 5 →	Blue/White	6 →	2	Pin 5 →	Blue/White
Pin 6 →	Green			Pin 6 →	Orange
Pin 7 →	Brown/White			Pin 7 →	Brown/White
Pin 8 →	Brown			Pin 8 →	Brown

MAKING THE CABLE ENDS

1. Locate the wire stripper.

2. Hold out one end of the cable.

3. Use the wire stripper to strip off a length of the cable jacket, leaving the pairs of twisted wires inside intact.

Remember the necessity of stripping off the correct amount of the cable jacket, as you learned in Task 3.6.

4. Untwist the exposed twisted pairs.

5. Refer to your pin-out diagram to order the colors of the wires correctly.

Since both ends are pinned out differently, choose one pin-out from the diagram and start with it. Just remember to switch to the other pin-out when constructing the other end of the cable.

6. Trim the wires straight across about half an inch from the wire jacket.

7. Locate an RJ-45 connector.

8. Locate pin 1 in the connector.

Refer to Task 3.6 to find out how to locate pin 1.

9. If you selected the left-hand pin-out scheme in the previous diagram, orient the correctly colored wires to their pin numbers as follows:

    - Orange/White to Pin 1
    - Orange to Pin 2
    - Green/White to Pin 3
    - Blue to Pin 4
    - Blue/White to Pin 5
    - Green to Pin 6
    - Brown/White to Pin 7
    - Brown to Pin 8

10. Insert the wires into the open end of the RJ-45 connector, making sure the wires are straight across about half an inch from the wire jacket.

11. Locate the crimp tool.

12. Insert the RJ-45 connector into the crimp tool.

13. Press the handles of the crimp tool firmly together and hold with the RJ-45 inside the tool.

14. Release the pressure on the handles and remove the connector.

15. Look closely at the RJ-45 connector and verify that the wires are in the correct order and that the pin connectors are making good contact with the wires.

16. Locate the other end of the cable and repeat steps 1 through 8.

17. If you pinned out the first end of the cable as described in step 9, orient the correctly colored wires to their pin numbers as follows:

    - Green/White to Pin 1
    - Green to Pin 2
    - Orange/White to Pin 3
    - Blue to Pin 4
    - Blue/White to Pin 5
    - Orange to Pin 6
    - Brown/White to Pin 7
    - Brown to Pin 8

18. Repeat steps 10 through 15.

 The pin-out in step 9 represents the ANSI/TIA/EIA 568A standard.

The pin-out in step 17 represents the ANSI/TIA/EIA 568B standard.

TESTING THE NEWLY MADE CABLE

1. Locate two PCs to use for the test.

2. Verify that they both have been manually configured to have IP addresses on the same subnet.

Since these computers are currently not networked, they will not be able to receive dynamic addressing from a DHCP server.

3. Connect one end of the crossover cable to the first computer's NIC port.

4. Connect the other end of the cable to the second computer's NIC port.

5. At one computer, open a command emulator and ping the other PC's IP address.

See Task 3.5, "Installing a Network Printer," and review steps 1 through 7 in the section "Verifying the Printer's Network Connection" if you aren't sure how to ping another computer.

Criteria for Completion

You will have successfully completed this task when you have completed steps 1 through 5 in the section "Testing the Newly Made Cable" and were able to ping the other computer.

See Task 3.8, "Testing Network Cables," for more information.

Task 3.8: Testing Network Cables

A wide variety of network-cable testers is available. Depending on how detailed a test you want the equipment to run, they can cost anywhere from $35 to $3,500. The simplest device is a single unit that both ends of the cable connect to and that verifies the point-to-point wiring of all eight wires in the cable. You can also purchase adapters to test cross-over cables. This sort of device allows you to test a cable's functioning without having to connect it to a computer or switch.

Objective

This task covers objective 220-802:4.5.

Scenario

You have made several straight-through cables to be used to connect some new servers to the patch panel in the server room. (See the scenario for Task 3.6.) You now need to test them to make sure they are functional.

Scope of Task

Duration

This task should take you only a few minutes.

Setup

No special setup is needed, except you will need at least one of the cables you constructed in Task 3.6.

Caveat

This task shows the use of a generic cable tester. The device you use may function differently. Refer to the manual for your device for details.

Procedure

This task will teach you how to use a cable tester to test the functioning of a straight-through cable.

Equipment Used

In addition to a straight-through cable, you'll need a cable tester. You can purchase such a device at any computer- or electronics-supply store.

Details

This task will walk you through the process of testing a straight-through patch cable to determine if it functions correctly.

Using a Cable Tester to Test the Straight-Through Cable

1. Locate the cable tester.
2. Power up the unit.

 Most of these devices require a 9-volt battery to operate. The battery has to be purchased separately.

3. Locate the cable you want to test.

4. Insert one end of the cable into an RJ-45 port on the tester.

5. Insert the other end of the cable into the other RJ-45 port on the tester.

6. Review the operation of the eight LED lights on the front of the tester.

If all eight lights flash continually in sequence, the cable is sound. If a light fails to light up, it indicates that the wire number of that light does not have a connection.

If one of the LED lights fails to illuminate, the most common cause is that the numbered wire for that light was not secured to the corresponding RJ-45 pin in one of the connectors.

Criteria for Completion

You will have successfully completed this task when you have used the tester to determine whether all eight pins of the cable are connected.

For this task, the cable doesn't have to be functional for you to be successful. You just need to be able to use the tester to determine the cable's status.

Task 3.9: Joining a Computer to a Domain

When a new user is assigned to a new computer, the computer will need to become a domain member in order to access all of the resources in the Windows Active Directory domain. This is pretty straightforward but it does require that you be at least an authenticated user and that you have the name of the domain for the computer to join. This is a fairly common task, so you'll quickly get used to doing this.

Objective

This task covers objective 220-802:1.6.

Scenario

A new employee has been hired in the Marketing department. A new computer has been installed for him but it needs to be joined to the Active Directory domain for the company. You have been assigned to perform this task.

Scope of Task

Duration

This task takes around 15 to 20 minutes.

Setup

You'll need Windows Server 2003 or Windows Server 2008 running on your network as a domain controller, and a client computer to successfully finish this task.

You can receive a free trial version of Windows Server 2008 Standard at http://www.microsoft.com/en-us/download/details .aspx?displaylang=en&id=5023

You can receive a free trial verson of Windows Server 2008 Enterprise at http://www.microsoft.com/en-us/download/details .aspx?displaylang=en&id=8371

This task was created using a Windows XP Professional computer and a Windows Server 2003 server, but the steps should be nearly the same if you are using Windows Vista or Windows 7 as the client computer and Windows Server 2008 as the domain controller.

Once you've installed Windows Server 2008 onto a hardware or virtual computer, you'll need to promote it to a domain controller. Click Start, and in the Search box type **dcpromo** and then press Enter. Follow the steps of the wizard to elevate the server to a domain controller. You will need to configure the server with the DNS server role during this process. For more detailed instructions, see the video tutorial at www.youtube.com/ watch?v=04PhcnV8gSs.

Caveat

Any authenticated user can add up to ten computers to a domain. To add more, you must have domain administrator rights.

Procedure

This task will show you how to join a client computer to a domain.

Equipment Used

No special equipment will be needed for this task.

Details

This task will show you the steps necessary to join a client computer to a Windows Active Directory domain.

Joining a Computer to a Domain

JOINING A WINDOWS COMPUTER TO THE ACTIVE DIRECTORY DOMAIN

1. Sitting at the computer you want to join to the domain, log on as the local administrator or have the user log on using his account.

2. Right-click My Computer.

3. Click Properties.

4. In the System Properties box, click the Computer Name tab.

5. Click Change.

6. Click the Domain radio button.

7. Type the name of the domain in the Domain field.

8. Click OK.

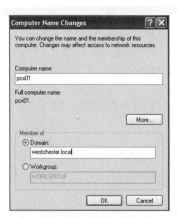

9. In the User Name field, type the name of an account with rights to join a computer to the domain.

10. In the Password field, type the correct password for that account.

11. Click OK.

12. When the Welcome to the Domain dialog box appears, click OK.

13. When you are prompted to restart your computer, click OK.

14. When the next dialog box appears, asking if you want to restart the computer now, click Yes.

The computer will reboot when you click Yes in step 14.

VERIFYING THAT THE COMPUTER JOINED THE DOMAIN

1. When the computer reboots, in the Log On to Windows box, click the Log On To drop-down menu and select the domain name.

2. Make sure your username and password are correctly inputted.

3. Click OK.

4. Once you are logged on, right-click My Computer.

5. Click Properties.

6. In the System Properties box, click the Computer Name tab.

7.   Notice that the Full Computer Name field now includes the name of the domain the computer has just joined.

Criteria for Completion

You will have successfully completed this task when you have joined the computer to the domain and have verified it as outlined in the last portion of this task.

Task 3.10: Creating a User in Active Directory

All resources in an Active Directory domain are considered objects. This includes computers, printers, groups, organizational units, and users. In order for a user to be identified in the domain (let's say another user wants to locate him using Active Directory), that user must be added to Active Directory on a domain controller (DC). This process can be done using the Remote Desktop Web Connection web interface or locally at any DC in the domain. This is a fairly routine task. Now that you have joined a computer to the domain for a new user, you add the user to Active Directory.

You can also install Remote Server Administration Tools and perform this task from a Windows 7 computer.

Objective

This task covers objective 220-802:1.6.

Scenario

Now that you have joined the new employee's computer to the domain (see Task 3.9), you must add him to Active Directory at a domain controller. You go to the server room and sit at the keyboard of a domain controller. You log on using the domain administrator's credentials and get to work.

Scope of Task

Duration

This task should take about 10 minutes.

Setup

You will need to be working with a domain controller to successfully complete this task. See Task 3.9 for instructions on how to acquire an evaluation copy of Windows Server 2008.

This task was created using a Windows XP Professional computer and a Windows Server 2003 server.

Caveat

Assuming you have rights to log on to the DC and you have all of the relevant information regarding the new user, this task should go smoothly.

Procedure

This task will teach you how to add a new user to an Active Directory domain.

Equipment Used

No special equipment is required to complete this task.

Details

You will be shown the proper steps for accessing a domain controller and adding a new user to the domain.

Accessing Active Directory Users and Computers to Add a User

1. Sitting at a domain controller, click Start ➤ Administrative Tools ➤ Active Directory Users and Computers.

2. Expand the domain name.

3. Click the Users folder.

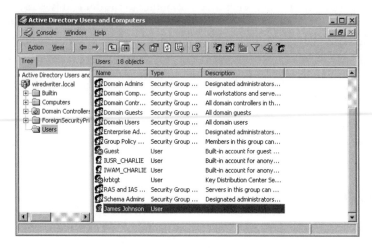

4. Right-click the Users folder.

5. Click New.

6. Click User.

7. In the New Object - User box in the First Name field, type the user's first name.

8. In the Last Name field, type the user's last name.

9. Verify that the user's first and last names are correct in the Full Name field.

10. In the User Logon Name field, type the user's logon name.

 If a user's full name is "Charles Emerson Winchester," for example, his logon name for step 10 could be "cewinchester."

 Notice that the domain name is appended in the field after the User Logon Name field in the System Properties box on the Computer Name tab after the computer has been joined to the domain.

11. Click Next.

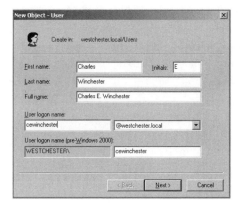

12. In the Password field, type the new user's temporary password.

13. In the Confirm Password field, type the password again.

 Make sure the password you enter in step 12 is of sufficient length and complexity to be accepted by the domain controller. If it isn't, you won't be allowed to complete the process of creating the user.

14. Check the User Must Change Password at Next Logon check box.

 Checking the check box in step 14 is a security precaution. You must inform the user of his temporary password and that the system will force him to change his password to one no one knows when he first logs in.

See Task 2.16, "Resetting Passwords," for more details about changing passwords.

15. Click Next.

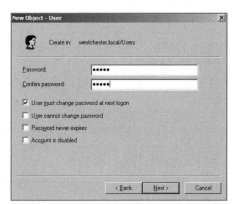

16. When the confirmation box appears, review your selections and click Finish.

17. The user is created and his name is displayed in the Active Directory Users and Computers main pane.

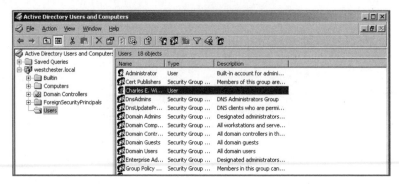

18. Close all open dialog boxes.

19. Log off the domain controller.

Criteria for Completion

You will have successfully completed this task when the domain controller confirms that the new user was added to Active Directory.

Task 3.11: Setting Up a Local User ID

Although it is important to know how to set up a user ID on an Active Directory domain, you must also know how to set up a user account on a local machine. For example, you may need to configure a computer for more than one end user to log on to locally. Alternatively, you may need to set up an account for IT staff to be able to log on to the local machine with administrator rights without using the account named Administrator.

Objective

This task covers objective 220-802:1.6.

Scenario

Two users in the Clerical department have a job-share arrangement with a single position. One user accesses the computer to do work in the morning, and another user needs a separate logon to do her work in the afternoon. You have been assigned to create the second user's local account ID.

Scope of Task

Duration

This task should take about 10 minutes.

Setup

There is no special setup for this task.

Caveat

In a production environment, it is unusual to create local accounts for users. Typically, all users log on to the domain and receive access to services via Active Directory. You are more likely to create a local administrator account under a name not obviously associated with an administrator account to allow IT staff access. In a smaller company or branch office, however, users may need access to the local machine to perform specific tasks.

Procedure

This task will show you how to create a local account on a Windows 7 computer.

Equipment Used

No special equipment will be necessary for this task.

Details

You will be taken through the necessary steps to create a new local user account on a Windows 7 computer.

Creating a Local User ID Account

SETTING UP THE NEW LOCAL USER ACCOUNT ON A COMPUTER

1. Sitting at the computer, click Start ➢ Control Panel.

 For this task, it is assumed Control Panel is in Small or Large Icon view.

2. Click the User Accounts icon.

3. In the User Accounts box, click Manage Another Account.

4. On the Manage Accounts screen, click Create a New Account.

5. On the Create New Account screen in the available field, type the name of the new account.

6. Select Standard User.

This user will not need to be the administrator of the local machine.

7. Click Create Account.

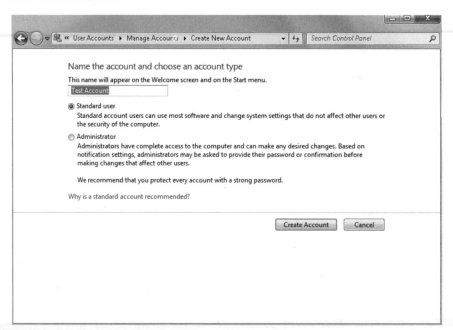

When you click Create Account, the user account is created and displayed in the User Accounts dialog box.

SETTING UP THE NEW ACCOUNT PASSWORD

1. In the User Accounts dialog box, click the new user's icon.

2. Click Create a Password.

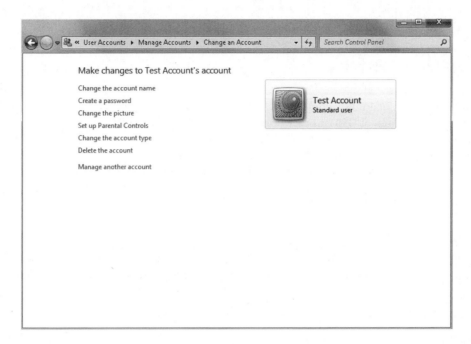

3. Type the user's password in the New Password field.

4. Type the same password again in the Confirm New Password field.

 Although it is available, I don't recommend that you use the Password Hint field because the hint would be visible to anyone who uses the computer.

5. Click Create Password.

 After you click Create Password, the password for the new account is created on the local machine and you are returned to the Change Account page for this user.

6. Close all windows on this machine.

7. Log out.

8. Have the new user log on to the local machine to verify her credentials.

Criteria for Completion

You will have successfully completed this task when you have created the new account and the user can log on using the credentials you have created.

Task 3.12: Adding a Multi-Port Card to a PC

Although most modern PCs come with ample peripheral ports for average use, sometimes a user needs additional USB or other port types added. Also, older PCs are outfitted with fewer USB ports, and a user might need to use additional USB devices. Today, users often have a USB cradle for their handheld, use a local USB printer, have an external USB hard drive for additional storage or backups, and attach additional devices as well. You will occasionally need to install additional peripheral ports on a PC to allow the user the ability to create a larger "local" network, or PAN.

A PAN, or personal area network, is usually composed of a collection of devices that are connected to a single PC via USB or wireless. A PAN gives an end user the ability to create simultaneous, short-range network connections to a computer for data storage, printing, and other tasks.

Objective

This task covers objective 220-802:1.6.

Scenario

A manager in Accounting needs additional USB ports on her PC to network several personal devices with her computer. Instead of choosing to install a USB hub, your supervisor gives you an internal five-port USB 3.0 adapter PCI card. You are to install the module into an open PCI slot, install the software, and test the unit. You gather your tools and proceed to the manager's office to do the install.

Scope of Task

Duration

This task should take about 30 minutes.

Setup

This task is somewhat similar to Task 1.4, "Installing a PCI Express Card." However, this task also requires you to install the driver software and test the unit by attaching multiple USB devices to the module's ports.

Caveat

The example in this task uses a USB 3.0 device. While USB 3.0 is generally backward compatible with USB 2.0, there are exceptions. For instance, USB 3.0 support on laptops with a USB 2.0 bus can only be added using an Express Card-to-USB 3.0 adapter. It is advisable to test all devices by attaching them to module ports and making sure they function properly before you call it "a job well done."

For more information about USB 3.0 and USB 2.0 compatibility, visit

www.datapro.net/techinfo/usb_3_explained.html#USB_Backwards_
Compatibility

Procedure

This task will teach you how to install the hardware and software for a network port module and how to test the device to make sure it works.

Equipment Used

You'll need one or two screwdrivers and your ESD equipment since you'll be installing the device inside the box. To properly test your success, you'll need a collection of USB devices (ideally) to attach to the PCI Express card once it's installed and operational.

Details

This task will take you through the steps required to install a multiport network peripheral device, install the drivers and any other required software, attach multiple USB devices to the ports of a multiport USB PCI Express card, and then test their functioning.

Installing and Testing a Multiport PCI Express Card

INSTALLING THE PCI EXPRESS CARD IN A PCI EXPRESS SLOT

1. Verify that the PC is powered down.
2. Unplug the power cord from the PC's power supply.
3. Remove the screws attaching the access panel to the PC.
4. Remove the access panel.

Take ESD precautions before working inside the machine.

5. Locate an available PCI Express slot in the PC.
6. Remove the screw or screws attaching the PCI Express slot cover to the PC's frame.

7. Remove the PCI Express slot cover.

8. Locate the PCI Express card, which should be stored in an antistatic bag.

9. Carefully remove the module from its packaging.

10. Examine the unit to determine if there is any obvious damage.

11. Assuming there is no damage, slowly guide the module into the PC case.

12. Orient the PCI Express pins on the module over the PCI Express slot.

13. Gently but firmly push the module in place.

14. Make sure the USB ports are correctly aligned at the back of the PC.

15. Use the screw you removed with the PCI Express slot cover to secure the PCI Express card in place.

16. Replace the PC's access panel.

17. Replace the screws securing the panel to the PC's frame.

18. Plug the power cord back into the PC's power supply.

INSTALLING THE SOFTWARE

1. Locate the driver disc that came with the card.

2. Locate the documentation that came with the card.

3. Read any special instructions on how to install the software.

Some devices require that you use the manufacturer's own installer rather than a Windows wizard to install the software.

4. When the PC powers up, Windows will detect the new hardware and display a message indicating that new hardware has been installed.

5. Open the DVD drive door.

6. Insert the disc.

7. Close the door.

When you close the drive door and the disc is detected, Windows 7 will display a selection box and ask you to run the program or explore the DVD.

8. Follow the instructions on the manufacturer's installer wizard.

9. When you have finished, you will be prompted to reboot the PC.

TESTING THE CARD

1. Once the PC has rebooted, locate the devices the user wants attached to the new card.

It is best if the user is present when you are attaching devices, because she will have to advise you of the exact setup she wants.

2. Plug in the first device.
3. Verify that it is recognized.

The process of verifying recognition will be different depending on the devices involved; no one method is used. A digital camera may be recognized differently than a USB printer.

4. Follow steps 2 and 3 with the next device.
5. As you add devices, verify that units previously connected to the module are still being recognized.
6. Continue to follow steps 2 through 5 with each device you attach to the network module until finished.
7. Have the end user access the devices and use them the way she normally does and make sure that she can operate them as required.

Criteria for Completion

You will have successfully completed this task when you have installed the module hardware and software and tested the performance of all attached peripheral devices, making sure they work.

Task 3.13: Setting Up VPN on a PC

VPN, or virtual private networking, is a method used by a computer to transmit data securely over a public network such as the Internet. It is often used by traveling businesspeople who need to connect to the home office from remote locations. It is also used by end users to telecommute or work while physically at home by connecting to the work network via VPN.

As a PC tech, you will be required to configure PCs and laptops to use VPN to connect to servers at the home office. From the users' point of view, it will be as if they were connected to the company's internal LAN when, in fact, over the Internet, they could be working 10 miles or one thousand miles away.

Objective

This task covers objective 220-802:1.6.

Scenario

One of the marketing executives needs to work from home several times a week. You have been assigned to go to his home and set up his PC to connect to the office LAN using VPN. You have been provided with all of the configuration information necessary to complete the task. You arrive at the executive's home and are shown to the computer you will be working on.

Scope of Task

Duration

This task should take about 15 minutes.

Setup

It would be ideal if you have a server setup that you could actually connect to using VPN, but this is not expected in most cases. You'll still be able to follow along with the steps, even if you cannot establish an actual VPN connection. In an actual scenario, a network technician or administrator would be responsible for setting up the incoming connection through their firewall.

Caveat

If you intend to set up a PC to actually use VPN, you must have the correct server setup at the home office. The server system will need to be configured with a VPN IP address pool so the connection has access to an address on the local network segment. A VPN "tunnel" will also need to be set up for the specific connection that the user will access using an encryption protocol such as Point-to-Point Tunneling Protocol (PPTP).

Configuring VPN on the server side is not a task usually assigned to a beginning PC tech, and therefore the procedure is not covered in this book.

Procedure

This task will teach you how to configure a VPN connection on a Windows 7 computer.

Equipment Used

No special equipment is required for this task.

Details

This task will take you step-by-step through the process of configuring a Windows 7 computer to securely connect to a VPN server over the Internet.

Configuring a Windows 7 Professional Computer to Use VPN

SETTING UP VPN ON A PC

1. On the Windows 7 machine, click Start, and in the Search box, type **VPN**.

2. In the menu that appears, select Set Up a Virtual Private Network (VPN) Connection.

3. On the Create a VPN Connection screen in the Internet Address field, type the domain name, IPv4 address, or IPv6 address of the server to which you want to connect (the domain name or address should be provided by the network administrator where you work).

4. In the Destination Name field, give the VPN connection a unique name or use the default name of **VPN Connection**.

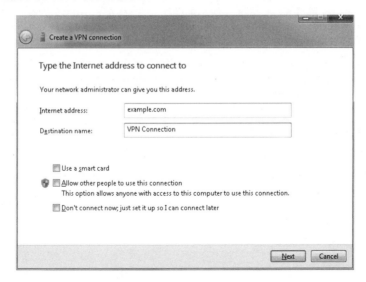

5. Click Next.

6. Under Type Your User Name and Password, type the username for this connection in the User Name field.

7. Type the password for the account in the Password field (if you want to see the password in plain text, select the Show Characters check box).

8. If you want the password to be automatically remembered when the customer opens the connection, select the Remember This Password check box.

9. You can optionally type the domain name in the Domain (Optional) field.

10. Click Connect.

11. Close all screens that were opened to create the VPN connection.

The connection will only be successful if you used the actual domain name, username, and password for a server set up to accept a VPN connection. Otherwise, the attempt to connect will time out.

TESTING THE VPN CONNECTION

1. Click Start and then click Control Panel.

2. In Large or Small Icon view, click Network and Sharing Center.

3. In the Network and Sharing Center under Change Your Network Settings, click Connect to a Network.

4. When the Currently Connected To box appears, under Dial-up and VPN, click the name of the VPN connection.

5. Click Connect.

6. If you did not configure the VPN connection to automatically remember the connection password, type the password in the Password field of the Connect VPN Connection box, and then click Connect.

TROUBLESHOOTING THE VPN CONNECTION

1. Click Start and then click Control Panel.

2. In Large or Small Icon view, click Network and Sharing Center.

3. In the Network and Sharing Center under Change Your Network Settings, click Connect to a Network.

4. When the Currently Connected To box appears, under Dial-up and VPN, right-click the name of the VPN connection, and then click Properties.

5. On the VPN Connection Properties box on the General tab, verify that the destination domain name or IP address is correct.

6. Click the Security tab and verify that the settings for the VPN connection are correct.

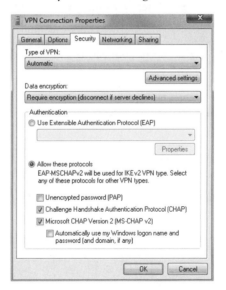

  The specific information for this connection required on the Security tab should be provided to you by the network administrator at your office.

7. When you have finished, click OK.

8. Close the Network and Sharing Center screen.

Criteria for Completion

You will have successfully completed this task when the PC has been configured to use a VPN connection and is able to successfully connect to the remote server.

 If you do not have access to a remote VPN server, the task is considered successfully completed when you have finished with the configuration and troubleshooting steps. Without a VPN server it is not possible to finish the configuration or troubleshooting steps.

Task 3.14: Connecting a PC to a Network Printer

Task 3.5 showed you how to install a network printer but stopped short of making the connection between a PC and the printer. This task will take up where Task 3.5 left off. As you recall, a network printer is equipped with its own network interface card (NIC) and a built-in print server. Once the printer is installed on the desired network segment, all that's left to do is to set up the PCs to connect to and print from the network printer.

Objective

This task covers objective 220-801:4.2.

Scenario

You have just finished successfully installing a new network printer in the Research department. Now you must verify that the PCs on the local network segment can connect to the printer and print from the device. You go to the first PC and begin the process.

Scope of Task

Duration

This task should take about 10 to 15 minutes.

Setup

Ideally, you'll have a PC on the same network segment as a network printer. This task was performed using a Windows 7 computer.

Caveat

With Windows XP, Windows Vista, and Windows 7 machines, it should be relatively simple to connect to a network printer. You will need to have the hostname or IP address of the print device. If you don't have that information or can't browse to the printer, you won't be successful at this task.

Procedure

This task will show you how to connect a PC to a network printer.

Equipment Used

No special equipment will be needed for this task.

Details

This task will guide you through the steps of connecting a Windows computer to a printer directly connected to the network.

Connecting a Computer to a Network Printer

CREATING A CONNECTION BETWEEN A PC AND THE NETWORK COMPUTER

1. Sitting at the computer, click Start ➢ Devices and Printers.

2. Click Add Printer.

3. On the Add Printer screen, click Add a Network, Wireless or Bluetooth Printer, and then click Next.

 If the automatic scan for printers on the network is unsuccessful, click Stop next to the scan bar if the scan is still running and then click The Printer That I Want Isn't Listed. Otherwise, click Next.

4. Under Select a Printer, select the printer name and IP address of the network printer and then click Next. Under Printers, scroll to the specific make and model of the desired printer and then select it.

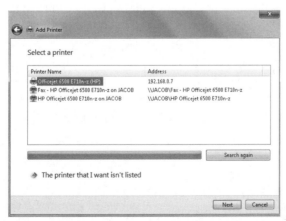

If the desired printer isn't in the list, click Windows Update on the Printers and Devices dialog box and then wait for the list to be refreshed.

 If you have the drivers disc for the specific make and model of the network printer, click Have Disk.

5. Under Type a Printer Name, type the desired name of the printer in the Printer Name box or accept the default name and then click Next.

6. On the Printer Sharing screen, click Do Not Share This Printer and then click Next.

7. On the success screen, verify that the Set as the Default Printer check box is selected.

8. After the test page successfully prints, click Finish.

MANUALLY LOCATING A NETWORK PRINTER

1. If, on the Searching for Available Printers screen, the automatic scan does not locate the desired network printer, click The Printer That I Want Isn't Listed.

2. On the Find a Printer by Name or TCP/IP Address screen, click the Add a Printer Using TCP/IP Address or Hostname radio button, and then click Next.

3. On the Type a Printer Hostname or IP Address screen, in the Hostname or IP Address field, type the IP address of the desired network printer (you should have this information because you set up the network printer during an earlier task in this chapter).

 The Port Name field will be automatically populated when you add the IP address. Allow the default check box selection of Query the Printer and Automatically Select the Driver to Use.

4. The remainder of the steps will follow steps 4 through 8 of the previous section, "Creating a Connection Between a PC and the Network Computer." Click Finish when you have finished.

Criteria for Completion

You will have successfully completed this task when you can print a test page from your computer to the network printer.

Task 3.15: Managing Windows Vista Outbound Firewall Settings

One of the issues with the Windows XP firewall was that it could only monitor activity going into your computer. If your computer was already potentially compromised, and an unauthorized application was trying to connect to the Internet, you would have no way of knowing this by using XP's onboard firewall. Third-party firewall applications would be your only way to discover this from within XP. Windows Vista corrected this but presented another problem. By default, all outbound settings are allowed, and setting outbound filtering to block specific applications, port numbers, or IP-address ranges requires that they be set manually. This task shows you a simple example of this process.

Objective

This task covers objective 220-802:1:4.

Scenario

One of your company's branch offices uses six Windows Vista computers. In addition to the firewall appliance used in the network closet at that office, the office's manager wants each computer's on-board firewall to block outbound traffic for all applications, allowing them to make connections using only specific port numbers. You will perform this task by creating a single new rule in the outbound firewall filter for each Vista computer.

It is possible to create numerous outbound filter rules, but the process is exceptionally detailed and beyond the scope of this book and the A+ certification requirements. This task shows you the level of complexity by describing the configuration of one simple rule.

You have been assigned to configure the outbound firewall filters of the Vista computers and have arrived at the branch office with the necessary instructions, including the specific list of port numbers to be used by the applications on the Vista computers to make outbound connections.

Although the scenario requires that you perform this task on six Vista computers, the requirements of this task are satisfied if you perform the steps on just one such computer.

Scope of Task

Duration

This task should take about 10 to 15 minutes per computer.

Setup

All you'll need is a computer running Windows Vista.

Caveat

There are extreme limitations to configuring the outbound firewall filters for Vista's on-board firewall. The configuration doesn't allow you to create an all-purpose rule that will block all potential malware connections. You can create a series of outbound filter rules, but you need to set up your filters for each specific type of malware, including name, port number, IP-address range, and so on. The process of manually configuring these filters for every possible known threat would take an enormous amount of time.

A good free third-party firewall application that will allow you to set up specific outbound firewall filtering is provided by ZoneAlarm. Find out more at www.zonealarm.com/security/en/trialpay-za-signup.htm.

Procedure

This task will show you how to access the Advanced Security dialog box for the Windows Vista firewall.

Equipment Used

No special equipment will be needed for this task.

Details

This task will guide you through the steps of accessing the outbound filters for Windows Vista's on-board firewall and configuring a new rule.

Configuring the Outbound Filter for Windows Vista Firewall

VERIFYING THAT WINDOWS FIREWALL IS TURNED ON

1. At the computer, click the Windows Vista button.
2. Click Control Panel.
3. Click Security.
4. Click Turn Windows Firewall On or Off. (When the UAC box appears, click Yes.)

5. In the Windows Firewall Settings dialog box, on the General tab click the On (Recommended) radio button.

6. Click OK.

ENABLING OUTBOUND FIREWALL FILTERING

1. Click the Windows Vista button.

2. Click Control Panel.

3. Click System and Maintenance.

4. Click Administrative Tools.

5. Double-click Windows Firewall with Advanced Security. (When the UAC box appears, click Yes.)

6. In the left-hand menu, click Windows Firewall and Advanced Security.

7. In the main pane, select Windows Firewall Properties.

8. Click the Private Profile tab.

9. Under Firewall State, select Block from the Outbound Connections menu.

10. Click OK.

ALLOWING APPLICATIONS TO MAKE OUTBOUND CONNECTIONS USING SPECIFIC PORTS

1. In the Windows Firewall with Advanced Security dialog box, right-click Outbound Rules in the left-hand pane and then select New Rule in the right-hand pane.

2. In the Rule Type pane, select Custom and then click Next.

3. In the Program pane, click All Programs and then click Next.

4. In the Protocol and Ports pane, select either TCP or UDP from the Protocol Type menu.

5. Select Specific Ports from the Local Port menu.

6. In the available field, enter the port numbers you were provided with, separated by commas.

7. When finished, click Next.

8. In the Scope pane, accept the default selection, Any IP Address, for both Local IPs and Remote IPs, and then click Next.

9. In the Action pane, accept the default selection of Allow the Connection, and then click Next.

10. In the Profile pane select any options that are available for the Private selections and then click Next.

11. In the Name pane, enter a name for your new rule in the Name field and enter an optional description of the new rule in the Description field.

12. Click Finish.

13. When the new rule appears in the main pane of the Windows Firewall with Advanced Security dialog box, close all of the dialog boxes you opened.

14. Repeat the process for the other five Vista computers in the office.

Criteria for Completion

You will have successfully completed this task when you have created a new outbound firewall filter rule and it has appeared in the main pane of the Windows Firewall with Advanced Security dialog box.

As you can see by performing these steps, there are many more options available in the configuration of Windows Vista's outbound firewall rule settings, but your duties as a PC tech aren't likely to require that you know how to configure this utility in great detail.

Task 3.16: Monitoring Network Activity with Windows Vista Firewall

One of the advantages of using Windows Firewall in Vista is that the firewall lets you monitor activity on the network. This allows you to detect potential threats and respond to them before an incident occurs that compromises your PCs (or at least soon afterward). This task involves enabling and then periodically reviewing the Windows Firewall log file. It is a manual rather than an automated process.

Objective

This task covers objective 220-802:2.1.

Scenario

One of your company's branch offices uses six Windows Vista computers. You recently completed an assignment, at the request of that office's manager, to configure Windows Firewall on each PC to block all outbound traffic on the computers except for a few specific applications. You receive a second request to enable the log file for Windows Firewall on each computer and demonstrate how to access and view the log files to the manager. In addition to the security applications that are functioning in that office's network closet, the manager wants to make sure that each computer is secure. Your supervisor verifies that this is a proper request and provides you with the information necessary to complete this task.

You make an appointment with the branch-office manager and meet him at the office. Seated at a Windows Vista computer and logged in as a local administrator on the machine, you begin the demonstration.

Scope of Task

Duration

This task should take about 10 to 15 minutes per computer.

> Although the scenario requires that you perform this task on six machines, for the purpose of this task you need only complete the steps on one Vista PC.

Setup

All you'll need is a computer running Windows Vista.

> The User Account Control (UAC) feature is turned off on the Windows Vista machine used to perform this task.

Caveat

Although enabling and viewing the log files for Windows Firewall isn't a complicated task, it may be difficult to successfully communicate how to properly view the log file, unless the individual has a basic familiarity with the contents of these files and some understanding of network security. While it may be more appropriate for IT staff to perform monitoring functions, you will sometimes see a request from nontechnical managers to be allowed such access as well.

You must be logged into the Windows Vista computer as a local administrator to have the authority to manage the firewall settings. Also, some settings may be unavailable if they are managed by Group Policy.

Procedure

This task will show you how to enable logging for Windows Firewall and how to view the log files.

Equipment Used

No special equipment will be needed for this task.

Details

This task will guide you through the steps of enabling and viewing the log files for Windows Vista Firewall.

Enabling Logging on Windows Vista Firewall

1. Click the Windows Vista button.
2. In the Search box, type **Administrative Tools** and then press Enter.
3. When the Administrative Tools dialog box opens, double-click Windows Firewall with Advanced Security.
4. Right-click Windows Firewall with Advanced Security in the left console tree.
5. Select Properties.
6. Select the desired tab, such as Domain Profile, Private Profile, or Public Profile.
7. Under Logging, click Customize.
8. Either accept the default path for the log or click Browse and navigate to the desired location.
9. Either accept the default maximum file size for the log of 4096KB or use the up- or down–arrow button to change this value.
10. Perform one of the following:
    - Create a log entry when Windows Firewall drops an incoming network packet by changing Log Dropped Packets to Yes.
    - Create a log entry when Windows Firewall allows an inbound connection by changing Log Successful Connections to Yes.
11. Click OK.
12. Click OK again.

Viewing the Windows Firewall Log File

1. Verify that you are on Windows Firewall with Advanced Security.
2. In the menu at the top of the screen, click Action and then click Properties.
3. On the Properties box, select a profile tab such as Public Profile.
4. Under Logging, click the Customize button.
5. When the Customize Logging Settings dialog box appears, in the Name field, copy the path to the location of the log files to the location of the log files, paste it in the Search box, and then press Enter.
6. Review the data and then close the log file and all open boxes and screens.

Criteria for Completion

You will have successfully completed this task when you have enabled logging in Windows Firewall and have successfully demonstrated how to view the log file.

Viewing the log file right after you enable logging will not show much in the way of information, since the firewall has not been able to collect much data. Waiting a few minutes or an hour will produce more results, depending on the level of network activity.

Task 3.17: Configuring MAC Filtering on a Wireless Router

A MAC address, or Media Access Control address, is the unique identifier for the network interface card, whether wired or wireless, in a computer. These unique NIC addresses can be used to help in wireless security.

A wireless router can be configured to recognize specific MAC addresses and allow only computers with certain MAC addresses to connect to the Wi-Fi network. All other MAC addresses will be rejected. If you know the MAC address of a computer you want to connect to the wireless network, you can configure your wireless router to recognize and allow a connection from the computer with that address.

Objective

This task covers objectives 220-801:2.6 and 220-802:2.5.

Scenario

You just bought a new Windows 7 laptop with a wireless network card and, as part of setting up the connection between your laptop and your home wireless router, you want to configure the MAC filter on the router to accept a connection from the MAC address of the wireless network card in the laptop. The first task is to find out what the MAC address of the laptop is, and the second task is to configure the wireless router's MAC filter.

MAC filtering is only one method of Wi-Fi security and it's not particularly foolproof. An unscrupulous person trying to connect to your wireless network may able to spoof the MAC address of a computer that has been configured to be accepted by your wireless router. For the safety of your Wi-Fi network, make sure you set up multiple methods of security and don't depend on MAC address filtering alone.

Scope of Task

Duration

This task should take about 10 to 15 minutes maximum.

Setup

You will need a wireless router, wireless access point, or broadband router with wireless capabilities. Connect to the device using a Windows computer and an Ethernet cable to set up MAC filtering. This exercise was written using a Windows 7 desktop machine, but you should be able to use any computer with a web browser to perform this exercise.

Caveat

An older Actiontec DSL modem with wireless capabilities was used to write this task, so the steps for configuring the MAC address filter will probably be somewhat different than on your wireless router or access point device.

Procedure

This task will show you how to find a computer's MAC address and then use that MAC address to configure a wireless router's MAC address filter.

 MAC filtering works by configuring the wireless router to deny connections from all MAC addresses except those that are added to an exceptions list.

Equipment Used

No special equipment will be needed for this task beyond what is described in the setup.

Details

This task will guide you through the steps of first locating a computer's MAC address using the command prompt and then connecting to a wireless router and setting up the MAC filter.

Finding a Network Card's MAC Address

1. On the Windows 7 laptop, click the Start button, and in the Search box, type **cmd**.
2. In the menu that appears, double-click cmd.exe or just press Enter to open the utility.
3. At the command prompt, type **ipconfig /all** and then press Enter.
4. If you have more than one network card on your computer, locate the wireless network card name and then locate the entry for Physical Address (it is written in hexadecimal and will look something like 00-26-78-B9-DB-AB).

5. Write down the MAC address on a piece of paper and keep it handy, since you'll need it to configure the MAC filter on your wireless router.

6. Type **exit** at the prompt and then press Enter to close the command prompt.

Configuring MAC Address Filtering

1. On the desktop computer with a direct wired connection to the wireless router, open a web browser.

2. In the web browser's address window type the IP address for the wireless router's control console (most likely it is http://192.168.0.1, and if not, consult the documentation for your wireless router) and then press Enter.

3. On the Main Menu page for the device, click Setup/Configuration.

4. On the Setup/Configuration page, click Advanced Setup.

5. On the Advanced Setup page, click Begin Advanced Setup.

6. On the Configuring the Advanced Settings page, click Wireless MAC Authentication in the sidebar menu.

7. On the Wireless MAC Authentication page, select the Enable Access List check box.

8. Select the Deny All Clients radio button.

9. In the Client MAC Address field, type the MAC address you wrote down in the previous exercise, and then click the Add button.

10. Verify that the MAC address was added to the Exception List field.

11. In the sidebar menu, click Save and Restart.

Criteria for Completion

You will have successfully completed this task when you have added the MAC address of the wireless network card to the exceptions list of the wireless router's MAC address exceptions list, saved your settings, and restarted the wireless router.

Task 3.18: Turning Off SSID Broadcasts on a Wireless Router

An SSID, or Service Set Identifier, is the 32-character unique name of a wireless network configured on a wireless router or access point. While the SSID helps you locate your own wireless network, it can also let unscrupulous people locate your Wi-Fi network as well. As a security precaution, you can turn off SSID broadcasts on your wireless device so that others can't find your network and possibly hack into it.

Objective

This task covers objectives 220-801:2.6 and 220-802:2.5.

Scenario

You want to improve security on your home wireless network, and as part of that effort, you plan to turn off SSID broadcasts on your wireless router.

 The wireless router or access point will still possess an SSID that identifies the network so you can connect a wireless laptop or other Wi-Fi–capable computer to the router or access point manually. To find out more about this process, go to www.windowsreference.com/windows-vista/how-to-manually-connect-to-wireless-network-not-broadcasting-ssid/ or enter the search string "how to connect to a wireless network not broadcasting ssid" into your preferred search engine.

Scope of Task

Duration

This task should take about 10 minutes or less.

Setup

You will need a wireless router, wireless access point, or broadband router with wireless capabilities. A Windows 7 desktop machine with an Ethernet connection to the modem was used for the actual configuration task.

Caveat

An older Actiontec DSL modem with wireless capabilities was used to write this task, so the steps for turning off SSID broadcasts on your wireless router device will likely be different than those presented here.

Procedure

This task will show you how to turn off SSID broadcasting on a wireless router or access point.

Equipment Used

No special equipment will be needed for this task beyond what is described in the setup.

Details

This task will guide you through the steps of connecting to a wireless router and turning off SSID broadcasts.

Turning Off SSID Broadcasts on a Wireless Device

1. On a computer connected to the wireless router, open a web browser.

2. In the web browser's address window type the IP address for the wireless router's control console (most likely it is http://192.168.0.1, and if not, consult the documentation for your wireless router) and then press Enter.

3. On the Main Menu page for the device, click Setup/Configuration.

4. On the Setup/Configuration page, click Advanced Setup.

5. On the Advanced Setup page, click Begin Advanced Setup.

6. On the Configuring the Advanced Settings page, click Wireless Settings.

7. On the Wireless Settings page, next to ESSID, verify the name of the SSID, which you'll need to use to manually connect wireless devices to the wireless router (you won't be performing an actual wireless connection in this exercise).

8. In the sidebar menu, click Wireless Advanced Settings.

9. On the Wireless Advanced Settings page, next to SSID Broadcast, select the Disable radio button.

10. Click Save and Restart.

Criteria for Completion

You will have successfully completed this task when you have disabled SSID broadcasting on your wireless router or access point, saved your changes, and restarted the device.

Task 3.19: Changing the Default Username and Password on a Wireless Router

Most wireless routers and access points come from the factory with a default username and password, and most users don't bother to change that name and password. Often, this default information is available on the Internet, and anyone who knows the default username and password to such wireless devices can easily enter into the control console and hack wireless networks, including yours. It is always best practice, as part of wireless security, to change the default authentication credentials as soon as you purchase a wireless router.

This is also true for any broadband modem device, so it is good practice to change the default authentication credentials on your modem.

Objective

This task covers objective 220-802:2.5.

Scenario

You want to improve security on your home wireless network, and as part of that effort, you plan to change the default username and password for the control console of your wireless router.

Scope of Task

Duration

This task should take a few minutes.

Setup

You will need a wireless router, wireless access point, or broadband modem. Technically, it doesn't even have to be a wireless device since the process of changing the authentication credentials will be the same. A Windows 7 desktop machine with an Ethernet connection to the modem was used for the actual configuration task.

Caveat

An older Actiontec DSL modem with wireless capabilities was used to write this task, so the steps for changing the authentication credentials on your device may be somewhat different.

Procedure

This task will show you how to change the default username and password on a wireless router or access point.

Equipment Used

No special equipment will be needed for this task beyond what is described in the setup.

Details

This task will guide you through the steps of connecting to a wireless router and changing the default username and password.

Changing the Default Username and Password on a Wireless Router

1. On a computer connected to the wireless router, open a web browser.

2. In the web browser's address window type the IP address for the wireless router's control console (most likely it is `http://192.168.0.1`, and if not, consult the documentation for your wireless router) and then press Enter.

3. On the Main Menu page for the device, click Setup/Configuration.

4. On the Setup/Configuration page, in the sidebar menu, click Admin Username/Password.

5. On the Change Admin Username/Password page, in the New Username field, enter the new username for the device.

6. In the New Password field, enter the new password.

7. In the Re-enter New Password field, enter the new password again.

8. Click Save and Restart.

9. After the device has completely rebooted, in your web browser, type **`http://192.168.0.1`** and press Enter.

10. If you are prompted for a username and password, enter the new username and password you configured in this exercise and verify that you can log in to the device.

Criteria for Completion

You will have successfully completed this task when you have changed the default username and password on the wireless router and verified that it has been changed.

Task 3.20: Setting Up a Mobile Phone to Use Email

Today's mobile devices are capable of a dizzying number of different functions, but one task they all support is the ability to send and receive emails. Although email is an older technology, it is still required for most personal and business tasks, and the person "on the go" most likely needs to be able to read and send emails from her mobile.

Objective

This task covers objective 220-802:3.2.

Scenario

You have a client who has a very basic cell phone and wants to be able to send and receive emails. She has already contacted her mobile network provider and received the mail server settings required. You have been tasked to perform the actual setup operation on the phone.

Scope of Task

Duration

This task should take 10 to 15 minutes depending on the make and model of the phone being used.

Setup

Since there are so many types of mobile devices available, recommending a single specific setup is all but impossible. You will need to have some sort of mobile phone, but it doesn't have to be a smartphone. You may or may not have email already set up on the device, so when you go through the steps in this task, you may not actually change anything on your phone but simply verify the current settings on your device.

Caveat

If you don't have email services set up through your mobile network provider, depending on the device type you use, you may not be able to follow along with this task. The web interface on your phone may block the setup routine unless you have requested email services from your provider.

Also, these steps are extremely generic, and it is a foregone conclusion that the steps used to set up email on your mobile device will be different than those presented here. Contact your mobile service provider for the actual steps required for setting up an email account on your phone if you desire this service.

Procedure

This task will show you how to set up an email account on a generic mobile device.

Equipment Used

You will need to have some sort of mobile phone to perform this task. Also, read the "Setup" and "Caveat" sections of this task for additional information.

Details

This task will guide you through the steps of setting up an email account on a simple mobile device.

Configuring an Email Account on a Mobile Device

1. On your mobile phone, open the menu and locate the Email or Messaging menu.

2. If necessary, manually configure the username and password for the email account.

3. If required, enter your name in the Full Name field.

4. If required, enter your email address in the Email Address field.

5. In the Incoming Mail Server fields, use the information you acquired from your service provider to set up the port number for the POP or IMAP server. The settings will be one of the following:

   - IMAP without SSL: 143
   - IMAP with SSL: 993
   - POP without SSL: 110
   - POP with SSL: 995

6. In the Outgoing Mail Server fields, use the information you acquired from your service provider to set up the port number for the SMTP server.

   - Without SSL, 25
   - With SSL: 465

7. If required, select Use Authentication.

8. Select Save or Done when finished.

Criteria for Completion

You will have successfully completed this task when you have set up an email account on your mobile phone and can send and receive emails.

Task 3.21: Setting Up Windows Live Mobile

In Tasks 2.26 and 2.27, you learned how to install Windows Live Mail and configure mail accounts on a PC. This task teaches you how to set up Windows Live on a mobile device.

As you learned in those previous exercises, Windows Live is a free, web-based service offered by Microsoft that lets you access messaging, calendaring, and contacts. Now you can take those services with you on your mobile device.

Objective

This task covers objective 220-802:3.2.

Scenario

You have created a Windows Live account by creating a Windows Live ID and an email account with Windows Live/Hotmail. Now you want to set up Windows Live on your mobile device.

Scope of Task

Duration

This task should take 15 to 20 minutes.

Setup

You will need a mobile device with a web browser and Internet access and a Windows Live account (see Tasks 2.26 and 2.27 for details about setting up Windows Live). If these requirements are not met, you will not be able to follow along with the steps of this exercise.

Caveat

Depending on the type of phone you have, the steps you will be required to follow may be different than those you see here in this exercise.

Procedure

This task will show you how to set up a Hotmail account on a mobile device using Windows Live.

Equipment Used

You will need to have some sort of mobile phone to perform this task. A Windows Phone 7 was used in the writing of this exercise.

 On a Windows Phone 7, when you first set up the phone, you are prompted to sign in using your Windows Live ID, so Hotmail would be set up after the initial setup process. This task assumes that setting up Windows Live/Hotmail was not performed during the initial setup of the phone.

Details

This task will guide you through the steps of setting up Hotmail account on a mobile device.

Configuring a Hotmail Account on a Mobile Device

1. On the Windows Phone 7, on Start, swipe left to the App list.
2. On the list, tap Settings and then tap Email and Accounts.
3. When the Before You Sign In screen appears, tap Next.
4. Tap the Windows Live ID field and then type in your Windows Live ID.
5. Tap the Password field and then type the password for your Windows Live account.
6. Tap Sign In.

Criteria for Completion

You will have successfully completed this task when you can sign in to Hotmail from your mobile device.

Phase

4

Troubleshooting and Restoring Computer Systems

Nothing will turn your hair gray faster than troubleshooting. Most textbooks serve up a canned set of problems that a five-year-old could solve in her sleep. Real-world problems are quite different, and some of them are unique, with no known cause. Nevertheless, when a cry such as "I can't print!" or "Where are my emails?" rings out, you will be expected to investigate and solve the problem.

Each of the tasks that follow is based on trouble tickets from an actual IT department. They are real problems that you could face at any time. This section not only presents the problems and their solutions; it also documents how the solutions were discovered. Computer-system problems come and go, but your problem-solving skills will be a constant in every situation you encounter. Pay close attention to what follows. These tasks could help save you a lot of time and frustration.

Task 4.1: Scanning for and Removing Viruses

Despite the best efforts of network-security engineers, occasionally a virus will invade the system and infect at least some of the computers on your network. Although medium- and enterprise-level antivirus and scanning products have the ability to limit network communications to and from a machine suspected of being compromised, once even one computer has been infected, that PC has to be scanned and the invader isolated.

One major difference between home-based and business-based antivirus systems is that an antivirus gateway scans all traffic coming into and going out of the corporate network, attempting to detect malicious software. Each individual business desktop also has the capacity to scan the local system for viruses. Also, although an individual home PC connects to the antivirus vendor's server to download virus definitions, in a business-based system you will have a server set up to download the definitions and then push them out to all of the Desktops.

Objective

This task covers objective 220-802:2.1 and 4.7.

Scenario

The main office network has been attacked by a virus. Although the threat was contained to just a few departments, numerous PCs were compromised. You have been assigned to the Design department to perform local virus scans on the Desktops and have the detected virus quarantined.

> Advanced antivirus solutions will send the virus to a quarantine folder on the local machine and then send a copy of the virus to a secure folder on the quarantine server.

Scope of Task

Duration

If you are running a scan on the entire hard drive, it could take quite some time. Once the scan is complete and the virus is detected, having it quarantined takes very little time.

Setup

You can easily follow these steps by using your personal computer's antivirus tool; however, you will not have the opportunity to detect and isolate a threat unless your computer has already been compromised.

Caveat

Regardless of the computing environment you are using, it is vital to keep your virus definitions completely current and to have your machines routinely scanned for possible threats.

> The computer you will use for this task must have an antivirus program installed, and the program must be configured to download the latest virus definitions and scan the computer on a daily basis.

> If you are not currently running an antivirus program on your computer (and shame on you if you aren't), you can access a free copy of the AVG antivirus solution at this URL: www.avg.com/us-en/free-antivirus-download.

Procedure

This task will show you how to run a virus scan and how to quarantine any detected threats.

Equipment Used

No special equipment is required for this task.

Details

You will be taken through the steps of scanning a networked PC for threats and isolating any viruses that are detected.

Scanning for and Isolating a Virus

PERFORMING THE SCAN

1. Log on to the computer as an administrator.
2. Double-click the antivirus product icon on the Desktop to open it.
3. Click the Scan for Viruses button.
4. Select the drive or partition you want to scan.
5. Click Scan.

> Even if the virus is detected early in the scanning process, allow the scan to run to completion in the event that there is more than one intruder on board.

DETECTING AND QUARANTINING A VIRUS

1. When the scan is complete, review the list of detected threats provided by the antivirus program.
2. Select all of the viruses detected. There may be a Select All button, or you can hold down the Ctrl key and use your mouse to click on each threat until they are all highlighted.
3. When offered the option, click Quarantine All.

> It's best to quarantine a virus rather than immediately deleting it. The virus may be "living" in a location that contains vital program files for the PC, and deleting the virus can also delete these files. The worst-case scenario is that you will be unable to reboot the computer and load the operating system if you delete the virus and associated files.

4. When offered the option to send a copy of the virus to the quarantine server, click Yes. You will receive a message stating that the virus was successfully quarantined.
5. Verify that the antivirus program is configured to contact the antivirus server and download any available definitions daily.
6. Verify that the antivirus program is configured to scan the computer daily.

Criteria for Completion

You will have successfully completed this task when you have completely scanned your computer's hard drive and, if any viruses were detected, you were able to quarantine them.

Task 4.2: Using Restore Point in Windows 7

In order to meet personal and business needs as well as keep your computer's operating system and application software current, it's necessary to make changes such as installing updates and brand-new software. However, sometimes things go wrong, causing unexpected and undesirable results. Like previous versions of Windows, Windows 7 has the ability to create restore points before critical changes and to let you recover your computer to a restore point should some change cause your computer to malfunction.

Although restore points are created automatically when software is installed or updated, you will have the opportunity to learn how to create a restore point manually and then restore your computer to a restore point later on.

Objective

This task covers objective 220-802:4.7.

Scenario

You are about to install a new version of a proprietary business suite onto a small-business customer's Windows 7 computer. As a precaution, you manually create a restore point before this operation. Later, you will notice that the computer is malfunctioning, making it necessary to recover the computer back to the restore point you created.

Scope of Task

Duration

Creating a restore point and then recovering to that restore point shouldn't take more than 15 minutes.

Setup

For the purpose of this task, you will manually create a restore point, download and install a small program, create a shortcut to that program on the Desktop, create a Notepad doc on the Desktop, and then immediately recover your computer to the restore point before the program and document were created. In this way, you'll not only get practice in using a restore point, but you'll also see the practical results. This task was written using Windows 7 Enterprise, but you can use any version of Windows 7.

Caveat

Creating and using restore points are fairly easy and safe, so there shouldn't be a problem putting your computer through this task. The program I used to illustrate how the restore point works is Paint.NET, found at www.getpaint.net/download.html, but you can choose to use any small software program you desire.

Procedure

This task will show you how to create a restore point in Windows 7 and then recover the computer to that restore point.

Equipment Used

No special equipment is required for this task besides a computer running Windows 7.

Details

You will be taken through the steps of creating a restore point and then recovering your PC to that restore point.

Using the Restore Point Feature in Windows 7

CREATING A RESTORE POINT

1. Click the Windows Start button.
2. On the menu that appears, right-click Computer and then click Properties.
3. On the System screen, in the left sidebar, click System Protection.
4. On the System Protection tab of the System Properties dialog box, near the bottom, click Create.
5. In the Create a Restore Point dialog box, type a brief description of the restore point in the available field, and then click Create.
6. When the success message appears after the restore point is created, click Close.
7. Close all other open dialog boxes and screens.

CREATING A NOTEPAD DOCUMENT AND THEN DOWNLOADING AND INSTALLING PAINT.NET

1. Right-click the Desktop of your Windows 7 computer, and in the menu that appears, click New and then click Text Document.

2. Give the document a name such as **test**.

3. Double-click `test.txt` to open it.

4. Type some text in the document, click File, click Save, and then close `test.txt`.

5. Open a web browser and go to `www.getpaint.net/download.html`.

6. Click the Download link to start downloading Paint.NET.

7. Follow the onscreen instructions to download `Paint.NET.3.5.10.Install.zip` in the desired directory.

8. Close the web browser and then navigate to the location of `Paint.NET.3.5.10 .Install.zip`.

9. Click `Paint.NET.3.5.10.Install.zip` to open the zip file in a separate window.

10. Double-click `Paint.NET.3.5.10.Install.exe` to launch it, and click Yes if prompted by UAC to run the program.

11. When the Paint.NET installer launches, select Quick and then follow the on-screen instructions to install Paint.NET.

 A system restore point will automatically be created as part of the installation process, so you can use this restore point or the one you created manually earlier in this task.

12. When the installation is done, click Finish.

13. If the program launches, close the program.

14. Go to the Desktop and verify that Paint.NET created a shortcut to the program on the Desktop.

15. Close any dialog boxes or other programs that may be open.

RECOVERING TO A RESTORE POINT

1. Click the Windows Start button.

2. Click All Programs and then click Accessories.

3. Click System Tools and then click System Restore.

 You can also type **rstrui** or **system restore** in the Search box and press Enter to launch System Restore.

4. When the System Restore screen appears, click "Recommended restore."

5. When the Confirm Your Restore Point screen appears, click Finish.

6. When the confirmation dialog box appears, click Yes (it may take some time for System Restore to initialize and restore previous files and settings).

7. Once your computer reboots, log back into the system.

8. If the restore was successful, a System Restore success message will appear. Click Close.

Criteria for Completion

You will have successfully completed this task when your Windows 7 computer has completed the system restore process to the restore point you created at the beginning of this task. On the Desktop, you will notice that the Paint.NET shortcut is gone, indicating that it was removed when you restored the computer to an earlier point, but the test.txt document is still present, indicating that the restore point process did not affect the Notepad document.

Task 4.3: Troubleshooting in Windows 7 Using the Action Center

The Windows 7 Action Center is the central location where you can view and act upon important notices regarding maintenance and security on your computer. The easiest way to see if the Action Center has any current alerts is to look at the notification tray at the bottom right of your screen. If you see what looks to be a small flag, hover your cursor over it to see how many messages the Action Center contains.

These messages can indicate a problem with your Windows 7 system or simply be notifying you of routine maintenance requirements such as setting a backup schedule. Although the Action Center isn't a complete cure for all of your Windows 7 computer's woes, it can notify you of problems and often solve them using automated systems.

Objective

This task covers objective 220-802:1.5.

Scenario

You are providing routine maintenance for a small-business customer's Windows 7 computer. As part of this process, you open the Action Center to see what important or critical notices may be present; then, upon reviewing the notices, you take the required action to correct any faults and perform necessary maintenance tasks.

Scope of Task

Duration

The duration of this task cannot be adequately estimated and depends on what notices you find and choose to act upon in your Windows computer's Action Center.

Setup

There is no particular setup for this task. It relies upon whatever maintenance and security issues have been detected by your Windows 7 computer's Action Center.

Caveat

The steps in this task may not match the actual steps you will take on your computer beyond opening the Action Center. The steps in this task were based on the state of the Windows 7 Enterprise computer used to write this task and may not reflect the state of your computer.

Procedure

This task will show you how to open the Windows 7 Action Center and respond to any notices you may find there.

Equipment Used

No special equipment is required for this task besides a computer running Windows 7.

Details

You will be taken through the steps of opening the Action Center in Windows 7 and responding to any notices you find present.

Using the Action Center Feature in Windows 7

OPENING THE ACTION CENTER

1. Click the Windows Start button.
2. On the menu that appears, right-click Computer and then click Properties.
3. On the System screen, in the left sidebar near the bottom, click Action Center.

4. Click the arrow next to Security to expand this section, and review any items listed in this area, as shown here.

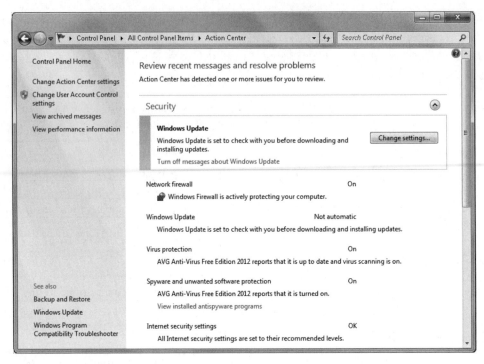

5. Collapse the Security section.

6. Expand the Maintenance section and review any items listed in that area.

7. Collapse the Maintenance section.

CHANGING A SECURITY SETTING IN THE ACTION CENTER AND CHECKING FOR SOLUTIONS TO MAINTENANCE PROBLEMS

1. In the Left sidebar, click Windows Update and then in the left sidebar, click Change settings.

2. When the Choose a Windows Update option box appears, click Install Updates Automatically (Recommended).

3. Expand the Maintenance section again.

4. In the Check for Solutions to Problem Reports section, click Check for Solutions.

5. After the Problem Reporting process runs, if the result is No New Solutions Were Found, click Close.

6. Close the Action Center.

As you can see from your brief examination of the Action Center, there is a wide variety of tasks you can perform here. Most likely, the notices you saw in your own Action Center were colored yellow for caution. Immediate threats are colored red, and it is recommended to attend to these matters first.

Criteria for Completion

You will have successfully completed this task when you have opened and reviewed the notices in the Action Center and when you have responded to one or more security or maintenance notices present.

Task 4.4: Scanning for and Removing Malware

Malicious software, or *malware*, is more than just viruses, Trojan horses, and worms. It also includes keyloggers, spyware, zombies, web-browser hijackers, and any other software types that are designed to be installed on your computer without your knowledge and permission. This software is intended to damage or disrupt as many computers as it can access. The process of scanning for and quarantining malware is substantially similar to the process for using an antivirus program (see Task 4.1). You can use a malware scanner from the same vendor that produces your antivirus solution, or you can use a completely different vendor's product.

Objective

This task covers objectives 220-802:2.2.

Scenario

You receive a trouble ticket from a user in your company complaining that the web browser on his laptop is "going crazy." You discover that the home page for his browser has been mysteriously changed to an adult-content website and the browser resists all efforts to change it back to the corporation's main web page. Also, multiple web-browser windows pop up every few seconds without end, filling the screen and making it impossible to work.

The user had his laptop with him on a recent business trip, and you suspect he may have downloaded some software that included a web-browser hijacker. You are able to gain control of the web browser's behavior only when the laptop is not connected to the network.

 You may have to run antivirus software in Safe Mode since often, a compromised computer will not allow the antivirus application to operate. You also may need to turn off System Restore in order to clear out any infections stored in a restore point.

At this point, you should advise the IT department that a compromised machine had temporarily been connected to the network so they can determine if any other devices have been affected.

You proceed to log on to the laptop and access the anti-malware program. To update the definitions, you access the anti-malware server from a separate computer, download the latest definitions to a prepared folder, and then transfer those files to a USB thumb drive.

Scope of Task

Duration

Just as in Task 4.1, the scanning process can be lengthy if you are scanning the entire hard drive, but once the scan is done, any detected threats can be quickly selected and isolated from the rest of the system.

Setup

You will need to have some sort of malware scanner installed on your computer. Here's a list of websites where you can download free versions of the vendor's malware scanner:

- AVG Anti-Virus and Anti-Spyware: `http://free.avg.com/us-en/free-antivirus-download`

- Spybot—Search & Destroy: `www.safer-networking.org/en/download/index.html`

- Ad-Aware Free Antivirus+: `www.lavasoft.com/products/ad-aware_se_personal.php`

If you have the free version of AVG Anti-Virus already installed, the anti-spyware software is also present. There is no need to download and install AVG's software a second time.

This task uses the free version of AVG 2012 on Windows 7, but you can use any other reliable antivirus/anti-malware software you desire.

Caveat

If you use an antivirus/anti-malware solution other than AVG 2012 when performing this task, the steps will most likely not be the same as those listed in this task.

Procedure

This task will teach you how to scan for malware on a computer and how to quarantine it if found.

Equipment Used

You will need a USB thumb drive onto which you will download the virus/malware defini-tions. In a real-world scenario, you would need access to an uninfected computer connected to the Internet from which you would download the definitions, and a separate, infected computer, disconnected from the network, on which you would manually update the AVG free applications with the definitions.

Details

This task will walk you through the steps of scanning for and quarantining any malware found on a computer.

Scanning for and Quarantining Malware

MANUALLY DOWNLOADING MALWARE DEFINITIONS USING AN UNINFECTED COMPUTER

1. Plug the USB thumb drive into an uninfected computer that has an Internet connection and wait for the removable drive to be recognized by the system.

2. Open a web browser and go to the AVG update download page at `http://free.avg` `.com/us-en/download-update`.

 This URL may have changed by the time you read this task. If the URL is unavailable, use a search engine to search for **downloading avg definition update to a thumb drive** or a similar string.

3. Click Iavi, which should be the latest virus and malware definitions.

4. When the Save As screen appears, navigate to the location of the USB thumb drive.

5. Save the Iavi file to the thumb drive (this may take a few seconds depending on the size of the file and your Internet connection speed).

6. Safely remove the thumb drive from the computer.

7. Close the web browser.

MANUALLY UPDATING MALWARE DEFINITIONS

1. Click the Windows 7 Start button.

2. Click All Programs and then click the name of your antivirus/anti-malware solution such as AVG.

3. Click AVG User Interface.

4. In the User Interface console, click Tools, and then click Update from Directory.

5. When the Browse for Folder dialog box opens, navigate to the update file on the USB drive and select it.

6. After the Update Completed Successfully message appears in the AVG console, safely remove the USB thumb drive.

SCANNING FOR MALWARE

1. In the AVG console, click Scan Now. The scan will begin.

 Just as in Task 4.1, allow the scan to complete even if malware is detected early in the process. You want to make sure that all threats on your computer are detected.

2. When the scan is complete, if any threats were detected, select all of those displayed in the list. In your program, there may be a Select All button, or you can select multiple names in the list by holding down the Ctrl key and clicking each item with your mouse.

3. Click Next.

4. When offered the option, click Quarantine.

5. Click Next.

6. If offered the option, click Send Copy to Quarantine Server.

7. Click Next.

8. Click Finish.

TESTING THE MALWARE REMOVAL

1. Open a web browser.

2. Set the default home page for the browser to the corporate website.

3. Close the web browser.

4. Open the browser again and note which site opens in the window.

5. Note if any other windows open without being specifically opened by you.

Criteria for Completion

You will have successfully completed this task when you have scanned for malware, quarantined any discovered threats, and tested the computer to verify that the aberrant behavior has been neutralized.

Task 4.5: Scanning for Rootkits

A rootkit is more than a single malicious program designed to compromise your computer. It's a tool or collection of tools covertly installed on your PC for the purpose of gathering your private information and even taking complete control of your machine, turning it into a spam-transmitting or a virus-spreading "zombie." Your standard antivirus and anti-malware solution may not detect the presence of a rootkit on your 32-bit Windows XP, Windows Vista, or Windows 7 computer, but there are other ways to find and remove this menace.

Objective

This task covers objectives 220-802:2.2 and 4.7.

Scenario

You receive a trouble ticket stating that a user's Windows XP laptop, which he often takes on business trips, has been frequently accessing the Internet and transferring data across the network for long periods of time when the computer was supposed to be idle. The user has run all of the usual antivirus scans, and his machine appears to be clean. You consult with your supervisor and she suspects that a rootkit may have been installed on the user's laptop. She advises you to attach the laptop to a test network that's isolated from the company's production network but that has Internet access. You're to download and install the Microsoft Security Essentials tool and scan the computer using it, to see if her suspicions can be confirmed. Once you have run the scan, you are to contact your supervisor again so she can evaluate the results and take further action.

She provides you with the necessary URL and instructions on how to use Microsoft Security Essentials. You take possession of the laptop, take it to your workbench, and connect it to the test network. You then go to the URL you have been provided, download the tool, unzip the compressed file, and get ready to work.

Go to http://windows.microsoft.com/en-US/windows/products/security-essentials to download this tool onto your Windows XP system.

Scope of Task

Duration

The Microsoft Security Essentials scan can take some time, depending on the number of files that need to be scanned.

Setup

No special setup is necessary. Just download the zip file from the previously referenced URL, unzip the file, open the folder, and launch the utility.

Caveat

Microsoft recommends that you close all files and applications prior to running Microsoft Security Essentials to avoid false positives. Also, it's recommended that no other antivirus program be installed on the computer when you install and run Microsoft Security Essentials. The tool has no pause function, so once the scan is started, you must either allow it to complete or click Cancel to stop the scan.

The process of removing a rootkit is beyond the scope of this task and book. The removal process can vary widely depending on the type and nature of the rootkit located.

Procedure

This task will show you how to install and launch Microsoft Security Essentials and read the results.

Equipment Used

No special equipment is required.

Details

This task will take you through the steps of installing, updating, and launching Microsoft Security Essentials and observing the results.

Downloading Microsoft Security Essentials and Scanning a Windows XP PC

1. Open a web browser and navigate to http://windows.microsoft.com/en-US/windows/products/security-essentials.

2. Click Download.

3. On the Download Microsoft Security Essentials page, next to your language, use the Windows version drop down menu and select the version of Windows running on your computer.

 If you don't know if your computer is running a 32-bit or 64-bit version of Windows, click the 'Is my PC running the 32-bit or 64-bit version of Windows?' link on this page and then follow the instructions.

4. Save the mseinstall.exe file to the desired location on your computer's hard drive.

5. Close your web browser and navigate to the location of mseinstall.exe.

6. Double-click mseinstall.exe to launch the program and then click Run.

7. When the Welcome to Microsoft Security Essentials Installation Wizard launches, click Next and then follow the onscreen instructions to install the application.

8. When the wizard is finished, make sure the Scan My Computer for Potential Threats After Getting the Latest Updates check box is selected, and then click Finish.

The Microsoft Security Essentials screen will open, and virus and spyware definitions will be downloaded and installed. Afterward, a quick scan is automatically performed on your computer.

In the described scenario, you would summon your supervisor at this point, allow her to examine the results, and then take whatever further action she advises. In our task, you can either close the tool now or run a full scan if you so choose.

Criteria for Completion

You will have successfully completed this task when you have used Microsoft Security Essentials to scan for rootkits and other threats on your Windows XP, Windows Vista, or Windows 7 computer. You are not required to verify the presence of rootkits or to remove any you may find.

Task 4.6: Backing Up Outlook

In corporate environments that use Microsoft Exchange Server to manage mail, when you back up the Exchange Server, you back up the mail. However, if your company is small or administers small branch offices with no connection to the main office's mail server, it may be necessary to back up mail from individual computers at these offices.

This task is one you should rarely perform in an enterprise networking environment, but on the odd occasion when a request such as this comes in, you'll be glad you know what you're doing.

Objective

This task covers objective 220-802:1.7.

Scenario

You are at a small office and have been assigned to back up mail information from Microsoft Outlook mail clients. The data is stored on the local hard drives of each computer. You review the instructions for backing up Outlook files, log on to the computer, and get ready to work.

Scope of Task

Duration

Depending on the amount of information being backed up, this task should take about 20 to 30 minutes.

Setup

You will need access to a computer with Microsoft Outlook installed. A Windows XP Professional computer with Outlook 2007 was used to write this task.

Caveat

This should be a fairly straightforward procedure; however, make sure you remember the location where you stored the backup in case you need to restore the mail to Outlook.

Procedure

This task shows you how to back up Microsoft Outlook data from the local hard drive.

Equipment Used

No special equipment is needed to complete this task besides an external USB storage device.

Details

This task walks you through the steps of accessing and copying Outlook PST files from the hard drive of the local computer to an external USB drive.

Backing Up Mail Files from Outlook

ATTACHING EXTERNAL STORAGE TO THE COMPUTER

1. Locate the external USB drive you brought with you.
2. After logging on, attach the drive's USB cable to a USB port on the computer.
3. Verify that the other end of the cable is attached to the drive and that the drive is attached to a power source and is active.
4. Click Start ➢ My Computer.
5. Verify that the external USB drive is recognized and assigned a drive letter. An information balloon should appear from the Taskbar stating that a new hardware device has been recognized.
6. Close the balloon.
7. Close My Computer.

COPYING PST FILES FROM OUTLOOK TO AN EXTERNAL DRIVE

1. Open Microsoft Outlook.
2. In the Outlook menu bar, click Tools and then click Options.

3. In the Options screen, on the Mail Setup tab, click Data Files.

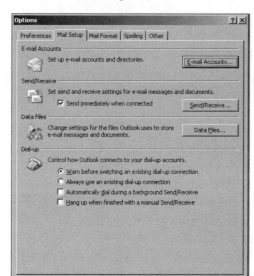

4. In the Outlook Data Files box, select the folder or folders you want to copy. The usual choices are Personal Folders and Archive Folders.

5. Click Open Folder.

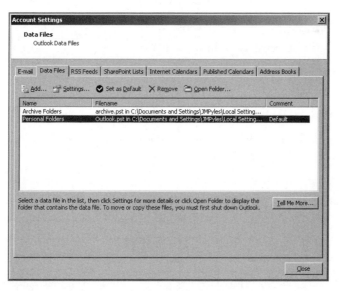

6. Click Edit ➢ Select All and then choose Edit ➢ Copy.

7. Click Start ➢ My Computer.

8. Double-click the icon for the USB storage device.

9. When you have opened the correct folder for the desired user/computer on the drive, right-click the empty space inside it.

10. In the menu that opens, click Paste.

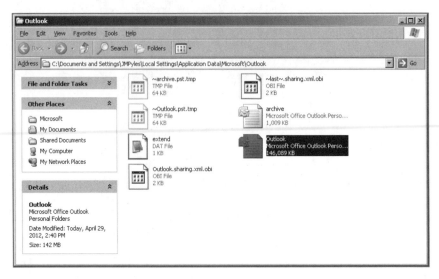

11. Close the USB drive window.

12. In Outlook, click Close.

13. In the Mail Setup dialog box, click Close.

14. Disconnect the USB drive from the computer.

15. Log off the computer.

Criteria for Completion

You will have successfully completed this task when you have copied Outlook PST files from the local computer to the external drive.

Task 4.7: Quickly Diagnosing Windows Vista Problems

Windows Vista comes with a utility that lets you quickly scan the system for problems and provides an easy-to-read report of any problems found on the computer. It's not a substitute for experience and keen problem-solving skills, but it does take a lot of the footwork out of tracking down whatever may be ailing a Vista PC.

Objective

This task covers objective 220-802:4.6.

Scenario

The HR manager calls you stating that her new Windows Vista computer doesn't seem to "work right." She isn't able to completely articulate what the issue seems to be but wants you to come to her office and check her computer. You contact your supervisor and she assigns you this task, suggesting you use Vista's Reliability and Performance Monitor to do a quick scan of the PC to see what sort of problems the computer may be experiencing. You are provided the instructions on how to locate and run the utility.

After arranging a time to meet with the HR manager in her office, you arrive, sit at the computer's keyboard, log in as an administrator, and begin your work.

Scope of Task

Duration

This task should take only a few minutes to complete, since the Reliability and Performance Monitor's scan of the system is very quick.

Setup

No special setup is required beyond access to a Windows Vista computer.

Caveat

Use this tool only as a necessary first step to locate or rule out potential problems. You will still need to use a wide variety of troubleshooting skills to successfully find and repair problems on Windows Vista computers.

Procedure

This task will show you how to use Vista's Reliability and Performance Monitor to scan a computer for problems.

Equipment Used

No special equipment is required except, of course, a Windows Vista computer.

Details

This task will take you through the steps of launching and reading the Windows Vista Reliability and Performance Monitor to discover potential problems on a computer.

**Using the Windows Vista Reliability and Performance Monitor
to Diagnose Problems**

1. Click the Windows Vista button and then click Control Panel.

2. In Control Panel, click System and Maintenance ➢ Performance Information and
    Tools ➢ Advanced Tools.

 You can perform this task on a Windows 7 computer if, in Control Panel,
click Performance Information and Tools in Small or Large Icon view, and
then follow the rest of the instructions in this task.

3. Click Generate a System Health Report. (If the UAC box appears, click Yes.)

4. When the report is generated, review the list of errors, indicated by red X's in the
    Reliability and Performance Monitor dialog box.

5. Make a note of the information presented in the Cause, Details, and Resolution fields
    for each error.

Criteria for Completion

You will have successfully completed this task when you have read the list of errors produced by the utility and noted the information related to each problem, including the potential solution. You can then use this information to devise a plan to investigate each error in
more detail and repair the problems.

Task 4.8: Troubleshooting a Randomly Rebooting PC

So far, many of the tasks that have been presented have been unambiguous in terms of a
solution. From this point on, you will be required to respond to issues with a cause and solution that aren't always apparent. As you gain experience, you will become more confident in
troubleshooting computer and network issues, but when confronted with a problem you can't
successfully diagnose, you can always rely on other IT staff to lend a hand.

A randomly rebooting computer is a classic troubleshooting problem. You will encounter
this problem only occasionally; however, being able to diagnose such an issue is a handy
skill to possess.

Objective

This task covers objective 220-802:4.2.

Scenario

You receive a trouble ticket saying that for the past several days, one of the computers in Accounts Receivable has been spontaneously rebooting. You are assigned to investigate.

Scope of Task

Duration

The amount of time required to accomplish this task will vary depending on the cause and solution. Under ideal circumstances, it should take an hour or so.

Setup

As you will see when you progress through the steps, this issue is difficult to simulate and requires that you be presented with a PC that is actually experiencing this symptom.

Caveat

Troubleshooting any computer problem involves both drawing on your experience and a certain amount of trial and error. As you gain experience, you will be able to assess a particular problem in terms of the most likely cause. You can then test to see whether your assumption is correct. If so, you can implement the solution and resolve the issue. If not, you can move on to the next most likely cause and test for that. Sometimes, however, the cause ends up being something unexpected.

> Another reason for spontaneous reboots is an overheating problem. To check this, open the computer and see if there is a lot of dust contamination. If so, use a can of compressed air to clean out the PC case, close the case, restart the computer, and observe its performance.

Procedure

This task will show you how to diagnose the cause of spontaneous reboots on a computer.

Equipment Used

Often when you begin a troubleshooting task, you don't immediately know what tools or equipment will be needed. In this case, in order to successfully resolve the issue, you'll need a screwdriver and ESD protection.

Details

This task will take you through the steps of diagnosing the cause of a computer spontaneously rebooting, determining the solution, and repairing the computer.

Diagnosing and Repairing a Spontaneously Rebooting Computer

INITIALLY INVESTIGATING A SPONTANEOUSLY REBOOTING COMPUTER

1. Locate the user of the computer.

2. Have the user explain in detail the nature of the problem. Before even touching the computer, it is important to get as many details about the issue as possible from the user. The following list includes some of the questions to ask in this situation:

   - When did the problem begin?

   - Were any changes made to the hardware, software, or configuration settings of the computer just prior to the problem occurring the first time?

   - How often does the computer spontaneously reboot?

   - What tasks is the user performing just prior to a reboot?

   - Is there anything that the user does on the computer that decreases or increases the frequency of the reboots?

> In this case, there seems to be no particular pattern to the reboot incidents. They occur at random, regardless of what the user is doing at the computer and even when she is away from the PC. No recent changes have been made to the computer, although the user has considered requesting a newer model since her PC is quite old.

3. Locate the PC.

4. Check all of the external power connections, including the connection on the PC's power supply, the connection of the power cord to the surge protector, and the surge protector's connection to the wall plug.

5. Perform a visual inspection of the power button on the outside of the PC.

> Occasionally, the power button will stick after being pressed and will create a partial connection that can cause the PC to reboot if the case is nudged or bumped.

> Your first assumption is that a loose connection inside the computer case may be causing the problem. The following set of steps attempts to address this assumption.

DIAGNOSING THE PROBLEM AT YOUR WORKBENCH

1. After powering down the PC, disconnect all of its connections at the user's work area and take the computer to your workbench in the IT department.

In this example, the problem cannot be resolved at the user's work area.

2. Place the PC on your workbench.

 Do not connect any power cords or peripherals to the PC.

3. Locate your tools and your ESD protection.
4. Using the appropriate screwdriver, remove the screws holding the access panel in place.
5. Remove the access panel.
6. Use ESD precautions.
7. Check the internal connectors from the power supply to the motherboard, all drives, and any other available connections to make sure they are secure.
8. Check to make sure the RAM sticks are seated properly, and reseat if necessary.
9. Check to make sure the CPU and the heat sink and fan are seated properly, and reseat if necessary.
10. Check to make sure all expansion cards are seated properly, and reseat if necessary.
11. Check the connections to the power button.
12. Secure any loose connections and replace the access panel.
13. Replace the screws holding the access panel in place.

 It's possible that a connection may have become just loose enough to cause an intermittent problem, even if it didn't feel particularly loose.

14. Check the movement of the power button to make sure it can be fully depressed.
15. Verify that the power button is in the off position (that is, the button is not pressed in so that it causes the computer to boot the moment power is applied to the power supply).

TESTING YOUR FIRST ASSUMPTION

1. Connect the PC to a monitor, keyboard, and mouse.
2. Verify that the monitor has power and is turned on.
3. Plug a power cord into the back of the PC's power supply and verify that the other end of the cord is plugged into a wall plug or surge protector that is powered.
4. Press the PC's power button.
5. Allow the PC to boot.
6. Observe the PC's behavior once the operating system has loaded.

The only way to test your solution is to leave the PC powered up for an extended period of time until you determine that it is not exhibiting its symptomatic behavior. You'll need to be present but can occupy your time with paperwork or other tasks that still let you pay attention to the computer.

CONTINUING TO DIAGNOSE THE PROBLEM

In this example, your initial assumption was not correct and the computer still exhibits symptomatic behavior.

1. Power down the computer.

2. Disconnect the power cord from the power supply.

3. Locate an appropriate replacement power supply and place it on your workbench.

4. Remove the screws holding the access panel in place.

5. Remove the access panel.

6. Take ESD precautions and prepare to replace the power supply with a new unit.

7. Once you have replaced the power supply, replace the access panel and the screws that hold it to the PC case.

TESTING YOUR SECOND ASSUMPTION

1. Reconnect the power cord to the power supply.

2. Power up the computer.

3. Continue to observe the PC's behavior once the operating system has loaded.

A spontaneously rebooting computer is often the sign of a dying power supply. Recall that the user mentioned that her PC was an older model.

Criteria for Completion

You will have successfully completed this task when the PC remains powered on for an extended period of time and the symptom does not reoccur.

Task 4.9: Troubleshooting an Intermittent Boot Failure of a PC

On the surface, this problem seems fairly similar to Task 4.8, but in fact it could be caused by a wide variety of circumstances. Problems that occur intermittently are some of the most maddening. It's like driving a car that has an intermittent knock in the engine. When you take it to the garage, the knock won't manifest itself. After you drive away again, the knock reappears. Under these circumstances, your job is to work with the computer and attempt to replicate the problem so you can observe and, hopefully, repair it.

Objective

This task covers objective 220-802:4.6.

Scenario

You receive a trouble ticket Monday morning stating that one of the users in the administrative office can't seem to power up his computer. The ticket states that when the user presses the power button, sometimes the unit powers up, but there's no image on the screen. On other occasions, when the user presses the power button the unit does not power up at all.

You suspect that the PC's power supply is failing, but your supervisor suggests that there could be a number of other causes, including a failing motherboard capacitor. You take your toolkit with you to the user's computer and prepare to begin the diagnostic process.

Scope of Task

Duration

The duration of this task depends on how quickly you are able to find the cause of the problem based on your diagnostic methods and the complexity of the problem.

Setup

As in the previous task, this issue is difficult to simulate and requires a PC that is actually experiencing this symptom.

Caveat

As previously stated, troubleshooting any computer problem involves both drawing on your experience and a certain amount of trial and error. The first step is to gather as much information as possible about the problem from the user and then logically proceed through several testing steps, eliminating possible causes until the actual cause of the problem is determined. This might take some time, but as you become more experienced with similar problems, you can more quickly home in on the solution.

Procedure

This task will show you the process of diagnosing a computer with intermittent boot problems.

Equipment Used

Since the scenario begins by suspecting a failing power supply, you'll need to take a paper clip with you to do a quick test of the power supply (see Task 2.3 for details).

Details

This task shows you the steps in diagnosing a computer that only intermittently powers up but never receives an image on the monitor.

Diagnosing a PC That Only Intermittently Powers Up

INITIALLY INVESTIGATING A COMPUTER BOOT PROBLEM

1. You contact the computer's user and begin the investigation by asking him questions regarding the problem.

   - When did the problem first occur?

   - Have there been any recent configuration changes to the settings on the PC?

   - Were any changes made to the hardware or software of the computer just prior to the problem occurring for the first time?

The user says he normally powers down his computer on Friday before leaving work for the weekend and then powers up his computer on Monday morning and leaves the computer powered all week. At the end of each workday during the week, he logs off his PC but leaves it in a running condition. When he came into work today, Monday morning, he discovered the problem described in the trouble ticket.

2. You sit at the computer and press the power button, but nothing happens.

3. After waiting a few minutes, you press the power button again and hear the computer powering up but see no images on the monitor.

4. You press the power button on the monitor several times and determine it is on.

5. You check the power-cord connections between the monitor and the power strip, but the connections are firm.

6. You check the connection between the monitor and the PC, but the connections are firm.

7. You check the power-cord connections between the PC and the power strip, but the connections are firm.

8. You power down the PC.

TESTING YOUR FIRST ASSUMPTION

1. You decide to test your first assumption that the power supply of the computer is failing, have an unfolded paper clip handy, and prepare to open the access panel to the PC.

See Task 2.2 to determine the specific type of a power supply and Task 2.3 to go through the steps of quick testing a power supply.

2. Based on your testing of the power supply, you determine that it is not the cause of the problem, although you are still convinced it is a power-related issue.

TESTING YOUR SECOND ASSUMPTION

1. Telling the user that you will return shortly, you go back to the IT department and find a spare power strip.

Although your supervisor suggests testing the power connection to the motherboard next, you suspect another cause, and it will only take a few minutes to test.

2. Returning to the user's cubicle with the spare power strip, you look under his desk at the existing power strip and verify that the power button on the strip is lit and that the strip is actively receiving power.

3. You ask the user to power down all devices that are connected to the power strip under his desk.

4. After the user has powered down all relevant devices, you go under his desk and disconnect all of the power cords connected to the power strip.

5. You disconnect the power strip from the wall power socket and plug in the replacement power strip.

6. You plug all of the power cords you removed from the old power strip into the replacement power strip, and verify that the power button on the strip is in the on position with the strip receiving power from the wall outlet.

7. You tell the user to power up all of the devices he powered down before you removed the old power strip.

8. You tell the user to power up the computer monitor and the PC.

9. You verify that the PC powers up and that the expected images appear on the computer screen.

10. After the computer successfully boots and the operating system loads, you have the user power down and then power up his PC a few times to make sure it operates normally.

Criteria for Completion

You will have successfully completed this task when the computer can be powered down normally and then powered up and operated normally.

Although this problem could have many different causes, in this situation a failing power strip providing intermittent power to the PC and monitor was the culprit. Testing the causes that can be accessed most easily and quickly can solve the problem or at least swiftly eliminate a potential cause.

Task 4.10: Troubleshooting a Failed RAM Upgrade

Installing and upgrading RAM is a very common task for a PC technician. Most of the time, it is a very routine operation, but occasionally things don't go as planned. In that event, you will need to troubleshoot why a RAM installation or upgrade doesn't work. Sometimes it's as simple as a bad stick of RAM, but occasionally the cause is more complex.

Objective

This task covers objective 220-802:4.2.

Scenario

You receive a trouble ticket to upgrade the RAM on two identical PCs in the Accounts Receivable department to 2GB. Both PCs are older and currently possess insufficient memory, resulting in significant work slowdowns by their users. Your supervisor provides you with four identical sticks of 1GB PC3200 RAM. You check the current specifications on the two computers in the IT department's records, and you find that the first computer has two sticks of 256MB RAM, while the other computer has two sticks of 128MB RAM.

By modern standards, the amounts of RAM we're discussing are very small, but you'll find that there are still plenty of legacy computers performing low-level tasks in many businesses that don't use significant resources.

You take your toolkit and the replacement RAM sticks to the Accounts Receivable department and locate the two PCs. The users are out to lunch, so you won't be disturbing their work while you do the upgrade. You plan to open each computer, remove the old sticks of RAM and replace them with the new sticks of RAM, and then boot up each computer to verify that the memory upgrade is successful.

See Task 1.2 for the specific instructions on opening a PC case and replacing RAM sticks.

You replace the two sticks of 256MB RAM with two sticks of 1GB RAM in the first computer, power up the PC, and verify that the new RAM is recognized and that the machine boots normally. You replace the two sticks of 128MB RAM in the second computer with two sticks of 1GB RAM, power up the computer, and discover that the beep codes indicate that the RAM is not recognized. The computer does not boot successfully. The two computers and four sticks of 1GB RAM are all supposed to be identical. You need to find out what went wrong and successfully upgrade the RAM in the second computer so that it will be able to run normally and not experience performance slowdowns.

Scope of Task

Duration

This task could take 30 to 60 minutes or possibly longer, depending on the number of steps taken to diagnose the problem and the extent of the research required to find the solution.

Setup

The problem being described is very specific, and you will not likely be able to duplicate it unless you are presented with a PC that is experiencing the same symptoms as the one presented in this scenario.

Caveat

While a RAM problem may seem to have a limited number of possible causes and solutions, occasionally the information initially presented about the computers you are working on may not be correct, resulting in a problem with an unlikely cause. It's important to recheck all of your records about machines you are working on to make sure your information is accurate.

Procedure

This task will show you the process of diagnosing a failed RAM upgrade.

Equipment Used

The equipment required includes a standard PC toolkit, including ESD-prevention gear and the RAM sticks necessary to perform the upgrade.

Details

This task shows you the steps in diagnosing a failure in upgrading the RAM in a computer.

Diagnosing a Failed RAM Upgrade

TESTING TO VERIFY THE COMPUTER WILL BOOT WITH THE ORIGINAL RAM

1. With the PC case of the second computer open, take ESD precautions and remove the two sticks of 1GB RAM, placing them in their antistatic bags.

2. Remove the two original sticks of 128MB RAM from their antistatic bags and replace them in the PC, making sure they are correctly seated.

3. Leaving the computer access panel off and verifying that the PC and monitor are connected to an active power strip, power up the PC.

4. Verify that the beep codes indicate that the original RAM is recognized and that the PC powers up normally.

5. After the operating system loads and you've verified that the computer behaves normally, power down the computer.

TESTING YOUR FIRST ASSUMPTION

1. Take the two sticks of 1GB RAM back to the IT department, believing one or both sticks are defective, and replace them with two other identical sticks.

2. Return to the Accounts Receivable department and to the PC you are attempting to upgrade.

3. Using ESD precautions, remove the two sticks of 128MB RAM and replace them with the two new sticks of 1GB RAM, making sure they are properly seated.

4. Verify that the computer and monitor are plugged into the active power strip, and then power up the computer.

5. The computer powers up, but the beep codes and monitor message indicate that the RAM is not recognized, so the original upgrade RAM sticks were not defective.

Alternately, you could simply take one of 1GB RAM out of the problem computer and reboot to see if that's the problem stick. Replace it with a second stick of 1GB RAM and reboot again to check the result. Then take a known good stick of 1GB RAM from the first machine you upgraded and check the boot to verify the result. The result is the same, but it saves you the time it takes to walk back to the IT department.

At this point, the user should be back from lunch and you'll need to replace the original sticks of RAM so that he can do his work. You arrange to return to his computer after normal working hours to perform the upgrade, assuming you are able to discover why the RAM upgrade was unsuccessful and solve the dilemma. You instruct the user to power down his computer when he leaves work for the day.

RESEARCHING YOUR SECOND ASSUMPTION

1. Returning to the IT department, you check your records to verify that both of the computers you are upgrading are actually identical.

2. You find out that both computers are the same make and model, but the second PC is older than the first PC.

3. You discover that the first PC supports 128MB, 256MB, 512MB, and 1GB non-ECC RAM up to 4GB.

4. You discover that the second, older PC supports only 128MB, 256MB, and 512MB non-ECC RAM up to 2GB.

TESTING YOUR SECOND ASSUMPTION

1. You acquire four sticks of 512MB RAM of the appropriate type for the computer you are attempting to upgrade.

2. You take the RAM sticks and your toolkit to the Accounts Receivable department after normal working hours and access the computer requiring the upgrade.

3. Making sure the PC is powered down, you open the computer's access panel.

4. Using ESD precautions, you remove the two sticks of 128MB RAM from the PC and install the four sticks of 512MB RAM.

5. Verifying that the computer and monitor are plugged into an active power strip, you turn on the monitor and power up the PC.

6. You verify that the normal beep codes sound and that the message on the monitor indicates the amount of RAM has increased by the desired amount.

7. Pressing Enter to continue, you watch as the PC boots normally and the operating system loads.

8. You replace the access panel on the PC and power it down and then leave a note for the user that the RAM in his computer has been successfully upgraded.

Criteria for Completion

You will have successfully completed this task when you have upgraded the RAM in the computer with the desired amount of memory.

Task 4.11: Troubleshooting a PC That Can't Print to a Local Printer

Diagnosing printing problems is an extremely common task. If the problem ends up being the printer's hardware, the problem will probably be turned over to the printer vendor's repair person since companies often have support contracts with a printer's manufacturer.

The sort of print problems you'll be asked to investigate involve faulty connections, configuration settings, and driver issues.

Objective

This task covers objective 220-802:4.9.

Scenario

You receive a trouble ticket stating that a member of the Accounting department can't print to her local printer. You pack up your toolkit and report to the accountant's cubicle. When you arrive, she shows you her computer and printer setup. You notice that there is one printer connected to the PC via a USB cable. The PC is powered up.

Scope of Task

Duration

Ideally, this task should take about 15 minutes.

Setup

You can simulate this task with a computer that is connected to a local printer.

 This task was written using Windows XP, so all of the instructions will be consistent with that operating system.

Caveat

There are an almost endless number of causes of a complaint such as "I can't print." It is important to gather all of the information available about the problem to try to narrow down the likely causes.

Procedure

This task will show you the process of diagnosing local printer problems.

Equipment Used

No special equipment is necessary for this task.

Details

This task shows you the steps in diagnosing a complaint of a user who prints to a local printer.

Diagnosing a PC That Can't Print to a Locally Connected Printer

INITIALLY INVESTIGATING A LOCAL PRINT PROBLEM

1. Ask the accountant what she knows about the print problem. Here is a list of some appropriate questions to ask in this situation:

   - When did the problem first occur?
   - Has the user ever successfully printed to the printer?
   - Have there been any recent configuration changes to the printer settings on the PC?
   - Were any changes made to the hardware, software, or configuration settings of the computer just prior to the problem occurring for the first time?
   - Do any error messages display when the user attempts to print?

 NOTE She tells you that she changed out her original local printer for a new one late yesterday right before she left work for the day. This morning, she discovered that she couldn't print to the new printer and called the help desk with a request for assistance.

2. Sit down at the keyboard and log on as administrator.
3. Click Start ➢ Printers and Faxes.
4. When the Printers and Faxes dialog box opens, verify that the new printer is available. You see that the currently attached local printer is not set as the default printer; the default printer is indicated by a white check mark in a black circle.

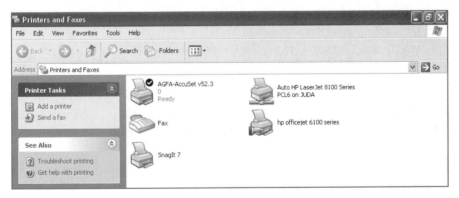

5. Ask the user the make and model of her previous printer.
6. Verify that it is the previous printer that is set as the default printer.

TESTING YOUR FIRST ASSUMPTION

1. Right-click the icon for the currently attached printer.
2. Click Set as Default Printer.

3. Verify that the check mark now appears next to the current printer.

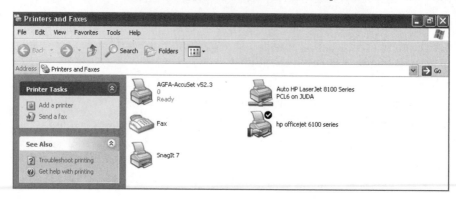

4. Log off the PC.

5. Have the user log on to her computer.

6. Once the logon is complete, click Start ➢ Printers and Faxes.

7. Verify that the currently attached printer is set as the default printer.

8. Right-click the default printer.

9. Click Properties.

10. When the Properties dialog box opens, click Print Test Page. A dialog box will appear asking you to click OK if the test page prints properly.

11. Remove the test page and verify that it printed properly.

12. Click OK in the dialog box.

13. Click OK in the printer Properties dialog box.

14. Close the Printers and Faxes dialog box.

15. Click Start ➢ All Programs ➢ Microsoft Word.

 You will want to verify that applications can also print correctly.

16. When a blank Word document opens, type a line of text.

17. Click File ➢ Print.

18. When the Print dialog box opens, verify that the local printer appears in the Name field.

19. Click OK.

20. If the Word document prints successfully, close the Word document without saving it.

21. Log off the computer.

Criteria for Completion

You will have successfully completed this task when you can print from the locally attached printer.

Task 4.12: Troubleshooting a PC That Can't Print to a Network Printer

As mentioned in the introduction to Task 4.11, print problems are among the most common ones you'll be called on to diagnose, and there are a large number of causes. Problems connecting to network printers can be even more difficult to troubleshoot than local printer problems because you need to factor in any problems on the local area network (LAN) as well as typical print-problem issues.

Objective

This task covers objectives 220-802:4.5 and 4.9.

Scenario

You receive a trouble ticket stating that a user in the Maintenance Systems department can't print to the network printer. You gather your toolkit and the network-configuration information for that department and report to the user.

Scope of Task

Duration

Ideally, this task should take about 15 or 20 minutes.

Setup

You can simulate this task using a computer that is connected to either a local or a network printer. This task was written using a Windows 7 computer.

Caveat

As always, gather as much information about the problem as possible to reduce the potential number of likely causes and solutions.

Procedure

This task will show you how to diagnose network printing problems.

Equipment Used

No special equipment is required for this task.

Details

This task will take you through the steps of diagnosing the cause of network printing problems.

Diagnosing Problems Printing to a Network Printer

INITIALLY INVESTIGATING A NETWORK PRINTING PROBLEM

1. You approach the user and ask him some questions regarding the issue. The following list includes some appropriate questions to ask in this situation:

   - When did the problem first occur?

   - Has the user ever successfully printed to the printer?

   - Have there been any recent configuration changes to the printer settings on the PC?

   - Were any changes made to the hardware, software, or configuration settings of the computer just prior to the problem occurring for the first time?

   - Do any error messages display when the user attempts to print?

   - Has the user experienced other networking problems?

   - Does anyone else in the department have problems printing to the network printer?

   - Does anyone else in the department have any networking problems?

 You discover that the network printer was installed late last Friday after everyone had gone for the day. This morning, everyone was able to print to the network printer except this user. He says he gets no error messages and that the print job just hangs.

2. You log on to the user's computer as a domain administrator and access the IT department's intranet site.

3. You navigate to the IT work logs for last Friday and find the work record for the network printer install.

4. You read the entire record and notice that access to the printer for this department is limited to standard business hours.

5. The user explains that the projects developed by the Software Systems department are highly confidential and printing is limited to normal work hours as part of the security measures applied to this department.

6. You close the IT intranet site and log off.

 At this point, your first assumption is that the issue is a network connection problem.

TESTING YOUR FIRST ASSUMPTION

1. Locate the PC.

2. Locate the patch cable attaching the PC to the Ethernet port.

3. Verify that the connection is secure at both ends.

4. Verify that the link light on the NIC is on.

5. Sit at the computer's keyboard again and log on as administrator.

6. Click Start.

7. In the Search box, type **cmd**.

8. Press Enter.

9. When the command-prompt window opens, type **ipconfig/all**.

10. Verify that the PC has an IP address and that the correct configuration settings are present.

 Although the user states that he is having no other network-related problems, it's still a good idea to make sure the network configuration is correct.

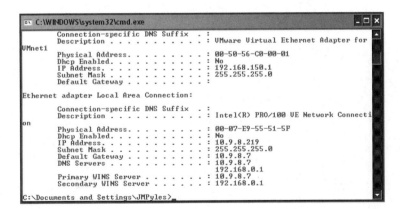

11. Refer to your information sheet for this network segment and compare the user's network settings to the data sheet.

12. Look up the IP address of the network printer.

13. Ping that IP address from the user's computer.

```
C:\WINDOWS\system32\cmd.exe                                           _ □ ×
       Physical Address. . . . . . . . . : 00-07-E9-55-51-5F
       Dhcp Enabled. . . . . . . . . . . : No
       IP Address. . . . . . . . . . . . : 10.9.8.219
       Subnet Mask . . . . . . . . . . . : 255.255.255.0
       Default Gateway . . . . . . . . . : 10.9.8.7
       DNS Servers . . . . . . . . . . . : 10.9.8.7
                                           192.168.0.1
       Primary WINS Server . . . . . . . : 10.9.8.7
       Secondary WINS Server . . . . . . : 192.168.0.1

C:\Documents and Settings\JMPyles>ping 10.9.8.200

Pinging 10.9.8.200 with 32 bytes of data:

Reply from 10.9.8.200: bytes=32 time=107ms TTL=128
Reply from 10.9.8.200: bytes=32 time=4ms TTL=128
Reply from 10.9.8.200: bytes=32 time=2ms TTL=128
Reply from 10.9.8.200: bytes=32 time=1ms TTL=128

Ping statistics for 10.9.8.200:
    Packets: Sent = 4, Received = 4, Lost = 0 (0% loss),
Approximate round trip times in milli-seconds:
    Minimum = 1ms, Maximum = 107ms, Average = 28ms

C:\Documents and Settings\JMPyles>
```

14. Type **exit** and press Enter to close the command-prompt window.

Your second assumption is that there is a fault with the printer configuration.

TESTING YOUR SECOND ASSUMPTION

1. Click Start ➤ Devices and Printers.

2. Verify that the network printer is the default printer by looking for the white check mark in the green circle.

3. Right-click the printer.

4. Click Printer Properties.

5. Click Print Test Page. A dialog box opens indicating that the test page has been sent to the printer.

6. Look for any error messages.

7. No error messages appear. You notice that the print-job icon appears in the right-hand corner of the System Tray but the job doesn't print.

8. Double-click the print-job icon. You see the print job in the queue but there is no activity.

9. Select the document by clicking it.

10. Click Document ➢ Restart.

11. When the document still doesn't print, click Document ➢ Properties.

12. Review the Test Page Properties dialog box. You notice in the Schedule area that the time the user is allowed to access the printer is misconfigured with a start time of 8:00 PM and an end time of 5:00 AM.

13. Click OK to close the Properties box.

14. Verify that the document is still selected.

15. Click Document ➢ Cancel. A dialog box appears asking if you want to cancel the print job.

16. Click Yes. The print job disappears from the printer window.

17. Close the Print job window and then close the 'A test page has been sent to your printer' window.

18. In the Properties box, click the Advanced tab. Notice that the time the printer is available is misconfigured with a start time of 8:00 PM and an end time of 5:00 AM.

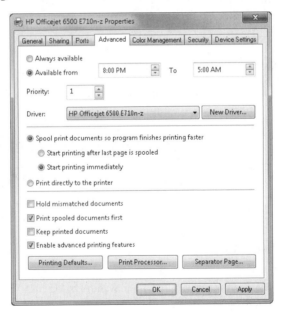

19. Click the PM next to 8:00 to select it.

20. Type **A**. PM will change to AM.

21. Click the AM next to 5:00 to select it.

22. Type **P**. AM will change to PM.

23. Click Apply and then select the General tab.

24. Click Print Test Page. After the page prints, close the 'A test page has been sent to your printer' window.

25. Click OK to close the Properties dialog box.

26. Close the Printers and Faxes dialog box.

27. Log off the computer.

 NOTE You are able to perform these tasks on the user's computer because you are logged in as a domain administrator. The user's normal login will not give him sufficient rights to make these changes independently.

VERIFYING THAT THE USER CAN PRINT FROM AN APPLICATION

1. Have the user log on to the computer.

2. Have the user open Microsoft Word.

3. Have the user type some text in the blank document.

4. Have the user print the document.

5. Verify that the document prints to the network printer.

Criteria for Completion

You will have successfully completed this task when the user can print to the network printer.

Task 4.13: Troubleshooting the Error Message "The Specified Domain Either Does Not Exist or Could Not Be Contacted"

Periodically, issues come up when trying to join a Windows PC to a Windows Active Directory domain. Virtually all medium and large companies use Active Directory Services to manage computers and resources on the network. If a computer can't join a domain, it can't be used effectively to do work in the business.

Objective

This task covers objective 220-802:4.5.

Scenario

You've been assigned to join a computer to the company's domain. A new user has been hired in the Design department and will be arriving tomorrow. You report to the Design department and are directed to the computer. You sit down at the keyboard and log on as administrator.

Scope of Task

Duration

This task should take about 30 minutes.

Setup

Ideally, you will need a client computer networked with a Windows 2003 Server or higher domain controller. The PC used for this task was Windows XP Professional. While you can use Windows Vista or Windows 7 (but only the editions that are capable of being domain members), the task steps will be somewhat different.

In this scenario, you are working at a smaller company that is using an older Windows 2003 Server as a domain controller, and the end user is on a Windows XP Professional computer.

See Task 3.9, "Joining a Computer to a Domain," for more information.

Caveat

This sort of problem can be especially frustrating because any number of different computer-, server-, or network-related problems can be contributing factors. Depending on the setup of your test computer and whether or not you have access to a domain controller on your test network, you may not be able to follow all of the steps in this task, but it does represent a real-world problem relative to joining a computer to an Active Directory domain.

Procedure

This task will teach you how to troubleshoot problems joining a computer to an Active Directory domain.

Equipment Used

No special equipment is needed for this task.

Details

This task will walk you through the steps in troubleshooting a problem of joining a computer to a Windows Active Directory domain.

Diagnosing a Problem Joining a Computer to a Domain

DISCOVERING THE PROBLEM

In most of the previous troubleshooting tasks, you already knew the outstanding problem when you received the trouble ticket. In this scenario, you are the one who discovers the problem.

1. Click Start ≻ Run.

2. In the Run box, type **cmd**.

3. At the command prompt, ping the IP address of the nearest domain controller and verify the connection.

4. Once it is verified, type **exit** and press Enter to close the command-prompt window.

5. Right-click My Computer.

6. Click Properties.

7. In the System Properties dialog box, click the Computer Name tab.

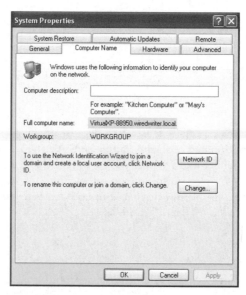

8. Click Change.

9. Click the Domain radio button.

10. In the Domain field, type the correct name for the domain.

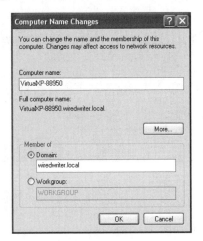

11. Click OK. An error message will appear.

12. Click Details to see more information.

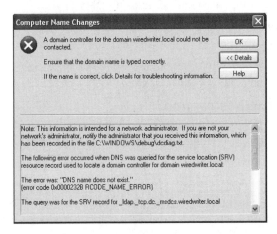

13. Click OK to close this dialog box, but leave the other dialog boxes open.

TESTING YOUR FIRST ASSUMPTION

You notice that in the Computer Name Changes dialog box under the Computer Name field, the full computer name is displayed with the DNS suffix `network.local`. This may be interfering with the computer joining the domain.

1. Click More. Notice the Primary DNS suffix displays here as `network.local` too.

2. Delete the entry in the Primary DNS Suffix of This Computer field.

3. Verify that the check box Change Primary DNS Suffix When Domain Membership Changes is selected.

4. Click OK.

5. You are prompted to reboot the computer.

6. Click OK.

7. When the second prompt appears, click Yes.

8. After the machine reboots, log on as administrator.

9. Repeat steps 2 through 7 in the "Discovering the Problem" section.

10. Verify that the full computer name contains no DNS suffix.

11. Verify that the Domain radio button is still selected and that the domain name is still in the Domain field.

12. Click OK. The same error message as before will appear.

13. Cancel out of all open dialog boxes.

TESTING YOUR SECOND ASSUMPTION

It is possible that the problem is a lack of network connection between the computer and the domain controller or a problem with name resolution of the domain controller's hostname.

1. Open a command-prompt window.

> See the first three steps in the section "Discovering the Problem" earlier in this task if necessary, for details about opening a command-prompt window.

2. Ping the domain controller's IP address.

3. Ping the domain controller by hostname.

4. Ping the domain controller by name and DNS suffix such as, `charlie.wiredwriter.local`.

5. Look at the datasheet for this job and verify the domain name for this task.

6. Call the help desk and verify that the domain name is correct.

7. Have the help desk verify that the domain controller and local DNS server are operating. The help desk reports that both servers are operating normally and that they have received no calls from anyone else on that network segment stating that they could not connect to the domain.

> Although the PC could use any domain controller to join the domain, it is better to use one on the same network segment so that the process doesn't have to cross one or more routers.

TESTING YOUR THIRD ASSUMPTION

There may be some error that isn't immediately obvious to you that has been recorded and can be reviewed in the Event Viewer of the computer. Also there may be a problem with the registration of DNS names on the network.

1. Click Start ➢ Settings ➢ Control Panel.

2. Double-click Administrative Tools.

3. Double-click Event Viewer.

4. When the Event Viewer opens, select System Log.

5. Double-click the most recent warning to read it.

6. Review all of the information available.

7. Click OK to close the Event Properties dialog box.

8. Close Event Viewer.

9. Close Administrative Tools.

10. Open a command-prompt window.

11. Type **ipconfig/registerdns**.

12. Press Enter.

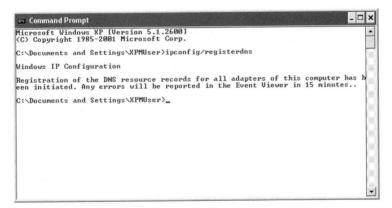

13. After the appropriate period of time passes, check the System Event logs in the Event Viewer for errors.

Follow steps 1 through 3 in this section to open the Event Viewer.

14. Close the Event Viewer.

15. Close Administrative Tools.

16. Open a command-prompt window.

17. Ping the domain controller by its hostname and DNS suffix.

18. Close the command-prompt window.

Follow the steps in Task 3.9, "Joining a Computer to Domain," to join this computer to the domain.

Criteria for Completion

You will have successfully completed this task when you discover the cause of the error, correct it, and join the computer to the domain.

If the issue had been with the domain controller, DNS server, or other high-level server or network problem, you would have handed off the task to a network technician or administrator to resolve before you attempted to join the computer to the domain.

Task 4.14: Troubleshooting the Error Message "Print Processor Unknown"

Here is yet another in a series of print-related problems. This one is characterized by a specific error message, which is a good thing because you can usually go to support.microsoft.com and search the Support Knowledge Base for the specific error and then discover the solution. No one can be expected to remember every single error message that a computer can deliver (with the exception of folks who write certification exams), so you will find yourself on the computer using your favorite search engine quite a lot.

Objective

This task covers objective 220-802:4.9.

Scenario

You have received a trouble ticket stating that several users in the Sales department have been receiving errors when they try to print documents. The error reads as follows:

```
Event ID: 61
Event Type: Error
Event Source: Print
Description: The document document_name owned by username failed to
   print. Win32 error code returned by the print processor: 63(0x3f)
```

The Sales department staff had been printing normally until this morning. Instead of reporting to the Sales department, you decide to first research the error message to see if you can narrow down the possible causes of the problem.

Scope of Task

Duration

Determining the cause of the problem should take less than 15 minutes. Correcting the problem could take a bit longer.

Setup

Ideally, you will need a Windows XP or higher server machine acting as a print server for one or more printers on a network. The network should have at least one client computer that you can print from.

Caveat

When interpreting an error message issued by Windows, you are better off searching the Microsoft support site than using a search engine such as Google. Google or any other search engine can cast too wide a net in its search, and you may end up spending a lot more time than necessary chasing down the answer to the problem.

Procedure

This task will show you how to research a printer error message and discover the solution to the printing problem.

Equipment Used

No special equipment is necessary to complete this task.

Details

This task will teach you the steps necessary to search for a specific error message, investigate your computing environment to determine how this error applies, and resolve the error.

Searching for and Discovering the Solution to an Error Message

SEARCHING FOR THE ERROR MESSAGE

1. Sitting at a computer connected to the Internet, open a web browser.
2. Type **support.microsoft.com** into the address field.

 Be sure to bookmark all of the links you frequently use to research problems.

3. When the Microsoft support page loads, locate the search field at the top of the screen.
4. "Type Win32 error cose returned by the print processor" along with the actual error code, into the Search field.
5. Press Enter.
6. Scroll through the results and select the one most likely to answer your query.
7. Click the link to open it.
8. Review the page to see if the information relates to your current issue.
9. Locate the specific answer to the problem (you may have to click other links and continue to do more reading if the answer involves accessing information on other web pages).

 You may receive an error message that can have a number of different causes so you may have to review a number of links on your search results page before finding the one that applies to your situation. Implementing a solution depends on the answer you find and how it applies to your circumstances, so the specific steps cannot be replicated here.

Criteria for Completion

You will have successfully completed this task when you have correctly found the resolution to the error message that applies to your circumstance.

Task 4.15: Troubleshooting a System Conflict with a Hidden Device

It's difficult to imagine that there may be "hidden" devices attached to your computer, but in this case, "hidden" means a device that is not reported by your Windows XP, Windows Vista, or Windows 7 Device Manager. Devices are not reported by the Device Manager if they are not Plug and Play devices. Since modern devices are Plug and Play, you should only encounter such a problem if older, legacy machines are connected to your computer. These older devices can cause problems if they result in device conflicts with other machines attached to a PC. Ironically, you normally use the Device Manager to diagnose device conflicts. How can you perform such a conflict diagnosis if the device is invisible to the Device Manager?

Objective

This task covers objectives 220-802:4.2 and 4.6.

Scenario

You receive a trouble ticket from a user in the Accounting department that states the speakers on his Windows XP computer aren't working. He can't use anything that plays music or other sound at all. You check the maintenance records for this computer and discover that a new sound card was installed just yesterday. You suspect that the sound card is defective and decide to replace it with an identical unit. Taking your toolkit and the sound card, you go to the user's cubicle and prepare to swap out the cards.

Scope of Task

Duration

Once the actual reason for the sound-card failure is discovered, it should take only a few minutes to resolve the issue.

Setup

No special setup is required.

Caveat

This is another example of assuming a problem has a specific cause when, in fact, the cause is very different. Since this troubleshooting task assumes a very specific cause, you are unlikely to be able to duplicate it on your test computer and follow along with all of the steps.

Procedure

This task will teach you how to diagnose problems related to hidden-device conflicts.

Equipment Used

Despite the initial assumption that the sound card is at fault, for the purpose of this task you do not need to remove and replace a PCI or PCI Express card on your test computer.

Details

This task walks you through the process of discovering a hidden-device conflict on a Windows XP computer.

Investigating and Resolving a Device Conflict

TESTING YOUR INITIAL ASSUMPTION

1. You report to the user's work area with your toolkit and the new sound card and advise the user that you believe his current card is faulty and plan to install a working card.

> See Task 1.3, "Installing a PCI Card," and Task 1.4, "Installing a PCI Express Card," for specific instructions on how to replace one extension card with another.

2. After having replaced the sound card and powering up the computer, you discover that the PC still cannot play sound from any application or from an audio disc in the optical drive.

3. You verify that the speakers are plugged into the correct port and that the connection is secure.

4. You verify that the speakers are turned to a sufficient volume for sound to be heard.

5. You go to Control Panel, double-click Sounds and Audio Devices, confirm that the volume slider is set to the High position, and confirm that the Mute check box is clear.

6. You reinstall the card you had earlier removed and verify that sounds still cannot be played.

7. You call the IT department and discuss the situation with your supervisor, receiving additional troubleshooting instructions.

TESTING YOUR SECOND ASSUMPTION

1. You click Start, right-click My Computer, and then click Properties.

2. In the System Properties dialog box, you click the Hardware tab and then click Device Manager.

3. When the Device Manager opens, you look but are unable to find any device conflicts.

4. Click View and then click Show Hidden Devices.

5. Verify that there is a device conflict present between a legacy scanner and the sound card.

6. With the user's permission, you right-click the scanner in the Device Manager, which the user hasn't needed for quite some time, and click Uninstall.

7. Close the Device Manager.

8. Physically disconnect the scanner from the computer.

9. Ask the user to open an application he expects to play sound.

10. Verify that the user's application plays sound appropriately.

Criteria for Completion

You will have successfully completed this task when you have resolved the hidden-device conflict and the user's computer can play sounds normally.

Task 4.16: Troubleshooting a Word Template Error Message

Microsoft Office Word is the world's favorite word processing application. For most people, creating a document is a relatively simple affair with Word, but Word is an extremely powerful tool with many different capacities. The use of templates is very common in the creation of documents, since a template can apply a preconfigured set of formatting, eliminating the need to create this formatting from scratch every time you need to produce a specific type of document, such as a book chapter for a particular series of books. However, not all templates work and play well together.

Objective

This task covers objective 220-802:4.6.

Scenario

You receive a trouble ticket stating that one of the content developers in the Documentation department of your company is experiencing a problem. Whenever he opens Word, he receives a warning message in a dialog box. When he clicks OK, more dialog boxes appear with different messages. The list of messages he receives in each dialog box is as follows:

```
The command cannot be performed because a dialog box is open.
Word cannot open this document template.
pToolbar_win_2.1.dot
The add-in template is not valid.
```

You go to the writer's cubicle and ask him to duplicate the error for you and see that it is happening just as stated in the trouble ticket.

Scope of Task

Duration

This task should take about half an hour or so, assuming you can locate the solution to the problem on the web right away and then implement that solution.

Setup

You probably will not be able to set up the circumstances for this error on your test computer since it requires that multiple templates be installed in Word and a number of .dot files be installed in the user's AppData/Roaming/Microsoft/Word/STARTUP directory. This task was written using a Windows 7 Professional computer and Word 2007.

Caveat

Exactly duplicating this situation is difficult because of the unusual combination of events that caused the problem.

Procedure

This task will teach you how to diagnose problems with Word templates.

Equipment Used

You will need no special equipment for this task.

Details

This task walks you step-by-step through the process of investigating and resolving a problem with Microsoft Word.

The following troubleshooting method isn't always effective but occasionally you are able to find a solution quickly.

Investigating and Resolving an Issue with Word

PERFORMING THE INITIAL INVESTIGATION AND IMPLEMENTING A SOLUTION

1. Open a web browser and using a search engine search for the string **the command cannot be performed because a dialog box is open word 2007.**

2. You click the first search result, which takes you to http://support.microsoft.com/kb/827732.

The path in step 3 is valid in Windows Vista and Windows 7 computers. For Windows X, the correct path is C:\Documents and Settings\username\ Application Data\Microsoft\Word\STARTUP.

3. Reading the information on the user's computer, you click the Start button and, in the Search box, you type **C:\Users\username\AppData\Roaming\Microsoft\Word\STARTUP** and press Enter (where *username* is the user's name on the computer).

4. In the STARTUP directory, you locate a number of files with .dot extensions, including pToolbar_win_2.1.dot.

5. Review the error messages that were reported in the trouble ticket and confirm that pToolbar_win_2.1.dot is in one of the error messages.

6. Press and hold the Ctrl key and then click each of the .dot files.

7. Right-click one of the selected files and then click Cut.

8. Navigate to another directory on the computer and paste the .dot files in that directory in case you need to replace them.

Although the Microsoft support page said to delete the files, you never know when you might need to replace something, so it's often a good idea to just put the offending files in a different directory where they can't get in the way.

TESTING THE SOLUTION

1. Close all Word documents.

2. Have the user repeat the actions that caused the original error messages.

3. Verify that the error messages do not appear.

4. Verify that the user can open all of his Word documents and templates and perform his normal routine.

This problem was likely caused by the user incorrectly installing one or more Word templates on his computer.

Criteria for Completion

You will have successfully completed this task when the end user can access Word documents and templates normally and perform all of his usual work assignments.

Task 4.17: Troubleshooting a Serious System Error in Windows 7

Microsoft Windows 7 is a very reliable operating system and I feel much more secure using it than the old days when the Windows 98 or Windows XP "blue screen of death" was an occasional but deadly problem. However, bad things can still happen to good operating systems when you least expect them.

Objective

This task covers objectives 220-802:4.3 and 4.6.

Scenario

You are under your desk trying to untangle the nest of power and network cables that attach to different computers in your small home office. You accidently hit the switch on the master surge protector, abruptly turning off the power to all of your electronic devices. You turn the surge protector on and reboot your computers. When your Windows 7 Professional machine boots, you receive a message that a serious error has occurred and you are prompted to boot into system recovery using the Windows 7 install disc to repair the damage.

The screen image is distinctly red and is full of static, the way old TVs in the 1960s used to display programs when the manual fine tuning was out of adjustment.

Scope of Task

Duration

This task should take about half an hour to an hour, depending on how long it takes to find the problem using a search engine and then implement the steps to recover the computer.

Setup

You probably will not be able to set up the circumstances for this error on your test computer since the original problem had a unique cause. The main purpose of this task isn't to test your ability to replicate this computer problem but to show you how to research and solve such a problem, especially under duress.

Caveat

Exactly duplicating this situation is difficult if not impossible because of the unusual combination of events that caused the problem.

Ultimately, the real problem turned out to be a bad hard drive, but I didn't know it at the time and the solution I am proposing actually did work but only temporarily. Eventually, I had to replace the hard drive and reinstall the applications and all my data from backups.

Procedure

This task will teach you how to diagnose and repair a serious error in Windows 7.

Equipment Used

You will need no special equipment for this task.

Details

This task walks you step-by-step through the process of investigating and resolving a problem with Windows 7.

Investigating and Resolving an Invalid System Partition Error in Windows 7

MAKING YOUR FIRST REPAIR ATTEMPT

1. After receiving the error message prompting you to boot into system recovery using the Windows 7 install disc, just reboot normally since occasionally a simple reboot will fix the problem.

2. When the computer reboots and the problem persists, click Start and in the Search box type **system restore**, and then press Enter to open it.

3. Run the System Restore Wizard to restore the computer to the Recommended restore point. See Task 4.2 for more information.

4. After reboot, the serious system problem is still present, so locate the Windows installation disc, insert it into the computer's optical drive, and reboot the computer.

 This assumes that the first drive the computer looks at to boot from is the optical drive.

5. On the System Recovery Options screen, click Startup Repair.

6. Run the wizard and allow the computer to reboot.

7. When the problem with the computer persists, follow the same steps as you did previously using Startup Repair, since this process sometimes requires several runs and reboots before the repair is complete.

8. After you run the tool again and reboot and the problem persists, shut down the machine.

MAKING YOUR SECOND REPAIR ATTEMPT

1. With the computer completely powered down, unplug the power cable that leads to the computer's power supply and then open the computer case.

2. Using ESD procedures, reach inside the machine and verify that all cable connections are secure, including the disk drive data and power cables.

3. Verify that all of the RAM sticks and the CPU are securely seated.

4. Close the computer case and plug the power cable back into the computer's power supply.

5. Power up the computer and notice that the problem still is present.

MAKING YOUR THIRD REPAIR ATTEMPT

1. Reboot the computer using the Windows installation disc and run the Startup Repair routine again.

2. At the end of the routine, click View Diagnostic and Repair Details and review the data presented, locating any messages indicating what the problem is.

3. Copy down the exact error message such as "couldn't find a valid boot partition," open a web browser on a different computer, and search for the error message.

4. In the search results, locate the solution to the "Couldn't find a valid boot partition" error and copy the instructions. In this case, the instructions say to use a command-prompt utility called Diskpart to set the active partition.

5. On your ailing Windows 7 machine, boot from the Windows installation disc, and on the System Recovery Options screen, click Command Prompt.

6. At the command prompt, type **Diskpart**.

7. When diskpart.exe launches a separate command prompt window, at the prompt, type **lis vol**.

8. When the results appear, locate the volume letter (probably C) or the volume number (probably 1) that contains the system partition.

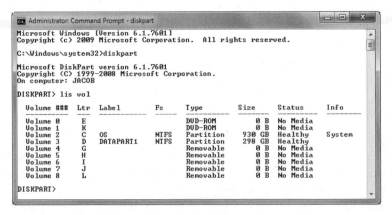

9. At the prompt, type **sel vol C** and press Enter.

10. Type **act** and press Enter.

> Diskpart only verifies that the partition is able to contain an operating system's startup files and does not check the contents of the partition. If you mark a partition as active and it does not contain the operating system's startup files, your computer is unlikely to start.

11. Type **exit** to close the command-prompt window.

12. Close all other open windows and dialog boxes.

13. Remove the Windows installation disc from the optical drive and reboot the computer.

TESTING YOUR FINAL SOLUTION

1. Verify that the computer boots and that Windows 7 loads correctly.

2. Verify that you can perform your usual activities on the computer without any problems.

Criteria for Completion

You will have successfully completed this task when you can boot into Windows and the machine behaves normally and exhibits no problems.

Task 4.18: Troubleshooting No Monitor Image When the PC Is Powered Up

Some problems seem very basic in terms of causes and solutions, but the occasional "head scratcher" can still make an appearance. However, there are still only so many reasons for a PC to be on and operating but have no image displaying on the monitor.

Objective

This task covers objective 220-802:4.4.

Scenario

You receive a trouble ticket stating that a user in Research says she powered up her PC this morning but no image appears on her monitor. Yesterday, the monitor was working fine. The user states that she's tried "everything" to fix the problem but with no success. You report to Research and locate the user at her computer.

If you have to perform a display diagnostic on a laptop, you can use the Fn <screen> button to cycle through internal, external, and both monitors.

Scope of Task

Duration

This task should take about 10 to 15 minutes.

Setup

No special setup is required. This task assumes a standard monitor and monitor cable connection.

Caveat

You can complete this task using either a CRT (yes, some people still use these dinosaurs) or an LCD monitor (not including laptops).

In the case of CRT monitors, *do not* open up the monitor case and attempt to probe inside. The risk of a dangerous and even fatal electrical shock is high *even if the monitor is unplugged!* This task only requires that you follow the subsequent steps, and none of them includes opening a CRT monitor.

Fortunately, the use of CRT monitors is very rare these days, but because the occasional home user still hangs onto their old monitors, I've included this information here.

Procedure

This task will teach you how to diagnose basic monitor and video issues.

Equipment Used

No special equipment is needed for this task.

Details

This task will go through the steps of diagnosing a nonresponsive monitor and providing a solution.

Troubleshooting a Problem with a Blank Computer Monitor

YOUR INITIAL INVESTIGATION AND TESTING YOUR FIRST ASSUMPTION

1. Push the power button on the monitor.

2. If no image appears, push it again.

3. Crawl under the desk, locate the monitor's power cord, and make sure it is securely connected to a power source.

4. Go to the back of the monitor and verify that the power cord is securely connected to the monitor.

5. Sitting at the computer, locate the brightness and contrast controls, adjusting them and seeing if an image appears.

 The first five steps in the first section represent the three most common causes of this complaint: the monitor is turned off, it has no power, and the brightness and contrast controls are not correctly adjusted.

6. Get permission from the user to take the PC to your workbench for further tests.

TESTING YOUR SECOND ASSUMPTION

1. Take the PC to your workbench.

 Most IT tech workstations include a working monitor, keyboard, and mouse to be used for testing computer problems.

2. Connect the PC to a keyboard, mouse, monitor, and power supply.

3. Verify that the monitor is connected to a power supply.

4. Turn on the monitor.

5. Power up the PC. A correct image appears on the monitor. You observe the monitor through the boot process and the loading of the operating system. There continues to be no problem with the image.

6. Return the PC to the user along with a monitor that is known to be in good working order.

 Only superheroes carry heavy objects over long distances. Get a cart to take any heavy equipment from and to the user.

7. Reconnect the PC, monitor, input devices, and power connections.

8. Power up the PC and monitor. A good image appears on the monitor.

9. Remove the old monitor from the user's work area.

Monitors get old and finally give out. If the issue had not been the monitor, the next most likely suspects would have been corrupted video drivers, an unseated video card, or a damaged video card.

Criteria for Completion

You will have successfully completed this assignment when the user can get a viable image on the computer's monitor.

Task 4.19: Troubleshooting the Inability to Connect to a Mapped Drive

One way to make it easier for users to access resources on servers is to map a network drive to the shared folder on the server. (See Task 3.1, "Mapping Drives.") Although the user could type the path in the Run box, it is easier for most people to open My Computer, click a drive, and have it open. If you tell a user that her Accounts Payable template is on her J drive, you don't have to explain that it's actually on the "such-and-such" server and can be accessed by entering the path \\server_name\share_name.

Occasionally, a user will complain that he or she can't access a mapped network drive, and it will be your job to find out why and to resolve the issue.

Objective

This task covers objective 220-802:4.5.

Scenario

You receive a trouble ticket stating that a user in the Payroll department can't access her J drive to retrieve her most recent accounting data. You check the work records for her computer and the server the J drive is mapped to and see no recent problems recorded. You access the relevant server using the remote web connection interface and are able to connect to the server and the share. You report to Payroll and locate the user. She is already logged on, so you sit down at the computer and start to work.

Scope of Task

Duration

This task should take you about 10 minutes.

Setup

Ideally, the computer you use for this task will have a mapped network drive that connects to a local or network shared folder. This task was written using a Windows 7 computer but should work just as well with Windows XP or Windows Vista.

Caveat

Sometimes a problem is relatively simple to solve. The only reason you might have a difficult time is if you overlook the obvious.

Procedure

This task will help you learn to solve problems with mapped drives.

Equipment Used

No special equipment is required for this task.

Details

This task will take you through the process of investigating a mapped drive issue and determining the solution.

Discovering and Resolving a Mapped Drive Problem

BEGINNING THE INVESTIGATION

1. Click Start ➢ Computer. You notice that the J drive is missing from the Network Drives area but see the drive letters for the hard drive, floppy drive, and optical drive.

2. Close Computer.

3. Click Start.

4. Right-click Computer.

5. Click Map Network Drive.

6. Use the drop-down arrow to expand the Drive menu and look for the J drive mapping. You notice that no drive letters are mapped, including the J drive.

7. Select the J drive.

8. Click the Browse button by the Folder field and browse to the required server share.

9. In the Browse for Folder window, select the network share.

10. Click OK.

11. Select the Reconnect at Logon check box.

12. Click Finish. The J drive window opens, showing you the contents of the shared folder.

13. Close the J drive window.

TESTING YOUR FIRST ASSUMPTION

1. Click Start ➤ Log Off.

2. When the Log Off Windows dialog box appears, click Log Off.

3. When the user is logged off and the Log On box appears, have the user log on.

4. Once the user is logged on, click Start ➤ Computer.

5. In the Network Drives area, the J drive appears.

6. Double-click the J drive to open it.

7. Close the J drive.

 The most likely explanation for this issue is that somehow the Reconnect at Logon check box had been cleared, and when the user logged off the computer, the drive mapping was lost.

Criteria for Completion

You will have successfully completed this task when the drive mapping is restored and the user can log off and log back on and still connect to the mapped drive.

Task 4.20: Troubleshooting the Inability to Access a Shared Folder on a Remote Computer

This task is similar to Task 4.19, "Troubleshooting the Inability to Connect to a Mapped Drive"; however, it is a bit more complicated. Although both tasks involve a user being unable to access a shared folder on the network, there is a wide variety of causes for such an event. It's a good idea to become familiar with this sort of problem because you'll encounter it often.

Objective

This task covers objective 220-802:4.5.

Scenario

You receive a trouble ticket stating that a user in the chemical lab located at a branch office can't access a shared folder on the local server. Recently, all of his data has been added to a single shared folder on a new server so he and his team members can share their work. Unfortunately, he and his coworkers can't get to those files in the shared folder.

You access the work record for that office and see that a new server was installed over the weekend. Data from several PC hard drives were consolidated into one shared folder on that server. There is no indication that there were problems with the installation and setup.

You report to the chem lab and locate the user.

Scope of Task

Duration

This task should take about 15 minutes.

Setup

For this task, you will need to have two computers networked together. One of the computers will need to have a folder shared on the network. This task was written using a Windows XP Professional client computer, but you should be able to use Windows Vista or Windows 7 as well. The server used was Windows Server 2008 R2.

Caveat

Network access problems can be many and varied. This is one of those situations where asking the user a few well-worded questions will help narrow your search.

Procedure

This task will teach you how to diagnose and resolve problems accessing network shares.

Equipment Used

No special equipment is required for this task.

Details

In this task, you will go through the steps necessary to investigate and resolve a problem accessing shared network folders.

Diagnosing and Resolving an Inability to Access a Network Share

PERFORMING YOUR INITIAL INVESTIGATION

1. These are some relevant questions to ask the user who first discovered the problem:
   - When did you discover the problem?
   - Do all users on your team have the same access problem?
   - Has there ever been a time when you were able to access the shares?

- Are you able to access other shared folders and devices?

- What exactly can you access and not access?

You discover that everyone in the office can open the shared folder and open documents but that no one can modify the documents, not even the document owners. This started after their data was moved off their local hard drives and into the shared folder on their office server. Everyone is able to access all of the shared folders and devices that were not moved during last weekend's server installation.

2. Sitting at the user's computer, click Start ➤ Run.

3. Ask the user for the path to the shared folder and type the path in the Run box.

4. Click OK. The shared folder opens, and you can see the documents the folder contains.

5. Double-click one of the documents to open it. You notice in the blue title bar over the Word toolbar that the name of the document and Microsoft Word are displayed along with "Read Only."

6. Close the document and open others to see if they're all read only. The user confirms that all documents in the folder are read only for everyone in the office.

7. Close all documents and the network share.

TESTING YOUR FIRST ASSUMPTION

1. Have the user show you where the server is located.

2. Sitting at the server's keyboard, log on as administrator.

In a large networked environment, specific administrator accounts are created on servers so IT staff can log on regardless of where in the network the servers are located and which departments they serve.

3. Navigate to the shared folder.

4. Right-click the shared folder, click Share With, and then click Specific People.

5. In the File Sharing dialog box, locate the username that is used by the chem lab staff to access the share. You notice that it is set for Read.

6. Right-click and then click Read/Write.

7. Click Share and then click Done.

8. In the Network Discovery and File Sharing dialog box, click Yes, Turn On Network Discovery and File Sharing for All Public Networks.

9. Click Done.

10. Log off the server.

11. Return to the user's computer and access the remote share.

12. Open a document in the shared folder. When the document opens, it is no longer tagged as Read Only.

13. Make some minor change to the document and save it.

14. Close the document.

15. Open the document again and notice if the modification is still present.

 There were two signs that the problem is resolved: when you attempted to save the changes and did not receive a message stating that the document is read only and when the document closed after accepting the saved modifications.

16. Have the user make changes to other files and save them.

17. Verify that all users in the office can access, modify, and save documents.

Criteria for Completion

You will have successfully completed this task when all users can open, read, modify, and save their own files and other shared files in the folder.

Task 4.21: Troubleshooting the Inability to Connect to the Network

In previous tasks, you've investigated problems with users having difficulty accessing some resource on the network. There are times when you will need to diagnose a situation in which the user can't connect to the network at all. If all users on a network segment lose connectivity, you can be reasonably assured that the problem lies with an internetworking device in the server room. When a single user has a connection problem, there can be any number of causes.

Objective

This task covers objective 220-802:4.5.

Scenario

You receive a trouble ticket stating that a user in the data-entry section of the Administrative department has lost her connection to the network this morning. She had a connection when she first logged on but lost it after working for about an hour. You check the service logs and see that no one else from her department has reported any networking problems. You check the switch that serves Admin's network segment and use the cabling documentation to locate the switch port assigned to the user's computer. The link light on that port is dark.

Your supervisor enters the server room and you explain the problem. She tells you to report to the user and investigate the problem at that end while she consoles into the switch to see if there is a problem with the switch port.

Scope of Task

Duration

Once you access the user's computer, this task will take about 10 minutes.

Setup

For this task, you will need two computers that are networked together through a switch.

Caveat

Since network-connection problems have many causes, this is another situation in which your investigation should begin by questioning the user.

Procedure

This task will illustrate how to diagnose a general network-connection problem.

Equipment Used

You will need no special equipment to complete this task.

Details

This task will walk you step-by-step through the process of investigating a general network-connection problem experienced by a single user.

Diagnosing a Network-Connection Problem

BEGINNING YOUR INITIAL INVESTIGATION

1. Here are some questions to ask the user:
   - When did the problem occur?
   - What were you doing right before you lost connectivity?
   - Are you experiencing a total loss of connectivity or is it intermittent?
   - Have you ever had this problem before?
   - Have any changes been made to your computer's hardware or software recently?
   - Have you made any changes to the computer or immediate networking environment recently?

The user reports that she logged on to the domain at 8 AM as usual and experienced no problems. An hour later, she was attempting to access a remote file share when she lost her network connection. She cannot access any network resource at all. She said that no changes have been made to her computer recently, but she needed a second network connection at her desk to accommodate her manager's laptop. At her manager's request, she is copying some files to the laptop in preparation for the manager's upcoming trip to a conference. She brought in a small five-port switch from home to split her connection. You discover that she installed it a few days ago under her desk.

2. Go under the user's desk and locate the switch.

3. Verify the network-patch-cable and power-cable connections. You notice that the patch-cable connections are secure and the cables are configured correctly but the power cable for the switch is disconnected from the switch. It's possible that the user accidentally kicked the switch or snagged her foot in the power cable, causing the cable to disconnect.

4. Reconnect the power cable and verify that the switch's power and link lights come on.

Your first assumption is that the computer needs to acquire a valid IP address.

TESTING YOUR FIRST ASSUMPTION

1. Sitting at the computer, click Start and in the Search box, type **cmd** and then press Enter.

2. When the command-prompt window opens, type **ipconfig/all**.

3. Press Enter.

The IP address for the computer is listed as 169.254.69.8 with a subnet mask of 255.255.0.0. You recognize this address range as belonging to Automatic Private IP Addressing (APIPA), which is usually assigned to a computer when it cannot connect to a DHCP server.

4. Type **ipconfig/release** and press Enter.

5. Type **ipconfig/renew** and press Enter. The computer receives an IP address from the DHCP server in the range assigned to the administrative network segment.

6. Type **ping** and then the IP address or hostname of the file server and press Enter. You receive a reply from the server.

You should start by pinging the IP address of the remote host rather than the hostname since DNS name resolution could be part of the problem.

7. Type **ping** and then the domain name of an Internet host such as www.google.com.

Some Internet hosts turn off echo replies for security reasons, so this test isn't always reliable. As of this writing, Google allows echo replies.

8. Press Enter. You receive a reply from the Internet host.

9. Close the command-prompt window.

When you return to the IT department, you will be obligated to report that an end user installed a piece of networking equipment without consulting with the IT department. Since this was done at the request of her manager, your supervisor will need to make appropriate contact with the manager and discuss proper use policy involving the installation of unsupported hardware.

Criteria for Completion

You will have successfully completed this task when the user is once again able to connect to the network.

Task 4.22: Troubleshooting Connection Problems with an External USB Hard Drive

USB devices are ubiquitous in today's computing environment. We quickly and easily attach all kinds of devices to our desktops and laptops via USB, and the vast majority of time the device "just works." Should a USB device ever fail to operate as we expect, I'm sure most people would be at least puzzled. As a PC technician, in this unlikely eventuality, you'll be expected to do something about it.

Objective

This task covers objective 220-802:4.3.

Scenario

You receive a trouble ticket from a user in Sales. He has been using an external USB hard-disk drive (HDD) to connect to his PC and temporarily store data from customer responses to a product demo that his department is using. Today, he plugged the device into his computer and immediately received the message "You may now safely remove hardware." He is unable to access the device at all.

You report to the salesperson's cubicle with your toolkit, sit at the keyboard, and open My Computer. You see the USB device listed as UNKNOWN, UNREADABLE. You double-click the drive icon and receive no response. You suspect a connection problem is the cause.

Scope of Task

Duration

This task should just take a few minutes.

Setup

For this task, you will need an appropriate USB hard-disk drive. A thumb drive will not be sufficient.

Caveat

The only concern you should keep in mind is to maintain standard precautions whenever opening any device. Also, the USB external drive used was an older device and the problem it presented will likely not occur on current USB external drives.

Procedure

This task will show you how to diagnose a connection problem between a computer and a USB hard drive.

Equipment Used

You should need only a screwdriver, a large-volume external USB drive, and a second USB device, such as a thumb drive.

Details

This task will take you through the steps of diagnosing a connection problem between a computer and a USB hard-disk drive.

Diagnosing a Connection Problem Between a PC and a USB HDD

1. Unplug the USB device from the computer, wait a few moments, and then firmly plug the device back into the PC.

2. Experiencing the same problem as the customer described, you unplug the device.

You can also try plugging it into a different USB port on the machine.

3. Take a thumb drive you brought with you, which you know to be good, and plug it into the PC.

4. When the thumb drive is appropriately recognized by the PC, safely remove the device.

5. Use an appropriate screwdriver from your toolkit to open the USB HDD, taking all necessary precautions.

6. You visually examine the interior of the device and discover that the drive's IDE pins are not making firm contact with the USB plug head.

7. Press the IDE pins firmly but gently into the USB plug head, verifying that the contact is complete.

8. Reassemble the USB hard-disk drive device.

9. Plug the device into the USB port of the user's PC and verify that it is appropriately recognized.

The external drive used was an older device that had an IDE-to-USB interface. Most large-volume USB external drives you'll encounter today will not use this sort of interface, but you'll need to be prepared to work on legacy devices when you encounter them.

Criteria for Completion

You will have successfully completed this task when the USB HDD is recognized by the PC and when the user can access and use the USB storage device normally.

Task 4.23: Troubleshooting a Scanner Problem

This task is an example of a problem that seems unique or idiosyncratic. Sometimes the "oddness" of a problem can throw off a PC tech and make locating the solution seem more difficult than it really is. Even with problems you've never encountered before, standard problem-solving steps are still the best way to resolve most issues.

Objective

This task covers objective 220-802:4.9.

Scenario

You receive a trouble ticket from a user in the Graphics department with an unusual problem. Normally the scanner in his department is attached to a Windows XP laptop and all scans are managed from that laptop. The user wanted to scan materials from his MacBook and so installed the drivers for the HP scanner onto his MacBook, disconnected the scanner from the Windows laptop, and attached it to his MacBook. He then successfully scanned materials to his MacBook.

Subsequently, the user reconnected the Windows laptop to the scanner, but now when he tries to use the laptop to initiate a scan, the Windows laptop isn't recognized by the scanner. When the user presses the Scan To button on the scanner, the options that appear are specifically for his MacBook, such as Scan to Adobe Photoshop and Scan to Mac Mail, and no options for the Windows laptop appear.

Other symptoms include being unable to initiate a scan from within a Microsoft Office application using the Scanning Wizard and being unable to open HP Director from the Windows laptop.

You report to the Graphics department and locate the scanner, which is connected to the Windows XP laptop as the user described.

The A+ exams do not require that you know anything about MacBooks or other Apple products, but real-world troubleshooting problems are not so forgiving.

Scope of Task

Duration

This task should take 15 or 20 minutes.

Setup

To exactly duplicate the situation described, you'll need an HP scanner or All-in-One imaging device, a Windows XP laptop, and a MacBook.

Caveat

Since the circumstances surrounding this problem are unique, you may not be able to duplicate the original issue; however, the solution is standard enough that you'll be able to implement it on a Windows XP computer.

Procedure

This task will show you how to diagnose and correct a scanner connection problem.

Equipment Used

No special equipment is required. You most likely won't be able to re-create the problem as described, so acquiring a MacBook (assuming you don't have one) isn't necessary. Having a scanner or printer will be handy when implementing the solution.

Details

This task will take you through the steps involved in diagnosing and solving a connection problem with a Windows computer and a scanner.

Diagnosing a Scanner Connection Problem

TESTING YOUR FIRST SOLUTION

1. Power down both the laptop and the HP scanner and wait a few minutes.
2. Power up the Windows laptop and then power up the HP scanner.
3. Place some media on the scanner bed and close the lid.
4. Use the laptop to start a scan.
5. The scanner continues to fail to recognize the laptop.

TESTING YOUR SECOND SOLUTION

1. On the laptop, click Start ➤ Control Panel.
2. Double-click Add or Remove Programs.
3. Locate the drivers for the HP scanner in the list and uninstall them and all related software.
4. Open a web browser on the laptop and go to www.hp.com.
5. On the HP site, click Support & Drivers.
6. Click Drivers & Software.
7. In the Enter a Product Name/Number field, enter the name and number of the scanner, and then click Search.
8. On the Step One: Select Your Operating System screen, use the drop-down menu to select the operating system of the user's computer and then click Next.
9. Under Step Two: Select a download, click Driver - Product Installation Software and download them on the laptop.
10. Once downloaded, install the driver and reboot the computer.
11. Once the laptop has rebooted, attempt to initiate a scan from the laptop.
12. Have the user perform all the usual scan functions with the Windows laptop attached and verify that they all perform as expected.

Criteria for Completion

You will have successfully completed this task when the Windows laptop can be used to completely manage the HP scanner as expected.

Although you may not know exactly what caused the problem, sometimes reinstalling the driver and other relevant software for a device will return it to working order.

Task 4.24: Troubleshooting a Laptop Wi-Fi Connection Failure

This task is deceptive in the sense that wireless networking, in spite of all its advances, still seems like half magic and half wishful thinking. A great many factors can affect a Wi-Fi connection, and since you can't see radio waves, it's difficult to tell what in the environment could be interfering with a computer's wireless connection. That said, sometimes the problem is right in front of you, waving at you in plain sight.

Objective

This task covers objectives 220-802:4.5 and 4.8.

Scenario

You receive a trouble ticket from a user on the Sales team saying that the he can't make a wireless connection, regardless of where he tries to connect, including on the office wireless network or at the local coffee shop. It was working fine yesterday, but this morning, he can't "see" any wireless networks.

In preparation, you go online and look up the specifications for the user's laptop, including any common problems regarding Wi-Fi connections, in the FAQs at the manufacturer's website. Then you visit his cubicle to test your assumption.

Scope of Task

Duration

This task should just take a few minutes.

Setup

No special setup is required. You'll just need a laptop that has a built-in wireless card and an available wireless network to which you can connect.

Caveat

As I previously mentioned, network connectivity problems, and wireless networking in particular, can be very difficult to solve. However, the best thing to do when in doubt is to start with the basics.

Procedure

This task will show you how to solve a wireless network connection problem.

Equipment Used

No special equipment is required, except for a laptop with a built-in wireless card.

Details

This task will walk you through the steps to discover the problem with a failed wireless connection.

Diagnosing a Wi-Fi Connection Problem

1. Have the user attempt to make a wireless connection as he normally would and observe the result.

2. Open a command prompt on the laptop and type **ipconfig/all**, press Enter, and observe that the wireless network card does not have an IP address.

3. Locate the notes you took when you researched the laptop on the manufacturer's website, and reread the information about the manual on/off switch for the Wi-Fi antenna.

4. Locate the switch and move it to the on position.

5. At the command prompt, type **ipconfig/release** and press Enter.

6. Type **ipconfig/renew** and press Enter, and observe that the wireless network card acquires an IP address.

7. Have the user attempt to connect to the office wireless network and observe that he is successful.

Many laptops with a built-in wireless adapter have a manual switch that allows the user to turn the Wi-Fi antenna on or off. This feature is included to save battery power when a user wants to work on the laptop but doesn't need a wireless connection. In this case, the user probably moved the switch to the off position by accident and didn't realize it.

Criteria for Completion

You will have successfully completed this task when the user can successfully connect to a wireless network.

Task 4.25: Troubleshooting the Failure of a Hard-Disk Drive

This situation is one that causes despair in many users, particularly those who have not backed up the vital data on their computers. It's also a great deal of work to troubleshoot, and the solution isn't a happy one. Nevertheless, a worst-case scenario is one that you will occasionally have to face as an IT technician.

Objective

This task covers objective 220-802:4.3.

Scenario

You receive a trouble ticket from a user who states that she is having multiple problems on her Windows 7 Professional computer. Applications like Word, Visio, and Chrome are continually hanging. Using Task Manager to close them is very difficult. When she is able to finally close an application such as Word, it won't reopen.

You check the work history for her computer and discover that another technician corrected an Invalid System Partition Error on her PC just a few weeks ago (see Task 4.17 for details). You suspect that a more serious hard drive problem is the cause, and you locate all of the necessary repair discs and other tools required to address this type of problem. Then you report to the user's cubicle.

Scope of Task

Duration

This task could take several hours and a great deal of effort.

Setup

Since the problem involves a failing hard drive, there is no way you can actually re-create this situation on your lab computer short of finding a drive that is just about to fail and installing it in the computer. This task is included to show you the steps in diagnosing a dying hard drive and pronouncing when death has occurred, which you will have to face someday.

Caveat

If you intend to follow along with some of the steps of this task, make sure you are prepared to go through different repair sequences on your lab computer. Do not use your production PC (the one you use in real life to surf the Web, game, and send email).

Procedure

This task will show you how perform multiple diagnostic and repair activities on a computer with a dying hard drive.

Equipment Used

No special equipment is required except for the Windows 7 installation disc (although many computer makers will only supply a repair or rescue disc instead) that comes with Windows 7. I also used Acronis since it is installed on my PC, but you don't have to purchase and install this software for the sake of the task (see Task 1.8 for more information on this application).

Details

This task will walk you through the steps required to diagnose and attempt to repair a serious hard-drive problem.

Diagnosing a Serious Hard-Drive Failure

RUNNING CHKDSK

1. Click Start and then click Computer.
2. Right-click the OS (C) drive and click Properties.
3. In the Properties dialog box, click the Tools tab and then click Check Now under Error-Checking.
4. When the Check Disk screen appears, make sure the Automatically Fix File System Errors and Scan For and Attempt Recovery of Bad Sectors check boxes are selected; then click Start.
5. When prompted with the message "Do you want to check for hard disk errors the next time you start your computer?" click Schedule Disk Check.
6. Reboot the computer.
7. Observe Chkdsk running on the machine (this will take some time).
8. You notice during the scan that Chkdsk says it corrected errors to the master file table's MFT bitmap attribute.
9. When Chkdsk completes its scan, have the user log in to the computer.

10. To verify that the problem is solved, run Chkdsk again, looking for a "No errors" report.

11. When Chkdsk finishes, it reports no errors but states that it failed to transfer logged messages to the event log with a status of 50, which usually indicates that a serious hard drive problem continues to exist.

RUNNING SYSTEM REPAIR

1. Insert the Windows 7 installation disc into the computer's optical drive and reboot the computer (this assumes the computer is configured to look to the optical drive for a boot sector first).

2. In the System Recovery Options screen, click Startup Repair.

3. Run the wizard and allow the computer to reboot. You reboot into a completely black screen, even though the monitor is receiving a signal.

4. Remove the installation disc and reboot.

RUNNING LAST KNOWN GOOD CONFIGURATION

1. As the system comes up, you press the F8 key repeatedly until the Advanced Boot Options screen appears.

2. Use the arrow keys to highlight Last Known Good Configuration (Advanced) and then press Enter.

3. When the computer boots and loads the Windows 7 operating system, have the user attempt to log in.

4. When the user attempts to click her username to log in, the applet vanishes and only a blue screen appears with the words "Windows 7 Professional" at the bottom, and no login method is offered.

5. You manually reboot the computer and boot into the Windows boot manager, noticing a message that states: "Status 0xc000000e, Info: The Boot Selection Failed Because the Required Device Is Inaccessible."

At this point, you excuse yourself and phone your supervisor to report on the situation, the steps you've taken to recover the drive, and the results. You are advised that the best way to proceed is to cease all recovery efforts, replace the hard drive with a new drive, and install Windows 7 from a preconfigured image.

Criteria for Completion

You will have successfully completed this task when you have performed all of the required recovery tasks. In this case, however, the drive is a lost cause, and the only way to repair the situation is to completely replace the hard drive.

Task 4.26: Troubleshooting a Persistent "Align Print Cartridges" Message after Cartridges Have Been Replaced and Aligned

This task is another example of a problem that seems more complicated than it really is and that standard problem-solving steps adequately address. Remember to try the most likely and the simplest solutions first. Often they will provide the answer you are looking for.

Objective

This task covers objective 220-802:4.9.

Scenario

You receive a trouble ticket from a user in Reception stating that after he replaced the black and color ink cartridges in his printer and completed the alignment procedure, he still is getting an "Align print cartridges" message. He also states that when he tries to print a color document, the only color that prints is red and the ink on the document fades at about a quarter of the way down the page.

After determining the make and model of the printer being used, you locate the proper replacement ink cartridges and take them with you when you go to Reception. You suspect that one or both cartridges are defective but will try a simpler solution before replacing them.

Scope of Task

Duration

This task should just take a few minutes.

Setup

No special setup is required.

Caveat

When working with printer ink cartridges, be careful to avoid creating any ink stains. Also, do not touch the contacts on the ink cartridges or printer carriage directly.

Procedure

This task will show you how to solve an unusual printing problem with a usual cause.

Equipment Used

No special equipment is required, except for access to a printer and print cartridges.

Details

This task will walk you through the steps required to diagnose a printing problem.

Diagnosing a Color Printing Problem

1. Open the panel on the printer to access the ink cartridges.
2. Carefully reach inside and unlatch the black ink cartridge.
3. Reseat the black ink cartridge and re-engage the latch.
4. Unlatch the color ink cartridge, reseat it, and then re-engage the latch.
5. Close the access panel.
6. Follow any instructions on the printer's control panel for aligning the print heads if required.
7. Have the user print the original document and verify that the printout is as expected.

Criteria for Completion

You will have successfully completed this task when the printer produces normal color printouts.

 Although the problem could have been created by defective ink cartridges or by dirty or damaged contacts on the cartridges or the print carriage, the cause, in this case, was a poorly seated color ink cartridge.

Index

Note to the Reader: Throughout this index **boldfaced** page numbers indicate primary discussions of a topic. *Italicized* page numbers indicate illustrations.

D